RUGBY UNION
Manual

Published in September 2008

A catalogue record for this book is
available from the British Library

ISBN 978 1 84425 503 0

Library of Congress catalog card no 2008926351

Haynes Publishing,
Sparkford, Yeovil, Somerset BA22 7JJ, UK
Tel: +44 (0) 1963 442030
Fax: +44 (0) 1963 440001
E-mail: sales@haynes.co.uk
Website: www.haynes.co.uk

Haynes North America, Inc.,
861 Lawrence Drive, Newbury Park,
California 91320, USA

Printed and bound by J.H.Haynes & Co Ltd,
Sparkford, Yeovil, Somerset BA22 7JJ, UK

Editorial Director Mark Hughes

Design Lee Parsons

Photography Getty Images
Except: 16–19 and 40–41, James Mann

Author's acknowledgements

Thanks to:

Louise, Elliott and Gabriel Johnson; Mark Hughes,
Lee Parsons and Iain Wakefield at Haynes; Martin
Johnson; everyone who gave their valuable time at
the RFU especially Jane Barron; Dick Tilley; Andy
and Claire Hunns; Stan and Moirya Brett; Marc
Slimak; James R Marshall at Excelsior Sports
Consultancy; Joy Walter, physiotherapist
specialising in sports injuries.

RUGBY UNION
Manual

ENGLAND RUGBY

THE OFFICIAL GUIDE TO PLAYING THE GAME
Howard Johnson
Foreword by England Team Manager Martin Johnson

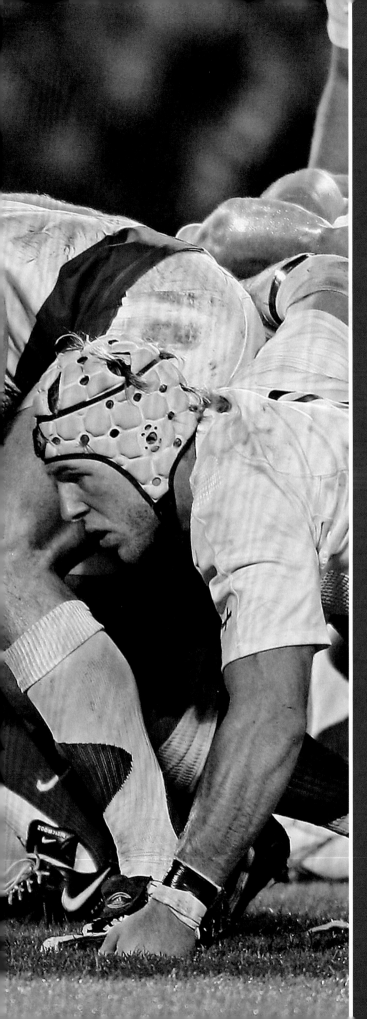

CONTENTS

ENGLAND
RUGBY

FOREWORD

Rugby is a fantastic sport that I've enjoyed for as long as I can remember. I was lucky enough to play for my country and to captain England to a Rugby World Cup Final victory over Australia back in 2003. But even if I hadn't been so fortunate I know I would still have loved every minute of playing the sport. My answer whenever I've been asked what I would have been if I hadn't become a professional rugby player is always the same. I'd have been an amateur rugby player, because I love rugby.

Now that my playing career is over I have the fantastic privilege of being England Team Manager. I work with the very best players in the country and our aim is to try to create a winning senior England team. There are many different elements that go into producing a great team, but the basics of individual technique, great teamwork and excellent communication are all vitally important.

The *Rugby Union Manual* is the perfect place to start if you want to get to grips with all of the underlying techniques that make for good rugby. The top players never forget that these basics form the bedrock of everything that they do on the field and that practising and honing these elements of their game is an absolute must, even at senior level. The *Rugby Union Manual* will give you everything you need to understand how to play in specific positions, how to develop key areas of the game such as the scrum, lineout, ruck and maul and how to develop specialist individual skills such as kicking, throwing, passing and tackling. Thanks to this book you can work on your technique using the same drills that the top young players in England practise within the England Academy structure, get expert advice on getting yourself in the shape of your life to compete in this most demanding of sports and also learn all about the laws of the game that will allow you to compete effectively and within the bounds of the law.

The *Rugby Union Manual* also gives you some exclusive content that you won't find elsewhere. You'll go behind the scenes at Twickenham to see what facilities we provide in the quest for excellence, see all the kit that helps the current squad perform at their very best and learn about the all-time great players who are considered masters of their art.

The *Rugby Union Manual* offers you everything you need to become a better rugby player. But it will also enable you to get more and more enjoyment out of this great sport of ours. And I hope that it will help you become as passionate about rugby as I am.

Martin Johnson
England Team Manager

ENGLAND
RUGBY

BEHIND THE SCENES AT
TWICKENHAM

It's the undisputed home of English rugby, a state-of-the-art 82,000 all-seater stadium that fans affectionately refer to as 'HQ'. Its recently redeveloped South Stand even includes a four-star Marriott Hotel, Virgin Active Classic Health Club and a Performing Arts Studio alongside its first class corporate hospitality facilities. And it dominates the West London skyline like nothing else. Twickenham Stadium reverberates with rugby. The unforgettable matches that have taken place

there, the legendary players who have graced its turf. And the country that gave the world the sport of rugby is rightly proud of its showpiece. Yet Twickenham rose from the humblest of beginnings, when the Rugby Football Union bought a ten and a quarter acre market garden in Twickenham back in 1907 for 5,572 pounds, 12 shillings and six pence. Committee member William Williams was largely responsible for acquiring the land in the face, it must be said, of some serious opposition, which is why

ENGLAND
RUGBY

Twickenham is also affectionately known as 'Billy Williams' Cabbage Patch'. Following the construction of the ground and its approach roads and entrances Twickenham's inaugural match took place on October 2, 1909 when Harlequins took on Richmond. Quins triumphed by 14 points to 10. Twickenham's first international featured England against Wales on January 15, 1910. England won by 11 points to 6. Since then Twickenham has undergone numerous changes and facelifts, especially behind the scenes as you'll see from our exclusive photographs over the next four pages. But it has always remained the home of the England national team and of the Union itself. Its vibrant heritage is celebrated everywhere you turn, but nowhere moreso than in the World Rugby Museum, housed within the stadium itself and packed with many priceless artefacts that brilliantly chart the sport's evolution. Twickenham is more than just a stadium. It's living, breathing rugby history.

①

④

The England changing room (*photo 1*) is laid out ready for the players before an international match. Each member of the matchday squad has his own personal plaque featuring his name fixed above his changing space. All players are given two match shirts, two match shorts, one pair of match socks, one warm-up kit featuring a T-shirt, a pair of shorts and a drill top, two bottles of water, two bottles of Powerade energy drink and three match programmes. The coaches' room (*photo 4*) is a little more spartan!

An individual player's 'cubby' (*photo 2*), in this case Jonny Wilkinson's. The corridor between the changing room and the bath and shower area (*photo 3*) also features a handy massage table. The baths (*photo 5*) were made by the London Allied Iron Foundry and were first used in 1932. When the West Stand was being redeveloped in 1995 the England squad at the time voted unanimously to keep the baths. On match days today four baths are used for ice and two for hot water, which means that showers (*photo 6*) come in handy. Doctors have just 15 minutes to get a deep cut stitched in the treatment room (*photo 7*) and the player back out on the pitch. There's no time for an anaesthetic, but adrenaline helps.

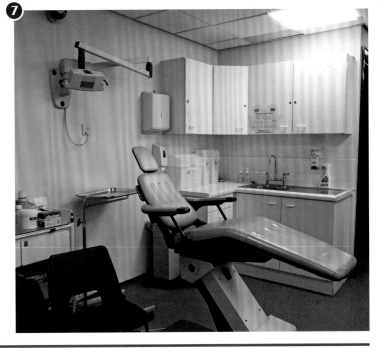

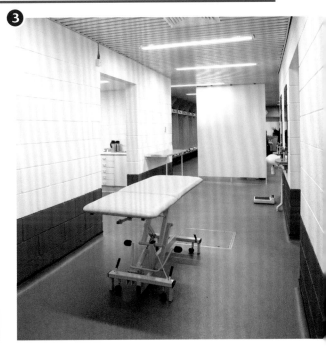

The National Fitness Centre in the bowels of the stadium (*photo 8*) is used by England players for pre-match warm-ups and post-match cool-downs, as well as for team training sessions, one-to-one fitness work and rehabilitation sessions with the coaches. There is a wide variety of fitness equipment available (*photo 10*), including free weights and cardiovascular ergometers.

Treadmills and static bikes (*photo 9*) also play an important part in maintaining fitness in training sessions and during warm-ups for matches.

ENGLAND
RUGBY

The Grunt Machine (*photo 11*) tests a player's ability to maintain leg drive, for example when carrying the ball into a tackle. Olympic lifts (*photo 12*) form a staple part of most players' training diet, all of which is designed to have athletes at maximum fitness when they walk down the famous tunnel (*photo 13*) and out onto the Twickenham pitch to represent their country.

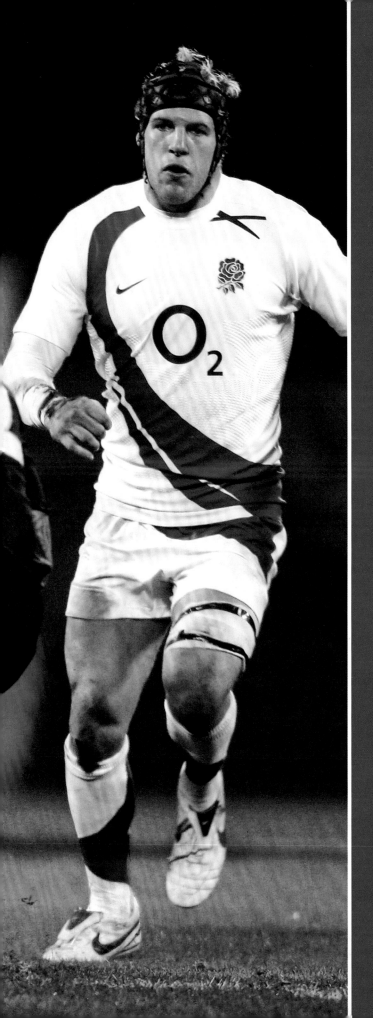

THE PLAYER

1

Rugby is a game that's become famous all over the world because of its physical demands, its ethics and its sense of sportsmanship. It's down to each and every player to stay true to this culture.

But before players can play rugby effectively and understand its joys and complexities, they must be both mentally and physically prepared to meet its challenges. From understanding the body's physical make-up, to developing strength and stamina, paying attention to diet requirements, knowing how to warm up and even getting the right kit, a rugby player needs a whole body of knowledge. But don't be intimidated. This section gives you all the advice you need to be in prime shape to play rugby.

PLAYERS' KIT

The selection of kit you see here was first introduced just before the 2007 Rugby World Cup. It helped England get to the Final.

Each England player receives everything on these pages for the autumn Investec Challenge Series, the RBS 6 Nations and the summer tour.

HOW IT HAPPENS

Sportswear manufacturer Nike have provided England's kit since 1997 and have a close relationship with both coaches and players. "We know that the opinions and views of the players and coaching staff are hugely important when it comes to putting together the right kit for everybody to perform at their best," says Nike's Sports Marketing Manager Barney Keeler. "For example, we were out with the England Saxons on their last tour testing products and looking at new designs. It's a crucial part of what we do and we take the players' comments very seriously." Once agreement is reached all of the design work is done at Nike's headquarters in Hilversum, Holland. Not everything you see on these pages is available to the public, especially the more expensive, technologically-advanced items. A range of England kit is available through the official Rugby Store at Twickenham. *www.store.rfu.com*

ENGLAND RUGBY

The equipment has a two-year life cycle. Nike have already been working on the new England kit which will first be seen in autumn 2009.

WHAT THEY GET

ITEM	QUANTITY
Presentation Warm-up Jacket	1
Warm-up Pants	2
Sideline Jacket	1
Short-Sleeved Training Jersey	2
Therma-fit	1
Long-Sleeved Training Jersey	3
Drill Top	2
Drill Pants	2
Rain Jacket	1
Training Shorts	3
Gym Shorts	2
Performance Socks	4
England Rugby Team Tee	2
Rugby Statement Tee	2
Blue Media Polo	1
White Media Polo	1
Travel Shorts	2
Hooded Fleece	1
Blue Performance Cap	1
White Performance Cap	1
Beanie Hat	2
Large Roller Bag	1
Large Duffle Grip	1
Gym Sack	1
Shoebag	1
Backpack	1

The majority of the England training kit is not stored at Twickenham, but in a warehouse in Basingstoke.

Every player in the senior England squad has his initials printed on each piece of his kit to avoid confusion.

"WHEN ENGLAND WENT TO THE RUGBY WORLD CUP IN FRANCE IN 2007 I HAD TO TAKE EIGHT TONNES OF KIT WITH ME"

DAVE TENNISON
Kit Technician

There are no medium sizes used in the senior England squad at all, but two special sizes, XLT and XXLT, are available for particularly tall players.

The England Coaching staff get similar kit to the players. The main difference is that their training kit (*below*) is grey rather than navy blue.

THE KIT MAN

England's Kit Technician Dave Tennison has spent the last six years making sure the nation's best rugby players are properly equipped to do their job. "I organise the materials needed by the senior squad, as well as all the other representative teams," he says. "It's quite a task." The senior squad alone needs 50 full sets of kit for any series of internationals. "When I give out the gear there are almost 2000 items, so making sure everyone has the right stuff is a real job." What does he do when a player comes and tells him he's lost everything? "They're pretty good as it happens – as long as they haven't moved house recently!"

PLAYER ANATOMY

BONES AND JOINTS (FRONT VIEW)

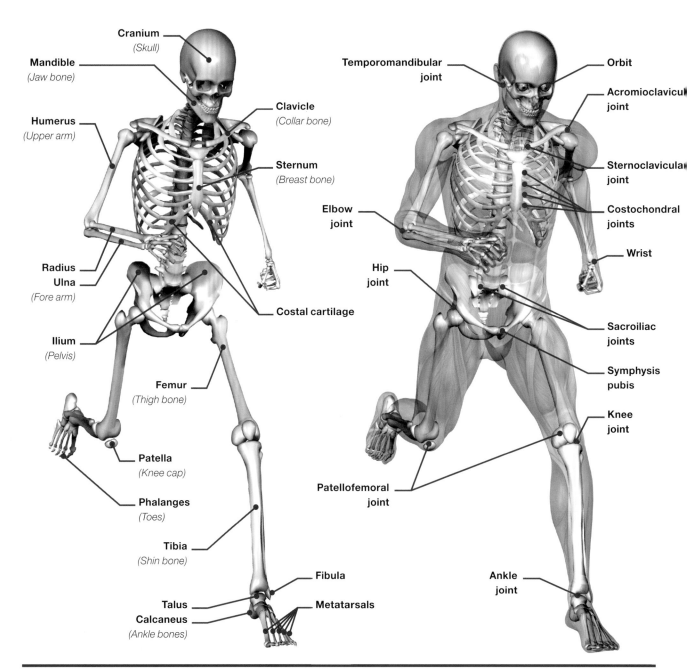

Cranium
(Skull)

Mandible
(Jaw bone)

Humerus
(Upper arm)

Clavicle
(Collar bone)

Sternum
(Breast bone)

Radius

Ulna
(Fore arm)

Ilium
(Pelvis)

Femur
(Thigh bone)

Costal cartilage

Patella
(Knee cap)

Phalanges
(Toes)

Tibia
(Shin bone)

Talus

Calcaneus
(Ankle bones)

Fibula

Metatarsals

Temporomandibular
joint

Orbit

Acromioclavicul
joint

Sternoclavicula
joint

Costochondral
joints

Wrist

Elbow
joint

Hip
joint

Sacroiliac
joints

Symphysis
pubis

Knee
joint

Patellofemoral
joint

Ankle
joint

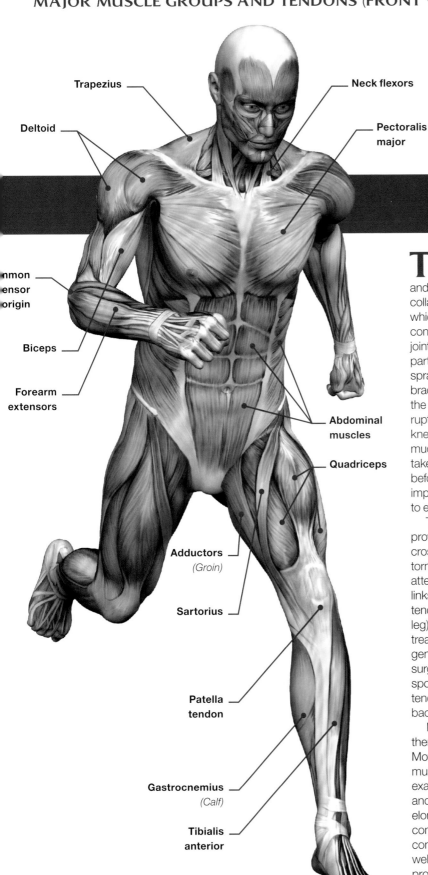

Trapezius

Neck flexors

Deltoid

Pectoralis major

Common extensor origin

Biceps

Forearm extensors

Abdominal muscles

Quadriceps

Adductors
(Groin)

Sartorius

Patella tendon

Gastrocnemius
(Calf)

Tibialis anterior

The skeleton of the human body is held together, supported and moved by the ligaments, tendons and muscles of the body. Ligaments are a type of collagen fibre, similar in make-up to the tendons, which hold the bones of the skeleton together and control the extreme (end) range of movement of all the joints. Failure of the ligament structures can be either partial or complete. A partial tear, eg a moderate ankle sprain, is usually treated with conservative measures – bracing, taping and then a controlled return to sport as the ligament tightens and heals. Total rupture, eg a rupture of the ACL (anterior cruciate ligament) in the knee, will generally require a surgical repair and a much longer graded return to exercise. ACL repairs will take a minimum of six to nine months recovery time before a player can begin rugby training again. It is important that high velocity joint sprains are checked to ensure that ligament ruptures are identified early.

Tendons attach the muscle to the bone. They often provide increased leverage for movement and may cross several joints. They can also be partially or totally torn. The effect of a tear will result in pain while attempting to use the muscle group which the tendon links to. Shoulder tendons (rotator cuff) and patella tendons (which attach the thigh muscle to the lower leg) are often affected and are slow to respond to treatment because the blood supply to tendons is generally poor. Ruptured tendons usually require surgical repair, especially in someone going back to sport, and they need a long recovery time. An Achilles tendon needs at least six months for a player to get back to fast running and directional change activities.

Muscles provide movement for the body and therefore provide force and power during activity. Movement involves the coordinated firing of many muscle groups. Some muscles act as stabilisers, for example core muscles such as abdominals, gluteal and spinal muscles. Other muscles contract or elongate to control movement. The thigh muscle contracts while the hamstring provides a counter control during running. Partial muscle tears respond well to a graduated flexibility and strengthening programme. Training muscle groups to maximise their stability and/or movement roles is an essential part of training conditioning.

> "UNDERSTANDING HOW THE HUMAN BODY'S LIGAMENTS, TENDONS AND MUSCLES WORK ALLOWS A RUGBY PHYSIOTHERAPIST TO GIVE SPECIFIC INJURY ASSESSMENT AND TREATMENT, WHICH IN TURN MINIMISES TIME OFF PLAYING"

JOY WALTER
Sports Physiotherapist

BONES AND JOINTS (REAR VIEW)

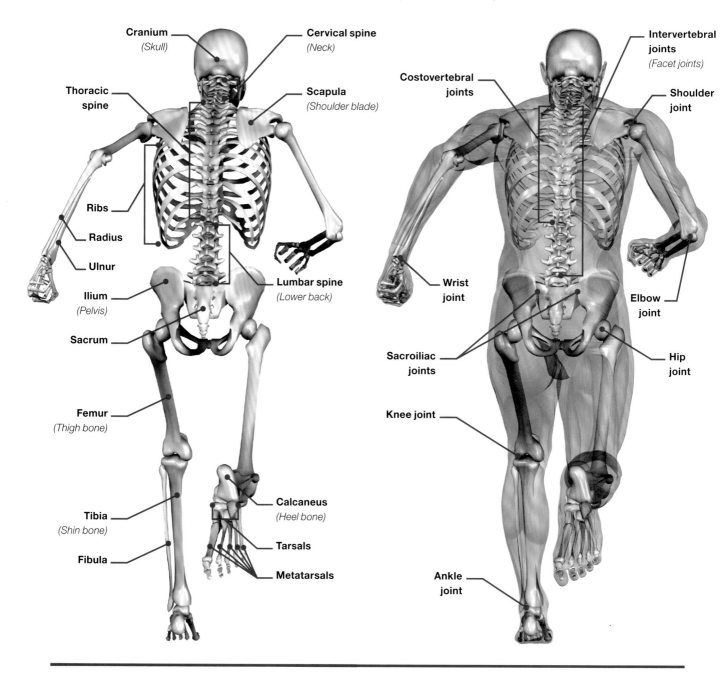

Cranium
(Skull)

Cervical spine
(Neck)

Thoracic
spine

Scapula
(Shoulder blade)

Ribs

Radius

Ulnur

Ilium
(Pelvis)

Sacrum

Femur
(Thigh bone)

Tibia
(Shin bone)

Fibula

Lumbar spine
(Lower back)

Calcaneus
(Heel bone)

Tarsals

Metatarsals

Costovertebral
joints

Intervertebral
joints
(Facet joints)

Shoulder
joint

Wrist
joint

Elbow
joint

Sacroiliac
joints

Hip
joint

Knee joint

Ankle
joint

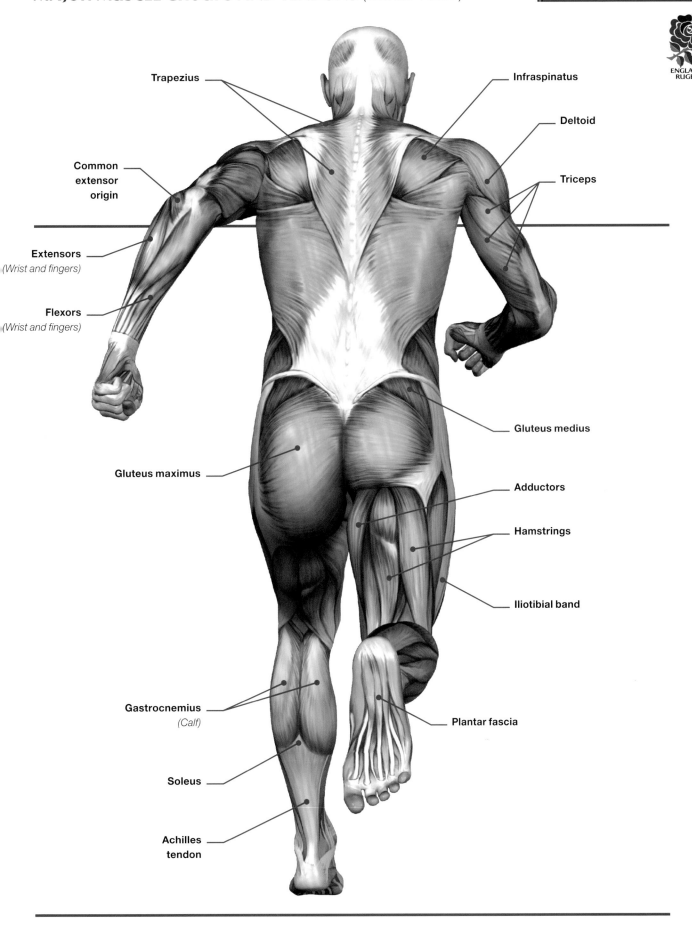

Trapezius

Infraspinatus

Deltoid

Common
extensor
origin

Triceps

Extensors
(Wrist and fingers)

Flexors
(Wrist and fingers)

Gluteus medius

Gluteus maximus

Adductors

Hamstrings

Iliotibial band

Gastrocnemius
(Calf)

Soleus

Plantar fascia

Achilles
tendon

THE PLAYER
HEALTH AND SAFETY

Health and safety compliance applies just as much to rugby as to any work environment and necessitates thorough planning for rugby training and games by the coach, the player and any support personnel. Players and coaches are familiar with the need to plan for tactics, skills acquisition and the physical/mental fitness to meet the challenges of training sessions and games. However, the preparation to ensure player and pitch safety can be overlooked. The preparation for any training and game has to have safety strategies defined and responsibility taken by the coach and players to ensure they are implemented.

The coach must consider players' safety as being a priority when planning. If the coach has the slightest doubt as to the safety of any aspect of a session he must halt or abandon the activity and seek advice from a more qualified person. This action must not be regarded as a sign of weakness or inexperience, but as good judgement and a chance for the coach and players to improve their level of knowledge as part of their development and understand more fully their role within the game.

Players and coaches should take personal responsibility for their own safety and the safety of others in their preparation before and during training and the game. Checking must be carried out to ensure that equipment to be used is in good repair, the pitch is safe (no debris or glass, goal posts protected etc), that there is an adequate supply of clean, fresh drinking water together with suitable drinking containers, a first

Left: Players must ensure they are physically ready and conditioned to train

Below: Coaches should always help players in all areas of health and safety

can increase the risk of exacerbating the problem. Players should ensure that they are physically ready and conditioned to train.

Training sessions need to be well planned for content and duration. Sessions lasting longer than 1.75 hours are more likely to result in player injury. Training planning also needs to recognise that player fatigue can contribute to match injuries so the coach must ensure that enough work is done in training to allow the players to cope with the physical demands of a full match. Post-training and post-match recovery strategies should also be agreed for the player.

The evidence of the benefit of using some items of protective clothing has not been proven. Scrum caps, while protecting the head and ears from cuts and light contusions, may not help prevent the more serious injuries resulting from direct or indirect trauma, for example concussion. But shin pads can provide good protection from a direct blow. If a player decides to use protective clothing it must adhere to IRB regulation standards in size, construction and material. Contact suits can be used by more experienced players for warm-up drills involving contact and in contact training to allow for simulation of real game situations.

aid kit that's correctly stocked and available and that there's access to a telephone in the case of severe injury, together with a list of all relevant emergency numbers. Coaches should have a plan for dealing with emergencies and members of the squad should be familiar with their support roles within this plan.

Players and their coach must know their physical limitations in order to train safely and coaches must respect the decision of a player to withdraw from training if the player feels he has sustained an injury or has aggravated an existing problem. It's not unusual for players to try to train through an injury and while progressive exposure to higher levels of training under professional guidance is acceptable, continuing to try to train through an injury without the correct guidance

POWER, STRENGTH, SPEED

A good rugby player will become better if he is more powerful, faster, stronger and able to reproduce work efforts throughout the game. Rarely in a match will there be a time when only one aspect of fitness is used. A 40 metre sprint may be followed by a tackle that requires strength and power, or a scrummage that requires static strength may have to be reset three or four times, requiring the ability to reproduce work. Training must reflect these demands of the game, so not only do the individual fitness components have to be addressed, but also how they work in conjunction with each other.

Having a balanced training approach can also help prevent training injuries that ultimately limit playing time. Warming up and cooling down are essential, as are exercising in different planes of movement, at different speeds and with different loads. Fitness adaptation is very specific, so only doing one exercise at one speed will make you good at doing just that.

Most aspects of fitness such as endurance, speed, flexibility, agility, muscular endurance and power can be developed without the use of equipment. However, a plateau may be reached that use of equipment can surmount as this can provide a mental and physical stimulus which promotes change and adaptation. Equipment in itself does not make a player fitter. Instead the principles of progression, overload and specificity should be applied to all your training sessions.

Two areas that are best developed with the use of equipment are strength and hypertrophy (increase of mass). Here weights such as dumbbells, barbells, medicine balls and asymmetrical objects such as sandbags or any heavy object can be used.

Young players can benefit from lifting weights, provided the weights are always kept light and that the correct technique for lifting is both taught and supervised. Young players should try to use as much variety of exercise in the gym as possible. Dumbbells are good because they promote symmetrical gains between the left and right sides of the body. Pushing, pulling, squatting and rotating exercises that use one arm or two arms and combinations of the four movements should be used. Great strength gains, however, will not be seen until puberty and as hormones change. Once players start to mature, lifting weights can help to increase both strength and power. It can also help with hypertrophy, using weights to make the body grow by placing it under load for more repetitions with short recovery periods.

Where lifting weights is concerned, however, understanding and teaching how to lift without damaging the body is absolutely crucial.

To develop speed players need to learn how to sprint effectively. This means working on acceleration, deceleration, changing pace, running on a curve and changing direction off either foot. By varying the rest time and distance of the runs, the emphasis of the session changes from pure speed to speed endurance. More rest allows for greater recovery and higher quality. Less rest means that the player learns how to run fast when fatigued.

Agility and suppleness are crucial for any rugby player if he wants to avoid opposition tacklers, create attacking opportunities and minimise the potential for injury. The body needs to be as lithe as possible. Obstacle courses, including slalom runs through cones,

To avoid opposition tacklers players must be agile and supple

AGILITY AND FLEXIBILITY

help to improve balance and allow a player to change pace and direction more easily. Progression can be achieved by changing the angles of the cones or shortening the distance between the poles so that the player has to make sharper and faster turns. Introducing passing, catching and evasion of opposition players will allow the drill to become game specific once the basic movement patterns have been established.

Rugby agility also requires a player to move up and down from the floor and around on the floor, so this should be trained too.

Integrating all the fitness aspects together makes training more fun. Once the basic skills have been taught, progression can be made by introducing a ball, opposition and tactical decisions. Changing the drill by allowing more or less space, more or less opposition and shorter or longer work periods changes the work and allows the players to develop different aspects of their fitness.

Lifting weights can benefit a player, but only when correct technique is used and supervised

ENGLAND
RUGBY

THE PLAYER
THE ENERGY SYSTEM

Rugby requires the ability to perform repeated efforts of both maximal and sub maximal work. Rest periods are built into the game, with scrummages, lineouts, penalties and injuries all providing opportunities to recover. The ability to produce high intensity work, recover and then repeat high intensity work is crucial and training needs to reflect this.

Forwards tend to work harder than backs with a work to rest ratio of 1:1.5 compared to 1:2.9. Total distance covered in the match is around 6–7km. Training can be split into two broad areas: sub maximal work is conducted as part of preparation and recovery; maximal work with repeated efforts can more accurately reflect the patterns of the game.

Sub maximal work primarily uses the aerobic energy system. This means that the body can utilise oxygen more efficiently to break down fuel within the body and provide energy to the muscles. Aerobic exercise is generally performed at an average level of intensity for a reasonable period of time, which helps rugby players develop endurance, an essential part of a player's fitness armoury. Regular aerobic exercise strengthens the heart muscle to improve its pumping efficiency and also helps to strengthen the muscles that help with breathing so air can be taken in and expelled more efficiently. It also helps to improve blood circulation efficiency and increases the number of red blood cells, which help transport oxygen. The increased storage of energy-giving carbohydrates allows for greater endurance and helps muscles to recover from exercise more quickly. A player's 'aerobic capacity' is defined as the maximum amount of oxygen the body can use during a period of exercise. The higher the aerobic capacity, the better the level of aerobic fitness.

Maximal effort work primarily uses the anaerobic energy systems. The body doesn't have the time to use oxygen efficiently so breaks down fuel more quickly. But this also produces more waste products and can't be maintained indefinitely. Anaerobic fitness is used to help produce better performance in activities that are high in intensity and short in terms of time expended. It's easy to see how this is a necessary ability that is complementary to aerobic fitness when playing rugby. An excellent all-round player needs to be able to keep going for a full 80 minutes and be capable of making a full-blooded,

high-intensity tackle at any point in the game.

There is no clear dividing line of effort or time that separates aerobic and anaerobic work, as both are generally used together, especially in rugby where the work is intermittent in both duration and intensity. High intensity work with repeated efforts develops both the anaerobic and aerobic energy systems. Low intensity work helps develop the aerobic system but has little or no effect on the anaerobic system.

Submaximal training can incorporate skill development and also non-specific movement patterns such as cycling and rowing. This may consist of repeated efforts of 5–10 minutes of work with 2–3 minutes rest or skill-based activity.

Maximal training can use rugby-related activities such as small sided games, down and ups, scrummaging or tackling drills against the clock and repeated sprints. The length of the interval can vary from 10 seconds to 120 seconds, the rest should increase accordingly. The movements involved can be team-related or position-specific. It is important to vary the duration and intensity of the sessions each week so that the body is continually adapting.

Left: **A great rugby player needs to keep going for a full 80 minutes**

Below: **The duration and intensity of a session needs to vary so the body adapts continually**

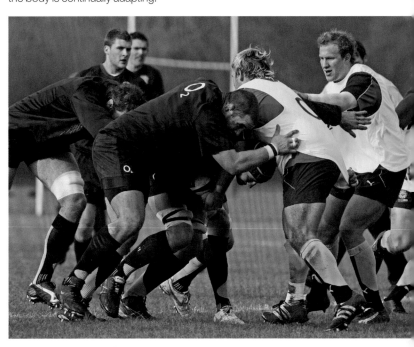

DIET AND NUTRITION

The old adage 'you are what you eat' has never been truer in modern sport. The ability to train hard and perform well doesn't happen by chance and having a good nutritional balance helps your body repair and refuel between training sessions and matches. Eating healthy foods in the right quantity at the right time will help you recover more quickly between sessions and also allow you to perform at higher intensities for longer.

There is no magic food that will allow you to perform better; instead a varied diet that consists of as much fresh, unprocessed food as possible is better than eating too much of any one food stuff. Your diet should be affordable, sustainable and suitable to your needs.

Rugby players' diets may differ from the normal

population in two main areas: volume of food and timing of the intake. If you're playing and training regularly then in order to maintain your current body weight you will need to eat more food than the average person. Eating fewer calories than you expend will result in weight loss, eating more calories than you expend will result in weight gain. Small changes that are able to be maintained will result in longer-lasting changes to body composition rather than drastic short term actions.

Fluid intake will also have to be increased both throughout the day and also during longer training sessions. A rough guide is to drink two litres of fluid a day plus one litre for every hour of exercise taken. This changes for every individual and also depends on the

ENGLAND
RUGBY

Left: Phil Vickery knows
that a varied diet of fresh,
unprocessed food is best

Below: There should
always be water available

Dairy – low fat varieties of milk, cheese, yoghurts.
Protein – beans, fish, poultry, soy, tofu, eggs.

Processed foods tend to have more sodium and preservatives in them than fresh foods. This can lead to excess fluid retention and a decrease in the quality of the nutrients in the food. Whilst convenient in the short term, they are detrimental in the long term.

Timing of the intake of food is important. It should be spread throughout the day to avoid spikes in blood sugar levels that will then lead to dips that make players feel tired and lethargic. Foods such as porridge, brown rice, apples and wholegrain bread have a Low Glycemic Index, which means that food is converted into glucose more slowly and over a longer period of time. These types of food should make up the bulk of your diet.

An exception to the timing of food intake may be immediately prior to training, during training and within 15 minutes after finishing training, as energy is then required as soon as possible. Foods such as rice cakes, watermelon, cornflakes and white rice have high a High Glycemic Index, which means that the food is converted into glucose more quickly.

Post training, a meal that contains both carbohydrate and protein has been shown to restore fuel in the body quickly and allow more work to be done the next day. Examples could be baked beans on toast, a jacket potato with broccoli and tuna, or a wholegrain banana sandwich.

climate and type of exercise being undertaken. Urine colour should always be a pale yellow or clear colour, darker than this or infrequent urination indicates dehydration. It is important to get used to taking fluid in training before you try to do so in matches.

VARIETY OF DIET

Include food from these groups:
Grains, bread and cereals – multigrain, wheat, oat and high fibre. Pasta – wholewheat.
Rice – brown, wild and basmati.
Vegetables – different colours and groups including cabbage, broccoli, cauliflower, carrots, tomatoes, green leafy vegetables.
Fruits – berries, citrus, apples, pears, bananas, melon.

Stretching is an
important part of both
the warm-up and the
cool-down

THE PLAYER
WARM-UP AND COOL-DOWN

In order to improve performance training needs to introduce stress to the body which will in turn adapt with the correct rest. Warming up with a set of physical activities helps the body to gradually adapt from a resting state to a state of readiness to train or play. By warming up properly a player can raise muscle temperature and increase blood flow to muscles and connective tissue and so reduce the chances of injury to the soft tissue. It also raises the heart, metabolic and respiratory rates, all of which are helpful in preparing the body for work.

Warm-ups need to vary slightly depending on whether they're taking place before a match or before a training session. In a match it's possible that players will need to work at maximum capacity from the start of the game. The warm-up therefore, needs to include a period of high intensity work for a short period. Muscle temperature can fall back to resting levels about 15 minutes after exercise has stopped and this should be taken into account when warming up pre-match. Additionally, special consideration must be given to substitutes' needs, particularly with regard to making sure they warm up throughout the match to avoid becoming cold and suffering muscle temperature drop.

Of course, because coaches can regulate the work done in a training session the warm-up can be less intense.

Warming up should start with general movement patterns such as jogging, skipping, lunging and squatting. Then either the range of movement should increase or the intensity or speed of the movements. Following this the specific movement patterns of the position should take place, such as getting up from the tackle or catching and passing the ball whilst running. As the warm-up progresses so should the specificity of the activity, so that by the end you're performing movements at match pace.

Dynamic stretching can form part of a rugby warm-up, where the stretching movements mimic the training elements a player is about to perform. Start with low intensity movements and gradually increase the speed and range, while remaining balanced and in control at all times. It's important only to simulate movements that will be needed during the game or session.

During intense rugby activity the body needs to produce energy quickly. Unfortunately the process of doing this also produces waste products. These products will stay in a player's muscles if he simply stops at the end of a training session or a match. The best known of these waste products is lactic acid. Light activity can help remove these waste products from the body so the body can recover more quickly. 5–10 minutes of movement at 50% of maximal effort has been shown to reduce lactate levels considerably. This period can be followed by 5–10 minutes of static stretching. This would consist of holding a stretch to the point of mild discomfort for between 10 and 30 seconds. Key areas to stretch may be the back and shoulders, hamstrings and groin, though some time should be allowed for individuals to work on their own specific areas.

Hot/cold contrast showers are also effective in removing waste products, so having 30 seconds of hot water followed by 30 seconds of cold water and repeating this three times will help recovery.

At some point during the cool-down fluid and fuel should be made available and this can be consumed in between each activity.

Remaining balanced and in control at all times is vital in the warm-up

THE PLAYER

INJURIES

Rugby is a collision sport, so injuries may occur. However, the chances of being injured can be reduced if a player has good all-round fitness, specific positional fitness and sound rugby technique.

It's essential that each club should appoint someone with relevant experience to be responsible for the management of player injuries. Records should be kept of all pre-training/pre-match injury assessments, treatments and tapings as well as any injuries assessed during and after training and/or playing. Post-training/match injuries should be reassessed and treatment and advice given on managing the injury. Information on injuries assessed by sport injury therapists/medical practitioners can only be given to coaches with specific player consent. Coaches who knowingly override the

advice given to players with regard to injuries take responsibility if the player is further injured.

Muscular injuries and contusions are the most common injuries, but knee ligament injuries and shoulder dislocations generally result in longer recovery times, so players are unavailable to train or play for longer.

Ligament injuries can be graded for severity and the amount of time needed before a player can return can be between four and 12 weeks if the ligament has not been completely ruptured. If surgical repair of the ligament is necessary a return to play could be between six and nine months later. As with soft tissue injuries, ice, compression and rest should form part of the immediate care. As a general rule massage, heat, alcohol and exercise of the injured area should be avoided, as these

Rugby is a collision sport, so injuries may happen

Records should be kept of all treatments and tapings

will most likely cause an increase in bleeding and swelling. With severe swelling and pain further advice should be sought as soon as possible.

Dislocations and partial dislocations (subluxations) are most likely to be of the shoulders or fingers. Shoulder dislocations are often caused by tackling with the outstretched arm. Immediate care following a dislocation should be through immobilisation and ice being applied if there is no sensation loss or circulatory compromise. Reducing a dislocation should not generally be attempted at the time of injury unless by an appropriately qualified practitioner. A dislocation of any joint, even finger joints if reduced at the time, should be referred for further assessment and an X-Ray as bone injuries are a common complication.

Injury recovery should include specific exercise programmes to restore strength and soft tissue flexibility around the injured area, range of movement of the joint, co-ordination, control and balance. A well-constructed rehabilitation programme should include all these elements, as well as maintaining general and rugby-specific fitness. Therefore a return to training and playing following an injury should be a progressive process, making sure that a player has completed the range of skills and fitness needed at each level of his recovery before increasing his participation.

Concussion can occur when there is a trauma to the brain. Trauma can be either direct or indirect. Concussion can and often does occur without loss of consciousness. If a player has lost consciousness in a contact situation he will be concussed and must be removed from the pitch. Even if there is only a suspicion that a player is concussed he should be removed from the pitch at once and medically assessed at the first available opportunity. It is important that players as well as coaches recognise the signs of concussion as player safety has to be paramount when these signs are observed. Signs of concussion can include loss of consciousness/impaired conscious state, poor coordination or balance, concussive convulsion/impact seizure, gait unsteadiness/loss of balance, vomiting, being slow to answer questions or follow directions, being easily distracted/poor concentration, displaying unusual or inappropriate emotions, vacant stare/glassy eyes, slurred speech, personality changes, inappropriate playing behaviour or significantly decreased playing ability. A player should not be allowed to return to play in the current game or practice. He should be monitored for possible deterioration and should not be left alone. As the player should continue to be monitored for the next 24 hours he and a nominated carer should be given verbal and written head injury instruction. Loss of consciousness for more than five minutes or signs of concussion lasting more than 30 minutes should always be referred to a hospital Accident and Emergency unit, as should any child with a concussive injury.

The International Rugby Board (IRB) has regulated that a player who has suffered a concussion cannot train or play for a minimum of three weeks afterwards and must have a medical practitioner give the player clearance to play. The player must also be symptom-free with each progressive increase in exercise before increasing training volume.

Spinal injuries are a rare occurrence, but it is essential to assume that a spinal injury has occurred when a player is unconscious and appropriate care must begin. Any player with a suspected spinal injury must not be moved on or from the pitch until trained personnel are present. An appropriate stretcher (spinal board) and neck immobiliser are used and it needs at least five people and appropriate instructions to complete the move from pitch to the stretcher. The only exception to this rule would be if other life-saving intervention were necessary. Coaches, managers and/or volunteers could be trained to assist if suitably qualified medical and paramedical people are regularly present at the pitchside.

REST AND RECUPERATION

It's an easy mistake to make and thousands of dedicated rugby players do so. But forgetting the importance of rest, sleep and relaxation as part of a complete rugby programme will inevitably result in a decrease in performance. In the rush to increase their physical capabilities players often neglect the fact that physical fitness is hugely dependent on the right amount of sleep. This is because sleep is the most basic source of a human being's recuperative power.

During sleep the body's immune system goes to work, human growth hormone is secreted, antioxidants work to repair DNA that's been damaged, testosterone is secreted and protein synthesis happens. In short, the body heals itself.

An average person needs eight hours sleep a night, but that figure varies greatly from person to person. If you can wake up in the morning feeling lively and full of energy, then the chances are you will have found your optimum sleep requirement. Then it's simply a case of getting that amount of sleep consistently. If you don't get enough sleep you'll feel tired, your levels of endurance will drop and your reflexes will be slower.

There are a number of ways to improve your chances of restful sleep. Caffeine-based drinks interfere with the process, but so does alcohol. Even though alcohol might help you fall asleep at first, it will disturb your sleep patterns later in the night. Eating too much just before sleep will also have a negative effect, as will eating too little. But certain

ENGLAND
RUGBY

Left: Finding time to relax
is important if you want to
perform at your best

Below: Resting properly
the day before a game is
a must

then lying still in a quiet room, or maybe listening to relaxing music can also help you take a break.

As well as sleep, the ability to relax is also very important in order to perform well on the rugby pitch. Reading or listening to music can help players to switch off from their daily rugby routines and England stars such as Jonny Wilkinson and Toby Flood even take guitars with them everywhere. They find playing instruments allows them to switch off mentally from rugby for a while. Keeping the mind fresh is a vital ingredient for any good rugby performance.

Players need to be particularly conscious of the need to rest up the day before a game. It's a mistake to train hard or play another sport energetically in those crucial 24 hours. Rest and sleep will do more to help a player perform at their peak at this point than any amount of extra work.

Sleep and relaxation really do go hand in hand in helping the body to heal and the mind to prepare for the tough, physical demands and the real mental intensity of rugby.

foods which are rich in magnesium – beans, wholegrain breads, nuts, lentils and green vegetables, for example – will help induce sleep more easily.

It may seem obvious, but the bed you sleep in must also be comfortable. Find the mattress and the pillows that you are most at ease with. You may have to try a few before you find some that really suit. Keep the room you sleep in well-ventilated, quiet and cool.

It's always a good idea to wind down before you hit the hay. Try to be completely relaxed for the last hour and a half of the day. Just as your body needs rest to repair, so does your mind. Indeed sleep may be more important for mental recovery than physical. An afternoon nap can help concentration on difficult tasks later in the day. If you find it difficult to sleep,

THE POSITIONS 2

One of the greatest joys of rugby is that there's a position on the field for everybody, regardless of shape or size. But whether you're a nippy wing or a giant lock, an elusive centre or an immovable prop, each position will demand fitness, skill and strength. This section will help you learn the differences – both major and subtle – between each position in a rugby side and give you the 'how to play' secrets and tips of England's top stars that will help you excel in your chosen role. Plus discover the greatest ever England stars in each and every position.

FIELD OF PLAY

THE POSITIONS

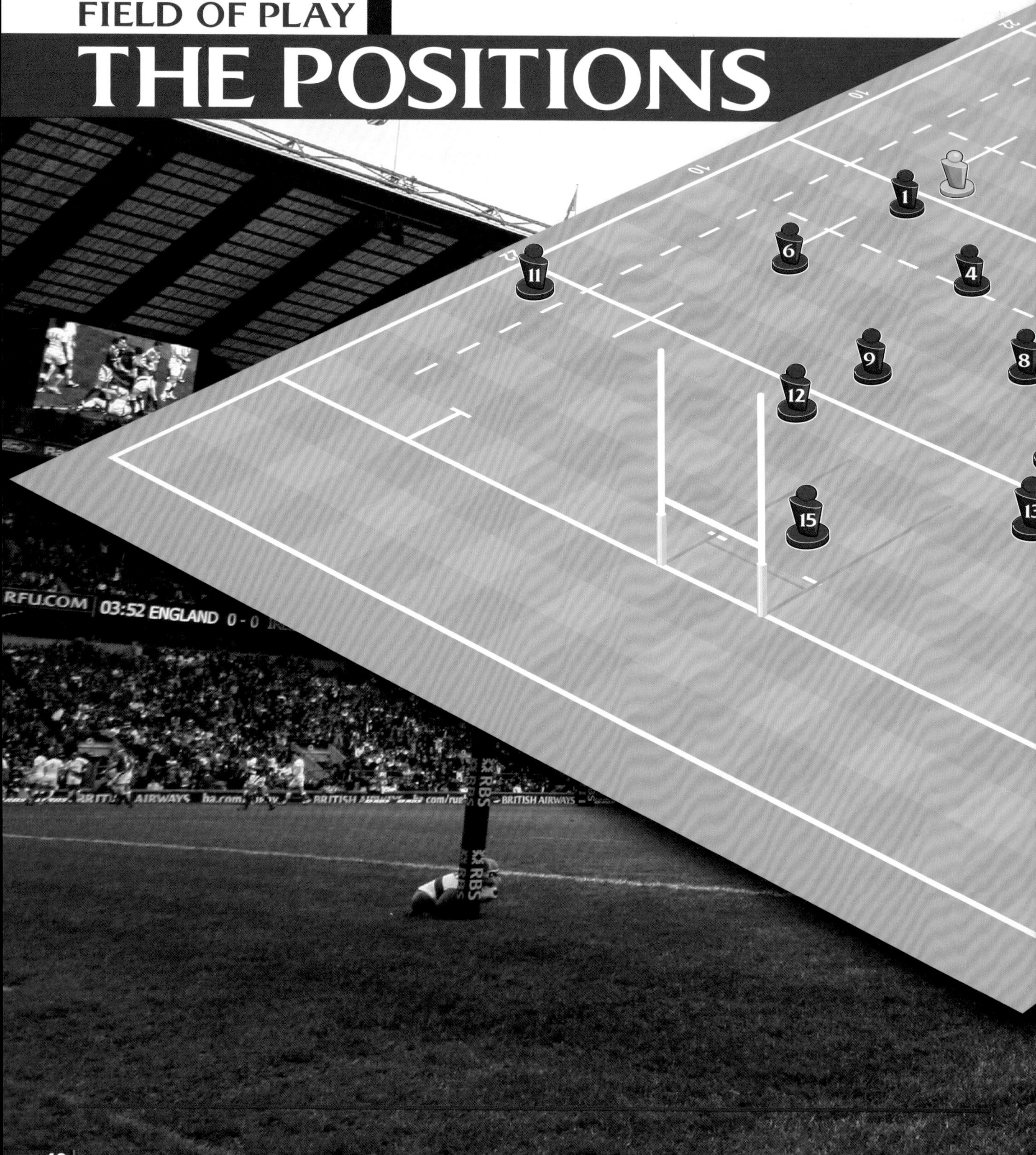

ENGLAND
RUGBY

1 **LOOSE-HEAD PROP**
Aggressive yet technically skilled

2 **HOOKER**
The director of the scrum

3 **TIGHT-HEAD PROP**
The scrum's anchor man

4 **LOCK**
Excellent lineout technician

5 **LOCK**
Good agility and aerial skills

6 **BLIND-SIDE FLANKER**
A tough defender

7 **OPEN-SIDE FLANKER**
The link between forwards and backs

8 **NUMBER 8**
Maintains forward momentum in play

9 **SCRUM HALF**
At the centre of everything

10 **FLY-HALF**
The key decision maker

11 **LEFT WING**
Good communicator in defence

12 **INSIDE CENTRE**
Link man who sets the tempo

13 **OUTSIDE CENTRE**
Has power as a strike runner

14 **RIGHT WING**
Genuine pace and evasion skills

15 **FULL-BACK**
Can deal with any type of kick

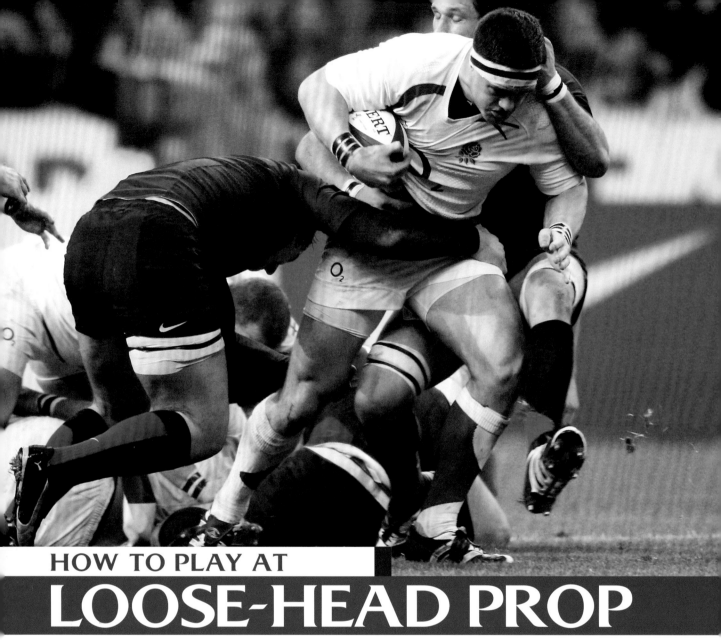

HOW TO PLAY AT
LOOSE-HEAD PROP

Andrew Sheridan is a classic loosehead. He's extremely strong in the neck, shoulders, upper body and legs

The loose-head prop forward wears the number 1, plays in the front row and packs down on the left-hand side of the scrum. Because players engage to the left of the opposition the loosehead will position his head outside that of the opposing prop, hence the name. He is the first to join the hooker in assembling the scrum.

Like their propping partner on the opposite side, the primary role of the loosehead is to support the hooker in the scrum and provide power when the scrum pushes forward. They should also be able to support or lift a jumper in the lineout to prevent the opposition winning the ball.

In order to scrummage effectively a prop must be extremely strong in the neck, shoulders, upper body and legs and must relish one-to-one contact. In the scrum the loosehead must be stable under pressure to make sure his own pack doesn't move backwards. Plus he must support his hooker by holding up his direct opponent. This allows the hooker to both see and strike the ball. The loosehead must resist pressure from the opposition and

be able to position himself in such a manner that the ball can go to the back of the scrum from the hooker's strike.

The moment of engagement with the opposition is crucial for the loosehead. The referee's instructions – crouch, touch, pause, engage – allow the props to prepare for the moment of contact. It's vital for the loosehead to work in harmony with the hooker to put pressure on the opposition tighthead in order to turn the scrum into an attacking weapon and drive the opposition back. Props also need to work to direct the movement of the scrum, moving side to side to prevent the other team from 'wheeling' (moving the scrum through 90 degrees) and forcing another 'put in' from the opposing side.

To achieve all these goals the loosehead must be extremely aggressive, yet technically skilled. The scrum is where much of rugby's mental battle is fought, because the team that dominates the scrum tends to dominate the match. Front row players have a unique role in this area. Because they must face their opposite number head-on they have to win a highly personal battle that requires a unique combination of physical and mental strength. Yet they must also work in unison with the rest of the pack so the group can deliver the maximum amount of power. If a member of the pack – and especially a member of the front row – pushes too early it creates an imbalance and the scrum won't function. To this end it's vital for the loosehead to make sure his weight is ready to move on the referee's call to engage and that feet are perfectly positioned parallel to the goal line, slightly more than shoulder width apart. The feet shouldn't move from this starting position until the scrum advances and even then feet shouldn't be lifted more than an inch off the ground as it shuffles forward.

While looseheads clearly come into their own in the scrum, the modern game demands greater all-round rugby ability than ever before. In the lineout the loosehead's role is to bind as closely to the catcher as possible so as not to leave a hole, to support the jumper at the top of the leap and to bind and drive to protect the ball in the follow-up. In open play props now need to get to the breakdown quickly in order to secure the ball for their side. This requires a loosehead to add speed, mobility and stamina to basic strength. The days of props making their contribution in the scrum alone are long gone. They now need to handle the ball, make quality passes and tackle effectively.

"YOU MUST HAVE GOOD PHYSICAL STRENGTH IN THE NECK, THE LOWER BACK AND THE LEGS. YOU HAVE TO MAKE SURE WHEN YOU ENGAGE IN THE SCRUM THAT YOU'RE IN THE STRONGEST POSSIBLE POSITION TECHNICALLY TO USE YOUR POWER. AND YOU NEED TO REALLY RELISH THE PHYSICAL CONFRONTATION"

ANDREW SHERIDAN

IN A NUTSHELL

- An attacking scrummager who dominates the opposition

- Must be flexible, agile and strong in lineout lifting and blocking

- Needs good core skills, game understanding and running fitness to contribute efficiently and effectively in rucks, mauls and broken play

- Offers strong driving and close quarter handling to be a dynamic ball-carrying option

The primary role of a loosehead like Tim Payne here is to support the hooker and provide power in the scrum

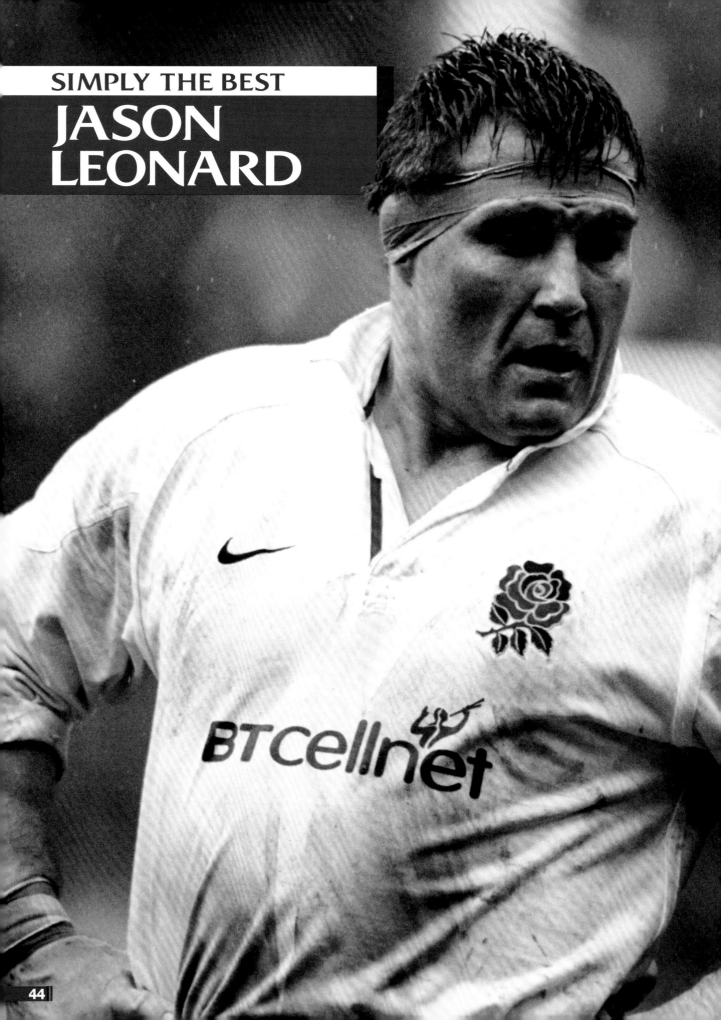

ENGLAND RUGBY

"WHO'S PROVED HIMSELF ON THE WORLD'S STAGE MORE THAN JASON? HE SEEMED TO GET FITTER WITH TIME AND HIS PRESENCE AND REPUTATION WERE ENOUGH TO INTIMIDATE ANY OPPONENT"

JERRY GUSCOTT
Legendary former England centre and BBC rugby commentator

It's not for nothing that Jason Leonard – or 'The Fun Bus' to his rugby mates on account of both his bulk and his ability to enjoy himself – holds the record for being the most capped England player of all time. His fully-committed front row performances in the famous white shirt throughout the 1990s made Jase a firm favourite with players and supporters alike. But it wasn't just his passion for the game and his love of the camaraderie that went with it that made Leonard such an indispensable figure. Jason's skill in being able to prop effectively on both sides of the scrum, of settling and focusing whatever pack he happened to be part of, together with his unlimited enthusiasm for going toe to toe and nose to nose with whoever the opposition might put in front of him, simply epitomised England's bulldog, never say die spirit. Whenever and wherever Leonard was on the field, everyone knew that England wouldn't go down without an almighty fight.

Born in Barking, Essex, on August 14, 1968, Jason grew up in an area that wasn't rugby-literate and didn't even start playing the game until the relatively late age of 10. "I was the first one in my family to get involved, though my brothers did play after me," he says. After taking both the plunge and his first serious steps in the sport at Barking Rugby Club, Jason moved first to Saracens, then to Harlequins, when the game was still amateur. His talents were quickly noticed and he made his full England début against Argentina in July 1990. Incredibly, Jason missed just one game for his country in the following five years and began collecting international championships with astonishing regularity. Eight Triple Crowns, seven Five and Six Nations Championships and four Grand Slams were won over the course of a career that ran to a massive 114 appearances for England and five British Lions caps. But Leonard is typically self-effacing about his achievements.

"I've not given the title of 'England's Most Capped

Player' much thought," he explains. "I've had people stopping me in the street cheering and clapping. But I tell my son they're all cheering for England."

Leonard's genius as a rugby player lay in the abilities he possessed, of course. There were very few who got the better of him when two packs engaged. And despite not being the most mobile of props, he had an uncanny and happy knack of always being there wherever the breakdown happened, working away at the coalface. Undoubtedly, though, what also contributed to his status as one of England's best-loved characters was his ability to embrace the dedication and commitment required of top players once the game went professional in 1995, while still retaining the sense of fun and sportsmanship that was so revered in rugby during the amateur era. His love of a post match drink was well-known, mainly because Jason did nothing to hide it. Yet during England's successful 2003 World Cup campaign, when his contribution was mainly made from the bench, Leonard was the only player of the entire 31-man squad not to miss a single day's training either during the tournament or the three months of preparation beforehand. He puts it all down to his absolute love of the game.

"Respect for my team mates, for the opposition and for the referee was always a big part of the sport for me. You never saw rugby players having a go at the ref or rolling around clutching their legs. That attitude really appealed to me and made me love the game all the more."

Jason announced his retirement from international rugby at the end of the 2004 Six Nations and soon afterwards stepped away from playing altogether, though he was back in the rugby firmament in the summer of 2006 when he was appointed to the RFU council. Wise move. A big man like Jason Leonard still has a huge contribution to make to the game.

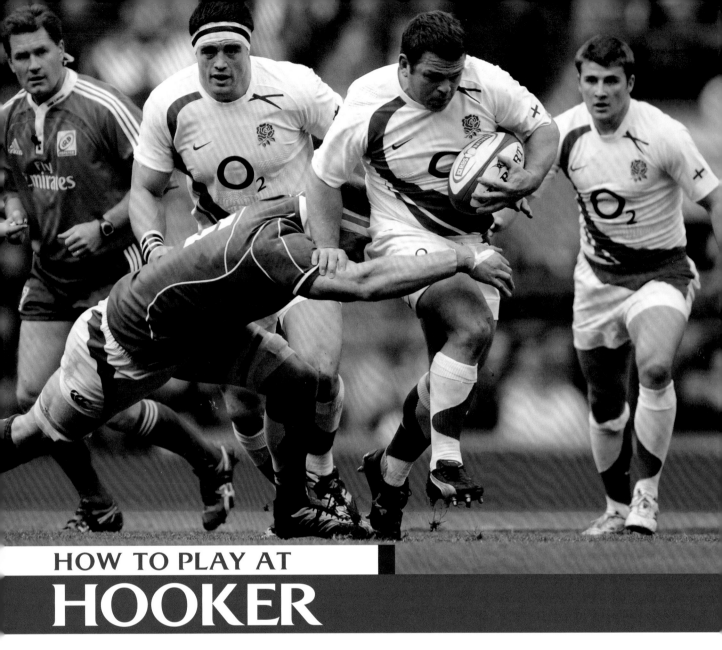

HOW TO PLAY AT
HOOKER

Hookers like Lee Mears need to be dynamic in open play and effective ball carriers

The role of hooker is one of the most demanding on the rugby pitch because of the variety of different skills a player needs to master. A hooker must co-ordinate the scrum and direct it, because it's their responsibility to strike at the ball – or 'hook' – when it's put in by the scrum half. They also need to dictate how the lineout unfolds by throwing the ball in from the sidelines to restart the game. Both roles are crucial to the success of a team, because the scrum and lineout are primary sources of possession.

Achieving an accurate throw takes constant practice so it becomes second nature. Whether the throw is pleasing on the eye is immaterial, so while many young hookers spend a lot of time trying to spiral the ball, the most important element is always to make sure the ball arrives safely and efficiently into the hands of the intended team mate in the lineout. If the hooker throws the ball end over end and it always reaches its target, then there's no problem. The development of a spiral throw will, however, allow the ball to be thrown a longer distance if required.

The hooker has a choice of where to throw the ball in

the lineout. Coded calls between the hooker and the jumpers indicate where the ball will be thrown and the hooker must deliver a precise throw every time. A throw to the front must be delivered as the jumper is getting into the air, to the middle just after they start jumping and at the back directly on the first movement. To deliver the ball effectively requires split-second timing. Practice used to involve simply grabbing a bag of balls and throwing them at a post, but the modern hooker spends time looking at his technique, how best to hold the ball and how to work on the core of his body to develop the necessary strength, power and control.

Because hookers aren't bound into the lineout they also have to be very aware of how play unfolds once the ball is delivered. They have to be alive to any loose ball that might appear after a deflection and be ready either to pounce on it themselves or offer protection to the half back if he's gathered the ball. When defending against an opposition lineout a hooker must mark the opposition hooker closely and always look to find an unimpeded line to the opposition's ball if it's deflected.

It's the hooker who leads the scrum into contact. The position requires concentration, bravery and technique. The way a hooker binds onto team mates and the position of the feet are essentials to work on. Hookers bind onto their props, usually by putting their arms over the shoulders and under the armpits and pull them in to ensure they act as a solid unit. One foot should rest slightly in front of the other and the player should be on his toes ready to hit, like a sprint start, in order to deliver explosive power at the engagement. In order to be able to hook effectively the hooker needs to develop an almost telepathic understanding with his scrum half so he knows where and when the ball will be put in. Then they must strike the ball – usually with the right foot – and propel it through the loose-head prop's legs at the right pace and in the right direction. The hooker must also put pressure on his direct opponent when it's the opposition's put in by driving on them or striking for the ball if they think they can reach it, in what is known as 'a strike against the head'.

As with all forwards the hooker must be dynamic in open play, be able to carry the ball effectively and use his power to provide 'go forward' in attacking positions. It's often the hooker who will have the responsibility of breaking the opposition's defensive line near the try line to go over for a score.

ENGLAND RUGBY

"ALWAYS THINK ABOUT THE NEXT PLAY. IF YOU'VE MADE A BAD THROW GET IT OUT OF YOUR HEAD AT ONCE AND FOCUS ON THE NEXT LINEOUT"

DAVID PAICE

IN A NUTSHELL

- ■ Must be an attacking scrummager with a clean strike of ball
- ■ Has an excellent and consistent throw over a variety of distances under pressure
- ■ A genuine footballer with a range of passing/ offloading skills and both game understanding and running fitness to employ their skill
- ■ Needs strong driving and close quarter handling ability to be a dynamic ball-carrying option
- ■ Is good over the ball at the tackle and has the ability to act as a second open side
- ■ Can defend the short side and midfield

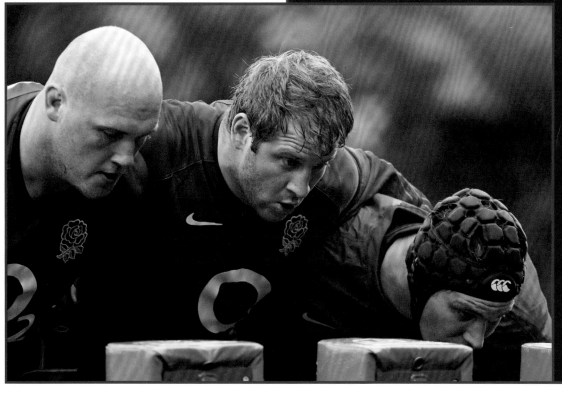

A good hooker like David Paice directs and coordinates the scrum

PETER WHEELER

ENGLAND
RUGBY

"A TOP PLAYER. PETER COULD THROW THE BALL AT A SIXPENCE, HE STUCK WELL AND WAS VERY MOBILE AROUND THE PITCH"

BILL BEAUMONT

Legendary former England captain and IRB vice chairman

England have been blessed with plenty of rumbustious hookers over the years. Brian 'The Pitbull' Moore. John Pullin. Steve Thompson. Rugby names to conjure with and just three of a number of proud Englishmen who've relished going into combat on the field to defend the country's good name. But of all the great 'never take a backward step' hookers to have worn the famous white shirt, many believe Peter Wheeler to be the finest of them all.

Wheeler didn't look the biggest or the most fearsome front row competitor on the international stage, but appearances can be deceiving. The Leicester Tigers man was tough as teak, as hard as nails and was always ready to stand his ground in the white heat of front row battle. Given that he possessed the irresistible combination of nigh on faultless technique coupled with perfectly controlled aggression, it comes as some surprise that London-born Wheeler only won his first cap in 1975, despite having already been selected for the England tour of the Far East four years previously, as well as receiving a call-up as a replacement for the 1974 British Lions tour to South Africa.

Perhaps he was ahead of his time. Wheeler's natural instinct was to be an all-round footballer rather than simply a brute at the engagement and a steady-as-she-goes lineout thrower. His work in the loose was as impressive as it was unusual for a player wearing the number 2 shirt. But with the game moving on and quickening up things were changing. And once he'd made the leap from squad player to full international Wheeler never looked back. Between 1975 and his last international appearance in 1984 he was a permanent fixture in the England starting line-up, notching up 41 appearances. Not only was he an England favourite but he won an impressive seven British Lions caps to boot.

Incredibly competitive by nature, Wheeler took immense pleasure in imposing himself on the

pitch. His delight at being an integral member of England's first Five Nations Grand Slam-winning team in 23 years in 1980 was obvious to all. But his combative nature – the very force of his game on the field – often brought him into conflict with the game's administrators. Always a strong advocate of the idea that it should be the players as well as rugby's authorities who should have a big say in the development of the game ongoing, Wheeler's outspoken views were not to everyone's taste. Indeed, some believe it was this that prevented him from being appointed England captain until very late in his career. No matter, when he finally got the

chance to lead the country a week shy of his 35th birthday in November of 1983, Wheeler grabbed it with both hands. An inspirational captain, he roused his troops to inflict the first English defeat on the All Blacks since back in 1975. The end of a ten season international career was just around the corner, however. After completing the 1984 Five Nations championship as first choice hooker, Wheeler then asked not to be considered for the forthcoming tour to South Africa and never played for his country again, bringing down the curtain on what was a truly illustrious international career.

This was far from the end of Peter Wheeler's involvement in rugby, though. After hanging up his boots at Leicester in 1985, having captained the club to one league title and three successive John Player Cup Final victories, Wheeler then entered the world of business. Fortunately for the world of rugby, however, he returned to the Tigers as Chief Executive in 1996 becoming a hugely influential figure in an area where he'd once been seen as something of a thorn in the side. Indeed, Peter Wheeler has been instrumental in helping build the club game in England and in working towards restructuring English rugby to the benefit of all.

HOW TO PLAY AT
TIGHT-HEAD PROP

Modern tightheads like Matt Stevens must have excellent energy levels to cope with the massive amounts of work they need to get through

While there are a certain number of players who have been able to operate on both sides of the scrum – Jason Leonard is perhaps the best-known Englishman to do so – nevertheless the challenge of playing tighthead is considerably different to playing at loosehead. The tight-head prop is the scrum's anchorman and leads the attack on the opposition's scrum. The role is primarily destructive on the opposition throw into the scrum. It's for this reason that tight-head props tend to be a little bit taller than looseheads, while remaining extremely well-built, solid and difficult to move.

The objective within the scrum is for front row players to beat their opponents into the best position in which to drive their opposite number back. The tighthead can maximise efficiency in this area by adopting a starting position where the feet are parallel to the goal line and the shoulders are in a square-on position.

The moment of engagement is the single most important time for a prop to gain the upper hand over their opposite number. Raw strength in both the neck and the shoulder areas will give a player a natural advantage at that moment of impact. But a player must add excellent technique to power to become an outstanding performer.

As with the loosehead, a tight-head prop's ability to achieve this goal of personal dominance on engagement depends equally on his ability to scrummage in harmony with the rest of the forwards as it does on his own technique and strength. If there's no cohesion between the prop and the lock and flanker directly behind them then the scrum won't function effectively as maximum power cannot be achieved without perfect cohesion.

While the skills required of a loose-head prop are different to those of a tighthead when it comes to scrummaging, prop responsibilities in the other

ENGLAND
RUGBY

areas of the game – in the loose, at the breakdown, at restarts and at lineouts – are very similar. An effective prop must have all-round aerobic capacity in order to be able to make first-up tackles at restarts, or to push with maximum force at a scrum, then be able to sprint to the next ruck or to make two or three high-intensity tackles in quick succession. The traditional prop was required to have density and bulk to give him power and stability in the scrum, but the modern prop must also be athletic and mobile. That's why this role has become increasingly both more varied and more demanding.

"SIMPLY BELIEVE THAT NOTHING IS EVER A LOST CAUSE"

JASON HOBSON

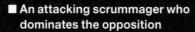

IN A NUTSHELL

- ■ An attacking scrummager who dominates the opposition
- ■ Is flexible, agile and strong at lineout lifting and blocking
- ■ Has good core skills, game understanding and running fitness to contribute efficiently and effectively in rucks, mauls and broken play and to be an enforcer
- ■ Offers strong driving and close-quarter handling to be a dynamic ball-carrying option
- ■ Needs to handle the ball, make quality passes and tackle effectively

It's vital for a tighthead like Jason Hobson to work on beating his opponents into the best position at the scrum to drive them back

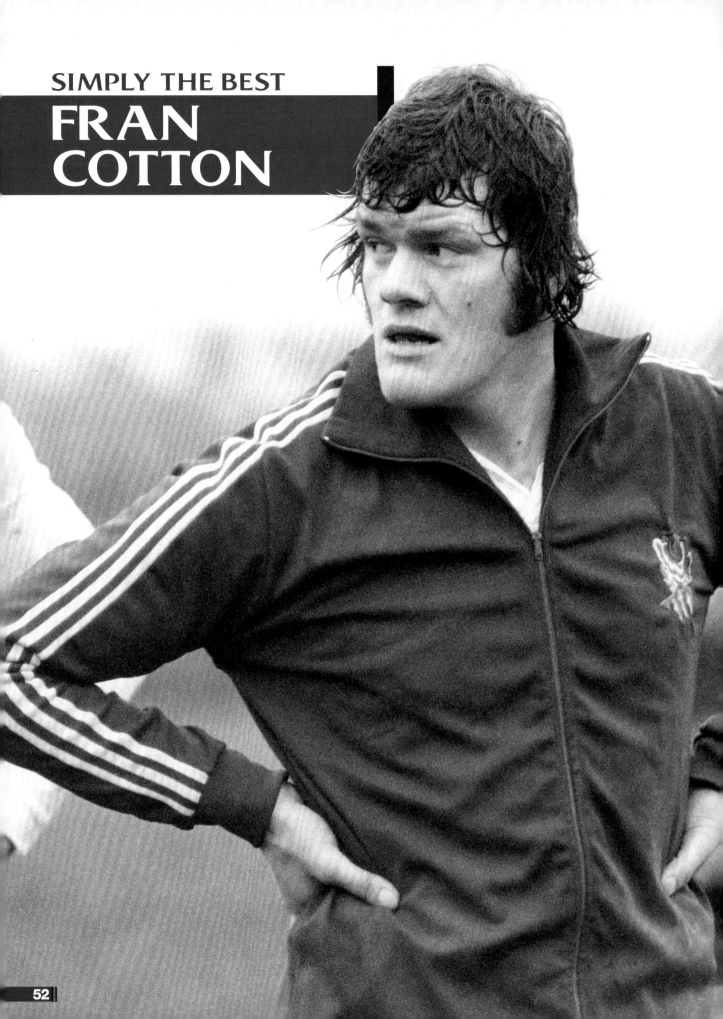

ENGLAND
RUGBY

> ## "I DON'T THINK WE'VE EVER SEEN FRAN'S EQUAL. HE COULD PROP BOTH SIDES AND FRANNY HAD GREAT HANDS TOO. I ALWAYS SAID HE WAS A FLY HALF IN A FAT MAN'S BODY!"

STEVE SMITH

Former England scrum half and Fran Cotton's business partner

While Fran Cotton looked every inch the traditional prop – the word 'craggy' simply didn't do justice to a heavy-jawed, weather-thrashed head that looked like it was hewn out of pure granite – there was far more to this giant of the front row than met the eye. In an era when rugby's amateur status meant natural ability got you a long, long way and diet and fitness regimes were eyed with suspicion, Cotton was truly ahead of his time. This Lancastrian son of a rugby league player – who found union fame with Coventry and Sale – had quickly decided that truly making the most of your talents required hard work and dedication. From the earliest days Cotton set about adding to what God had given him by relentlessly seeking to improve both the physical and the technical side of his game. Such a dedicated approach paid off. Not only was Cotton soon to establish himself as one of the toughest competitors in international rugby, but he also garnered a reputation as one of the most adroit. The number of front rowers who could truly perform with equal aplomb on both sides of the scrum can be counted on one hand. Cotton was one of them and for many was the best ever at both loose-head and tight-head prop.

Despite making his England debut while still a student at Loughbrough University in the RFU's centenary year of 1971 – an inauspicious 26–6 defeat against Scotland – it wasn't until two years later, in the Five Nations tournament of 1973, that Fran truly established himself in the England set-up. Here he played in all four matches and also featured in the England side that recorded a stunning and memorable 16–10 victory against New Zealand in Auckland that same year.

Despite England's poor showing in the following year's Five Nations where they finished bottom of the table, Fran's huge-hearted performances were rewarded with a place in the British Lions squad to tour South Africa, where he snaffled the tighthead spot for all four tests on a memorably successful tour. Besides the rugby and the entirely uncompromising Lions attitude on the field of play, Cotton himself wryly remembers the tour for other reasons too. "The British government at the time decreed that there would be no contact between the British Embassy and the team. You can imagine how distraught the boys were at missing those God-awful cocktail parties," he said. Despite this reluctance to play politics, though, Cotton was made England captain. But his tenure wasn't a successful one. His side lost all three games in the 1975 Five Nations before Cotton was injured and replaced by Tony Neary.

So despite being universally recognised as a giant of the world game, it was starting to look more and more likely that Fran was destined never to win honours wearing the white of his beloved England. All that changed in 1980, fortunately, when England finally came good and waltzed off with a Five Nations Grand Slam under the captaincy of Bill Beaumont. Cotton finally had some silverware to show for his inspired efforts wearing the red rose.

Buoyed by this new-found success, Fran confidently headed off to South Africa for his third consecutive Lions tour, but without playing a test he was diagnosed with a heart condition and his tour was curtailed as a precautionary measure. A nagging hamstring injury suffered in the first international of the 1981 season ended Fran's England career too. But his performances in amassing 31 caps – often in difficult circumstances for the national team – were never forgotten either by fans or players. The intelligence Fran showed on the pitch was mirrored later in life when he went on to develop a vibrant sportswear manufacturing business with his former England colleague Steve Smith, while also managing an enormously successful British Lions tour of South Africa in 1997.

HOW TO PLAY AT
LOCK

Locks like Steve Borthwick are key receivers in the lineout and need excellent jumping skills

The lock is a key ball winner in many areas of the field and a specialist both in the lineout and at restarts. But a lock is also a crucial component of the scrum. Locks provide the power that energises the scrum and so have to work closely with the props to produce the most effective drive possible. It's also their responsibility to ensure that the scrum remains stable – as the name suggests they 'lock' the unit – and it's for these reasons that they're often known as the scrum's 'engine room'.

To be able to both jump effectively in the lineout and provide 'go forward' in the scrum locks have to be tall, strong and athletic. They are often the tallest players on the pitch and are amongst the strongest, adding an extra dynamic to their team as strong ball carriers, able to punch holes in defences around the ruck and maul. This means the best locks are comfortable running with the ball in hand.

When a scrum is formed a lock needs sound scrummaging technique and perfect synchronicity with the rest of the pack. This can be achieved by developing a strong bind through the prop's legs and onto the waistband of the shorts, thereby pulling the prop onto the lock's own shoulder. The two locks must also bind together, around the body and onto the top of the shorts, so that they pull each other's hips close together and have a flat back ready to drive. To bind correctly locks often find it easiest to kneel down on one knee before binding onto the prop, although some players simply start off in what for them is a comfortable position and the props and hooker then let the lock in.

In the lineout the locks tend to be the key receivers, which means an ability to jump from a stationary position – as well as while moving both forwards and backwards – is absolutely essential. Practice is vital for all three methods of jumping, leading with both right and left foot. Once a player can spring effectively they have to be able to catch the ball in a variety of positions while in the air; one-handed, two-handed, in front of where they're jumping or arching backwards to take a lobbed ball. The added difficulty is that the opposition will also be competing for the ball themselves and so strength in the arms as well as the upper body is essential in order to resist the opposing locks. Being able to distribute the ball cleanly and accurately once it's been secured is also a prerequisite.

A successful lineout depends on the locks having all of these core skills honed to perfection, but it also demands split-second timing between all of the members of the group and a total understanding of pre-worked calls which allow the team to know where the hooker will aim to throw the ball without the opposition understanding.

The complete lock also needs to be able to catch the ball from his own side's restart kicks, as well as the opponent's. To be able to do this successfully requires aggressive chasing and absolute confidence in securing the high ball as early as possible. There are two ways of doing this; either by catching the ball cleanly and as high as possible, then moving forward into contact, or by catching and playing the ball back towards fellow players.

When defending a lock has to make his physical presence count by making big hits all over the field, particularly around the fringes, meaning he needs to display a voracious appetite for work and be prepared to cover huge amounts of ground despite his large frame.

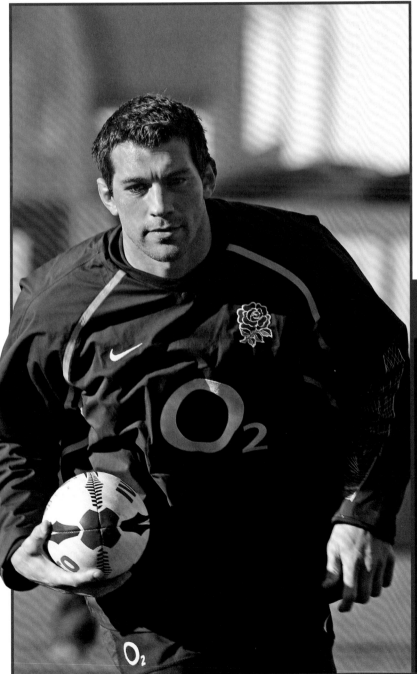

> ## "SPEAK TO MORE EXPERIENCED PLAYERS IN YOUR POSITION AS MUCH AS YOU CAN TO LEARN ALL OF THEIR SECRETS"
>
> ### NICK KENNEDY

IN A NUTSHELL

- Needs to be an excellent lineout technician and practitioner
- Has good agility and aerial skills for restarts
- Should be a rangy runner with solid core skills to contribute efficiently and effectively in ruck/maul situations and in broken play
- Shows good distribution and support skills
- Is both a powerful and strong scrummager

The best locks have a voracious appetite for work, as Nick Kennedy proves

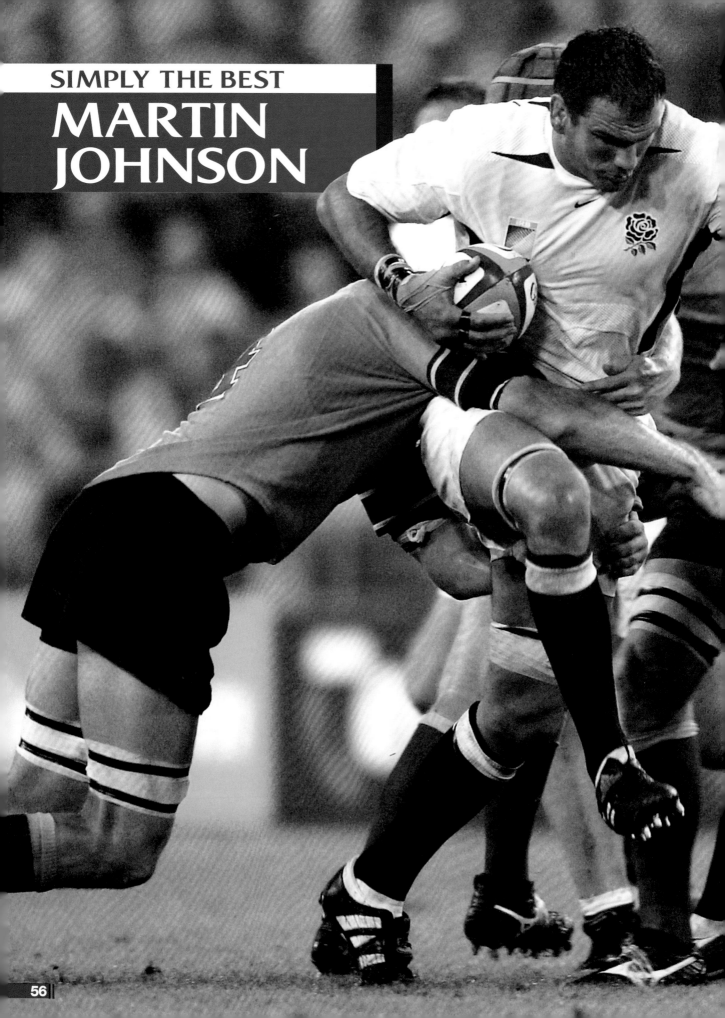

ENGLAND
RUGBY

"HE WAS THE STANDOUT PLAYER OF HIS ERA AND I DON'T THINK THERE ARE ANY PLAYERS OF THE LAST 20 TO 30 YEARS WHO CAN MATCH THE THINGS HE'S DONE"

TREVOR WOODMAN
England Rugby World Cup winner and fellow forward

Has anyone ever had a bad word to say about Martin Osborne Johnson? International opponents who've had to go eyeball to eyeball with him in the white heat of forward battle, no doubt. And they probably still carry the bruises to remember him by, too. But no single English rugby player has ever been so universally acknowledged as 'Simply The Best' in quite the way Johno has. A daunting 6' 7", 18st 9lb frame meant you could hardly ignore Johnson on a rugby field, yet his genius lay not in the flash and spectacular, but in performing the basics exceptionally well and exceptionally consistently. His work in the lineout and scrum was exemplary and the engine he possessed to haul his immense frame the length and breadth of the pitch was a thing of wonder. But what made Johnson more than simply an outstanding player and to many the greatest English rugby player who ever lived was his mental strength. Here was a man who never knew when he was beaten, who would lead his troops into battle safe in the knowledge that he would never ask a thing of them that he wasn't prepared to do himself. His physical presence was allied to a granite-hard mental approach that often seemed to force the opposition to buckle under nothing more than the strength of Johnson's will. No wonder. His mother Hilary was a tough cookie herself, both mentally and physically. She took part in 100km 'ultra distance' races for England and reckoned, according to Martin, "that if you couldn't run a marathon then you weren't fit." Her absolute focus and absolute determination rubbed off on her son.

"He had immense presence on the field at all times," said former England captain John Spencer. "He was a captain who led by example on the pitch rather than with a load of fancy rhetoric off it," claimed erstwhile England full back and RFU Coach Jon Callard. "He was simply a world class player," confirmed former England skipper Nigel Melville. "It's

absolutely impossible to sum up his contribution to England in just a few lines," enthused fellow World Cup winner Will Greenwood. We could fill up an entire book with eulogies, but that wouldn't be Johnson's style. Talking himself up isn't his thing. He'd much rather laugh about his less than lightning pace and his paltry return of just two international tries. And he'd get more pleasure out of discussing football trivia concerning his beloved Liverpool FC. But the statistics don't lie. An international career spanning 11 years, 84 England caps with 39 appearances as captain, eight appearances with the British Lions, six as skipper, five Six Nations victories including one Grand Slam, five league titles with his one and only club side Leicester Tigers and two Heineken Cups. And then there was the small matter of Rugby World Cup 2003, where Johnson led his England side to an incredible triumph with the same hard-headed pragmatism and unshakeable belief that victory really could be won that had served him so magnificently throughout this illustrious career.

"He'd say something to us. Maybe just one line," explained England's hero of the final against Australia Jonny Wilkinson. "It might be about the opposition, or us, or the occasion or the game plan. But it was always right and always so aggressive and ruthless. To see your captain like that made you think 'God, am I glad he's on my side'." Seeing Johnson leading out his troops often made England supporters think that it was actually God himself who was on their side. Given what Martin Johnson achieved in the white shirt of England, you'd have to say it was an easy mistake to make. No wonder, then, that England again turned to their mighty leader in 2008 when Johnson was appointed the country's Team Manager, a wide-ranging role that sees him in full control of our senior rugby sides. It's a position many believe is tailor-made for the man.

HOW TO PLAY AT
BLIND-SIDE FLANKER

Intelligence and brute strength are required from blind-side flankers like James Haskell to punch holes in the opposition's defensive line

While the blind-side flanker shares many of the same roles and responsibilities as the open-side flanker on the opposite side of the scrum, there are still fundamental differences in the ways the two players perform.

The blind-side flanker is primarily a defensive player on the blind side of the scrum – which will vary depending on the position of the scrum – with responsibility for cleaning out rucks when required and shutting down the opposition Number 8 or scrum half. Because his sphere of operation is more limited than that of the openside, and because his defence must be first rate, the blindside is often the more physically solid of the two flankers. He may have less electric pace, but his presence on the field will be more rugged and intimidatory.

If there's one player who will form the bedrock of the three back row positions then it will most likely be the blind-side flanker. He

needs to be a destructively-minded player who actively enjoys patrolling the advantage line, making sure that the opposition has little or no opportunity to cross it. A good blind-side flanker also needs to relish physical confrontation and must enjoy smashing opponents backwards.

But as the game has developed, so has the blindside's offensive role. Nowadays he must be comfortable carrying the ball all the way to the opposing defensive line and have the combination of intelligence and brute strength that will allow him to punch a hole in it and force his way through. In the modern game coaches often look to their mobile back row forwards to break through opposing defensive curtains, where this was once the job of the fly half and the two centres. Given that the blind-side flanker is a powerful ball carrier he is often able to draw two defensive players, thereby leaving

ENGLAND
RUGBY

holes elsewhere on the pitch that can be exploited by team mates.

The blindside must always be alive to the opposition's attacking options once the ball moves away from the scrum. The first segment of the pitch between the opposing scrum half and the fly half is the openside's responsibility, so the blindside must avoid the temptation to move across the field too early and wait until the chances of a move back infield have receded. A quality blindside will also have good defensive judgment. He must know instinctively when to cover behind the backs

and give himself more time to read the upcoming play or when he should attack the ball early to snuff out an opponent's forward momentum or try to win turnover ball. The former strategy is a greater risk, because if he doesn't manage to secure the ball the flanker is eliminated from play.

Any flanker, be it blindside or openside, must understand the other's role and be able to complement it. The blindside player is perhaps more of a workhorse than the openside, but both flankers need strength, speed, heart, courage and an instinct to be at the very heart of the action to be effective.

> "THE GAME IS GETTING FASTER. MAKE SURE YOU'RE FIT ENOUGH TO KEEP UP WITHOUT LOSING THE ABILITY TO HAVE AN IMPACT IN CLOSE PLAY"
>
> **CHRIS JONES**

IN A NUTSHELL

- Has a physical presence in the loose with strong driving and ball-carrying ability, coupled with strength over the ball
- Must combine good aerial skills and lifting/blocking ability at lineouts
- Will be a tough defender
- Has good distribution and support skills
- Needs good game understanding to be effective in wide, centre field and close quarter channels

A good blindside such as Chris Jones has the instinct to be at the very heart of the action

"THE FIRST NAME DOWN ON THE ENGLAND TEAM SHEET FOR MANY YEARS. HE JUST GOT ON WITH WHAT NEEDED TO BE DONE WITHOUT ANY FUSS OR BOTHER"

WILL GREENWOOD

England Rugby World Cup winner and Sky Sports rugby pundit

Not to be confused with the English international scrum half of the same name, this Richard Hill formed one third of the legendary back row – together with Neil Back and Lawrence Dallaglio – that formed the base of England's 2003 World Cup-winning pack.

His fellow internationals took enormous pleasure in telling the world that Hilly's biggest rugby attribute was being blessed with a skull that was significantly thicker than average! But Hill had far more to offer than a bash-proof bonce. His work on the blind side may have gone almost unnoticed to the casual rugby fan, but those who really know the game have never been in any doubt about the massive contribution he made to every team he played for.

Born in Surrey in 1973, 'Hilly' took his first steps in the game at Bishop Wordsworth's School in Salisbury, then at the town's rugby club, before Saracens recognised his potential and signed him in 1993. Four years later he was called up by England for the 1997 Five Nations tournament, making his début at openside against Scotland – ironically at the expense of Neil Back, who at the time was considered too small to play at international level. By November of the same year, however, Clive Woodward was England Head Coach and things were about to change. Woodward was a Back fan and moved Hill to the blindside to accommodate him. Lawrence Dallaglio took the No. 8 shirt and it quickly became apparent that England had found a back row combination capable of competing with the very best in the world. So it proved, when England went on to become World Champions in 2003. Injured during the very first game of the World Cup tournament against Georgia, it was no coincidence that England didn't truly click into gear until Hill was pronounced fit for the semi-final meeting with France and turned in a performance worthy of his status as a 'silent assassin' – despite an uncharacteristic error which allowed the French in for their only try of the game – to secure

a place in the final. Hill's calm, unflappable nature meant his reputation as an unsung hero suited him perfectly. Not that he would necessarily agree.

"I didn't call myself an unsung hero," he said. "I got the recognition that was warranted." Sadly for such a talented player the four years following the World Cup victory were blighted by injury, including an 18 month stint out of the game after two separate knee injuries. That he was able to come back and play high-level rugby at all is a remarkable tribute to the man's iron will and there's no doubt that England missed Hill's scavenging know-how and steadying influence during this period. Nobody would have been hurt more by the national side's problems at this time than Hill himself. Given his nature it's easy to see why.

"I hate failure," he said. "I don't like making mistakes and I particularly don't like making mistakes that affect the rest of the team. People think that only positive things should motivate you. But fear of failure's worked for me." And how. Three consecutive British Lions tours, a World Cup winner's medal and more than 70 appearances for England bear testimony to a career that is rich in highlights. Had Hill not been so desperately unlucky with injury it's perfectly possible that he would have passed the 100 cap mark, especially given his hard-wired mental strength.

"You don't rest on your laurels," he explained. "You've always got to be looking at your game to see where you can improve, talking to the coaches to see what amendments you can make." Of course, no player is without fault, but at the height of his powers Hill came as close to back row perfection as anybody. So it was with great sadness that English rugby fans said goodbye to Richard at the end of the 2007/08 season when he finally listened to his body and decided that the time was right to call it quits. No player could have possibly given more.

HOW TO PLAY AT
OPEN-SIDE FLANKER

Lewis Moody displays the kind of raw courage that's essential if you want to be a top-class openside

Flankers, as the name suggests, form part of the three-man back row of forwards, flanking the Number 8 on either side of the pitch. The openside flanker and his opposite partner, the blindside, act as an essential link in ensuring his team's play maintains forward momentum. The openside's primary function is to be first to the ball at the breakdown, always looking to secure possession and turn rucks and mauls into continuity play. Defensively he must be extremely aggressive, prepared to tackle himself to a standstill and have the necessary physical presence not only to hold up opposition play, but to win back possession for his own side. Given the fact that he has a larger amount of the pitch to monitor, the openside is often the quicker of the two flankers. Raw courage and speed of both body and thought are essential to fill this role effectively.

The openside flanker has an important role to play in all phases of the game. In open offensive play an openside needs to be comfortable with the ball in hand. He has to be able to make good decisions quickly, deciding whether to pick and go, send a pass, look to protect the ball by going over it or clear opposition players away. The ability to retain the ball is paramount in this role and opensides must possess a wide array of skills to achieve this, going to ground to protect the ball or staying on their feet to keep the attack going.

When defending the open-side flanker has to pressure the opposition inside backs and stop attacks with exceptional tackling. His aim is to disrupt possession by either stealing the ball on contact, stepping over the ball and driving off opponents if it's grounded, or by actually picking the ball up.

In addition to needing this wide variety of skills, the flanker also plays an important role at the lineout. Here, too, his tasks are many and varied. Given the amount of tackling he's expected to contribute during a game, it's reasonable to assume that the openside will be the faster of the two flankers, though this is not a hard and fast rule. At the lineout, then, the blindside will often be required to help support or lift the jumper, while the open-side flanker stands at the back of the lineout to support the attack and to sweep up. During a defensive lineout the flanker who's positioned at the back will look to put pressure on the opposition backs.

The open-side flanker plays a crucial role when defending at set plays. At the lineout his primary responsibility must be to tackle any opposing player coming around the end of the lineout and to try to drive them backwards or in towards the touchline. But if the opposition has moved the ball out to the backs quickly the openside must make sure there's no hole to exploit between the back of his lineout and the fly half. If the ball comes back inside, the openside will be in a position to make a tackle.

At scrum time, on engagement, he must both push and add stability to the pack. If it's an attacking scrum and the ball is being put in on his side, then the openside should be helping to control it if necessary once it's been struck by the hooker. He must watch the ball all the way through the scrum, be able to protect the scrum half as he decides what to do and then explode off the scrum himself once the ball is out to be the first away to support play. When defending at a scrum the openside must play a full part in the eight-man drive and be up quickly to defend once the ball is played.

Openside flankers need to be prepared to do the dirty work at the bottom of rucks and mauls, which means they often operate on the very edge of the law. The fact that they're so heavily involved around the ball throughout a game also means they'll be playing the game right under the referee's nose. That means excellent technique to avoid committing fouls is essential, along with a good understanding of the laws pertaining to the tackle and breakdown area.

> ## "GATHER AS MUCH EXPERIENCE AS YOU CAN, EVEN ABOUT POSITIONS THAT ARE NOT YOUR OWN. THAT WAY YOU CAN LEARN THE GAME INSIDE AND OUT"
>
> ### WILL SKINNER

IN A NUTSHELL

- An excellent defender with very good defensive knowledge and communication skills to lead the defence

- Has the ability to get over the ball on the floor in both attack and defence

- An intelligent link player between forwards and backs with excellent support skills

- Offers a good understanding of where to play after the first tackle area in attack

Quality opensides must be every bit as comfortable with the ball in hand as Will Skinner

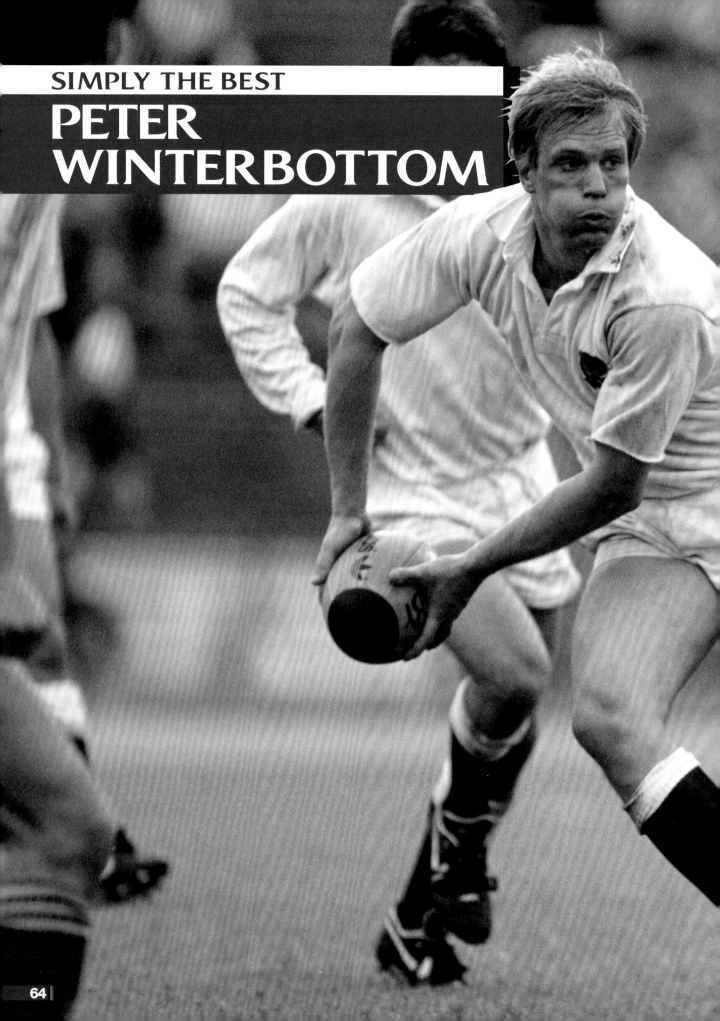

PETER WINTERBOTTOM

ENGLAND
RUGBY

"PETER PROVED HIS WORTH TIME AND AGAIN. HE WAS PLAYING JUST AS WELL AT THE END OF HIS CAREER AS HE WAS WHEN HE STARTED. AN AWESOME PLAYER AND THE HARDEST TACKLER I CAN EVER RECALL"

MIKE TEAGUE

Former back row team-mate and fellow Grand Slammer

There was every chance that Peter Winterbottom's international rugby career could have been eclipsed before it had even started. After all, the 21 year old had the misfortune to make his full England debut – against Australia at Twickenham – on the same January day in 1982 when the exceedingly buxom Erica Roe performed her famous streak. Not that Winterbottom had the slightest idea what was happening, though.

"Bill Beaumont was giving us the half time captain's talk," he recalls. "I noticed someone in a gorilla suit coming on from the other end and was looking at him, so I never even caught a glimpse of Erica."

Despite such headline-hogging competition Yorkshire-born Winterbottom did at least make enough of an impression to go on to become a hugely-respected forward amongst his fellow professionals. He collected an impressive 58 caps for England and cemented his standing as one of the most outstanding open-side flankers of all time. And all this despite having started his career at Number 8.

Winterbottom's reputation was made because he encapsulated the essential characteristics of the perfect flanker. He was hard as nails, worked like a Trojan, tackled anything that moved and was never once found wanting when courage was needed. "He was a wonderful competitor," explains Michael Lynagh, the Australian fly half who crossed paths with the blond-haired Englishman on a number of occasions. "He was a fantastic player, but he had a very physical presence and was always a problem. I always tried to stay well away from him!"

Winterbottom's physicality on the field may well have had something to do with his background. A Yorkshireman from farming stock, the young Winterbottom was recognised as an outstanding talent early in his career, representing neighbouring Lancashire Schools at both 16 and 19 age groups before making his mark with England's Colts wearing the Number 8 shirt. It was no surprise when 'The Straw Man' – as Winterbottom was known because of the shock of blond hair that was habitually perched on top of his head – stepped up to full international level. And step up he most certainly did. England hooker Brian Moore reckoned Winterbottom was the hardest man he had ever met. And when such a judgement is delivered by a man who was affectionately nicknamed 'Pitbull', then you know it simply must be true. But Winterbottom's game was about much more than sheer, naked aggression. He had an excellent appreciation of the technicalities of the sport, was lightning quick to the breakdown and could recycle ball all afternoon long.

It wasn't just the English selectors who recognised Winterbottom's sniping talents as a flanker, either. Despite the England team's unimpressive form in the early part of his international career, Winterbottom was selected for the first of his two British Lions tours in 1983. He performed in a losing side down in New Zealand, yet still managed to impress a notoriously discerning and hard-to-please Kiwi public.

Winterbottom eventually reaped the rewards his talents deserved when he was an integral part of the England side that won back-to-back Grand Slams in 1991 and 1992 under the leadership of Will Carling. He also gained a runners-up medal as England went down in the 1991 World Cup Final against Australia at Twickenham. At club level, meanwhile, Winterbottom captained Harlequins to three successive Pilkington Cup triumphs between 1991 and 1993, which certainly contributed to him being selected for another Lions tour, again to New Zealand, a full 10 years after his first selection. His powers undiminished, 'The Straw Man' was again inspirational throughout the tour, despite the series being lost by two tests to one.

Winterbottom never played another international after his return from New Zealand, but his place as a true legend of the English game has certainly endured.

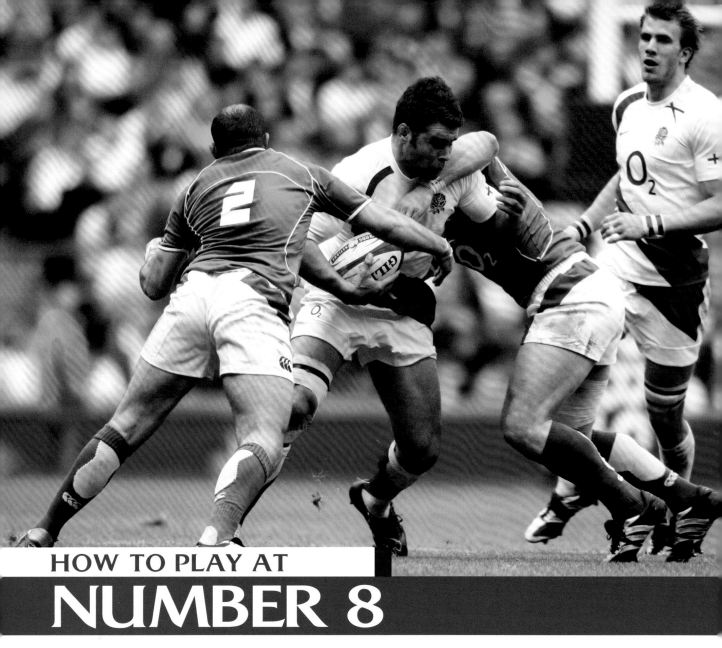

HOW TO PLAY AT
NUMBER 8

Nick Easter shows the kind of aggression a top Number 8 needs if he's to get over the gain line

The Number 8 is a ball carrier with good running and handling skills and an aggressive tackler. They pack down at the back of the scrum and act as a key figure in this area because they're responsible for controlling the ball with their feet, either while the scrum advances or before the next passage of play unfolds through the scrum half or via the Number 8 themselves.

As part of the back row forward unit, the Number 8 needs to work closely with the two flankers to provide the essential link that maintains forward momentum in play. They must retain possession, recycle the ball and give their team continuity. Normally tall and athletic, Number 8s can be used as a third lineout jumper behind the locks, but they are often required to lift or support a jumper. Meanwhile, in defence, the Number 8 is key in winning ball from the opposition.

In the scrum the Number 8 binds the two locks together by having his shoulders against each player, while his arms pull them both inwards. His driving helps to channel all of the power of the scrum forwards. While the Number 8 controls the ball at the back of the scrum with his feet he must always maintain his binding on the locks. As the hindmost player in the scrum his decision-making is crucial. He has the option to control the ball with the right foot to allow his scrum half to pass without interference from the opposing number nine. He may, however, opt to pick up the ball to start a move – which means he needs a real understanding of the backs' alignment and their timing – or to run like a back himself to break the line of the opposition defence. This means that a Number 8 must have plenty of aggression to get over the gain line, yet also possess strong ball handling skills in order to distribute properly. When defending at the scrum the Number 8 must act as the second tackler around the sides after the flanker.

In open field the Number 8 has to support the play as often as possible. He is frequently the second forward to the breakdown from scrums and so needs to be able to manage contact in the tackle area, go to ground to control the ball if required and yet stay on his feet to continue the attack if at all possible. He also needs to work in tandem with the flankers to provide defensive cover. If a flanker has been beaten on the inside it's down to the Number 8 to be in position to make a tackle and discussion amongst the back row will allow for an understanding of tackling responsibilities – who takes the first ball carrier, who takes the second and who looks after the third. A Number 8 needs to be an excellent decision maker in and around the tackle or breakdown area.

As the most important link man between the forwards and the backs a Number 8 must have an in-depth understanding of the specific roles of both sets of players and be able to knit them all together in a cohesive manner to ensure the whole team functions efficiently and effectively at all times. This requires a wide variety of skills, an ability to analyse what's happening on the field of play quickly, intuitively and accurately and a finely-honed decision-making capacity.

> # "MAKE SURE YOU HAVE TIME TO CONTROL THINGS AT THE BACK OF THE SCRUM AND ALWAYS WORK ON MAINTAINING EXCELLENT COMMUNICATION WITH YOUR SCRUM HALF"
>
> ## NICK EASTER

IN A NUTSHELL

- Has excellent distribution at the base of the scrum
- Needs good game understanding to be effective in wide, centre field and close quarter channels as a strong driving and ball-carrying option
- Offers excellent distribution and support skills
- Combines good aerial skills and lifting/blocking ability at lineouts
- Has very good tactical decision-making skills at the scrum

Luke Narraway remembers that a good Number 8 stays on his feet at the contact area if at all possible

LAWRENCE DALLAGLIO

ENGLAND
RUGBY

"HIS CHARISMA AND HIS ABILITY MARKED HIM OUT AS AN OUTSTANDING PLAYER OF HIS GENERATION. A BRILLIANT DEFENSIVE TALENT WHO ALWAYS STOPPED THE OPPOSITION GETTING QUICK BALL"

STUART BARNES

Sky Sports presenter and former England fly half

Alongside Martin Johnson, Lawrence Dallaglio is the most recognised England rugby player of recent times. His physical appearance – the prominent lantern jaw setting off the fixed stare of the warrior – became synonymous with the very best characteristics of English rugby. Steely determination. Refusal to take a backward step. Unflinching desire for combat. Dallaglio was a hero to everyone who loved the red rose and a pantomime villain to all those who hated it, especially when summoned by the referee for a ticking off following a supposed transgression. Dallaglio's ability always to look rather hurt that his integrity should be called into question delighted England fans and infuriated opposition supporters equally, as did his game. A hugely influential player when his team had forward momentum and an impressively disruptive force whenever England were on the back foot, Dallaglio's sheer will to win alone seemed to lift England out of some particularly tight spots and drag the side to victory.

Born in London on August 10, 1972 to an Italian father and an Irish mother, it was England's good fortune that Lawrence Bruno Nero Dallaglio opted to represent the country of his birth. Having joined London Wasps as a teenager, back rower Dallaglio first made strides on the international stage when he was an integral member of England's sevens squad that won the inaugural World Cup in 1993. He was then called up for the full England tour to South Africa in 1994, despite being unable to hold down a regular place with his club side. That situation changed in 1995 when Rob Andrew left Wasps for Newcastle and took a number of senior players with him. Dallaglio seized his chance, was soon appointed Wasps skipper and proved to be an inspired choice, leading the club to the 1996/97 Premiership title. Dallaglio had served notice that here was not only a rugby player of international calibre, but also a leader of immense stature.

His England début finally came from off the bench against South Africa in November of 1995, but when new national Head Coach Clive Woodward was appointed in the autumn of 1997 he immediately awarded Dallaglio the captaincy of his country in place of Phil De Glanville. Dallaglio was, in turn, replaced by Martin Johnson two years later after newspaper revelations about his private life forced him to give up the skipper's role. Yet Woodward not only kept faith with his powerhouse forward in his playing role, but he also helped to settle Dallaglio into the Number 8 shirt and watched him become an indispensable member of the England back row alongside flankers Richard Hill and Neil Back. The country's pack formed the backbone of the superb England side that would go on to achieve both a Six Nations Grand Slam and a World Cup victory in 2003. Dallaglio played every minute of every match in Australia, driving England to prevail.

When Martin Johnson retired from international rugby at the beginning of 2004 Woodward again turned to Dallaglio to skipper England, but by the summer of the same year he too had announced his retirement from the international game with 73 caps to his name, saying that he knew the time was right. Most England fans believed they had seen the last of Dallaglio's relentless work at the breakdown in a white shirt, but by the start of 2006 he'd had a change of heart and was back in the international fold, though no longer as an automatic first choice. No matter. At the height of his powers Dallaglio had an invaluable ability to galvanise all around him to perform at the peak of their game. It made him a crucial cog in the wheel of England's most successful side of all time. Following the 2007 World Cup and an appearance from off the bench in the Final against South Africa, Dallaglio retired from England for a second time. With 85 caps to his name and legendary status assured he finally hung up his boots for good at the end of the 2007/08 season.

HOW TO PLAY AT
SCRUM HALF

Richard Wigglesworth knows that a top scrum half should be able to produce a kick that deals with any situation

The scrum half is the key player in any rugby team, the player who's at the centre of everything that happens in a game. The fact that they have their hands on the ball more than any other player on the field proves this. While other team members play extremely important roles in linking forwards and backs – the Number 8, for example – nobody exerts as much influence in this department as the number nine. This player is the co-ordinator who dictates when the ball is to be produced from rucks, mauls and scrums and who most often decides where the ball goes and what happens next. They are also the key players when it comes to deciding the calls at lineouts and scrums, and as well as shouldering much of the tactical responsibilities on the field they must also have an impressive array of rugby skills. These include being an accurate passer of the ball and an effective tackler, with explosive speed off the mark and natural ability as an evasive runner. The best scrum halves are excellent readers of the game who have no qualms about making decisions and directing their team mates on the field of play.

A scrum half's stock in trade is his pass. Without a strong pass he won't be able to direct the game in an effective way. Therefore he has to be able to pass the ball both quickly and accurately off either hand. This is achieved by avoiding reaching for the ball, which makes it hard to swing it away, rather getting above the ball or taking a quick step back after the pick-up before distributing. Being able to be quick and accurate is more important than being able to throw the ball a long way. If a scrum half is too focused on getting a long pass away, more often than not he will end up slowing his own backline down. There are a number of styles of pass that a scrum half has to master in order to deal with any kind of situation; the standing pass, the pivot pass, the dive pass and the reverse pass.

A scrum half should be able to kick well with either foot and be able to produce high 'box' kicks over scrums, lineouts, rucks and mauls. Successful kicks are again produced by taking a step back beforehand, but also by using the protection of the breakdown, the scrum and the lineout. Time is tight in the areas where the scrum half operates, so he has to be able to kick facing in a number of different directions to work effectively.

The scrum half can be a hugely effective offensive weapon by having the vision to spot gaps in the opposition defence and possessing enough acceleration to instigate a quick break. But knowing when the break is really 'on' rather than simply running up a blind alley is also a crucial part of a scrum half's game understanding.

The scrum half also has a number of important roles to play defensively, not least of which is organising those around him at rucks and mauls. He needs to work closely with the back line, be one of the first players into the tackle and be able to decide where he can be most effective, either following the ball around if the opposition back row picks and goes, or harrying the opposite fly half if the ball is passed to him.

It's because a scrum half needs to master such a variety of skills and be tactically astute and confident enough to take a game by the scruff of the neck that many coaches feel he must be the best overall player in the team.

> ## "WORK AS HARD AS YOU CAN ON YOUR PASSING GAME. PESTER PEOPLE WHO HAVE GOOD KNOWLEDGE OF YOUR POSITION AND NEVER THINK YOUR JOB IS DONE"
>
> ### RICHARD WIGGLESWORTH

IN A NUTSHELL

- Clears the ball quickly and accurately from contact situations to the first receiver
- Drives the team and the forwards with his communication skills and tactical understanding
- Has good all-round footballing skills

Scrum halves like Peter Richards dictate when the ball is to be produced from rucks, mauls and scrums

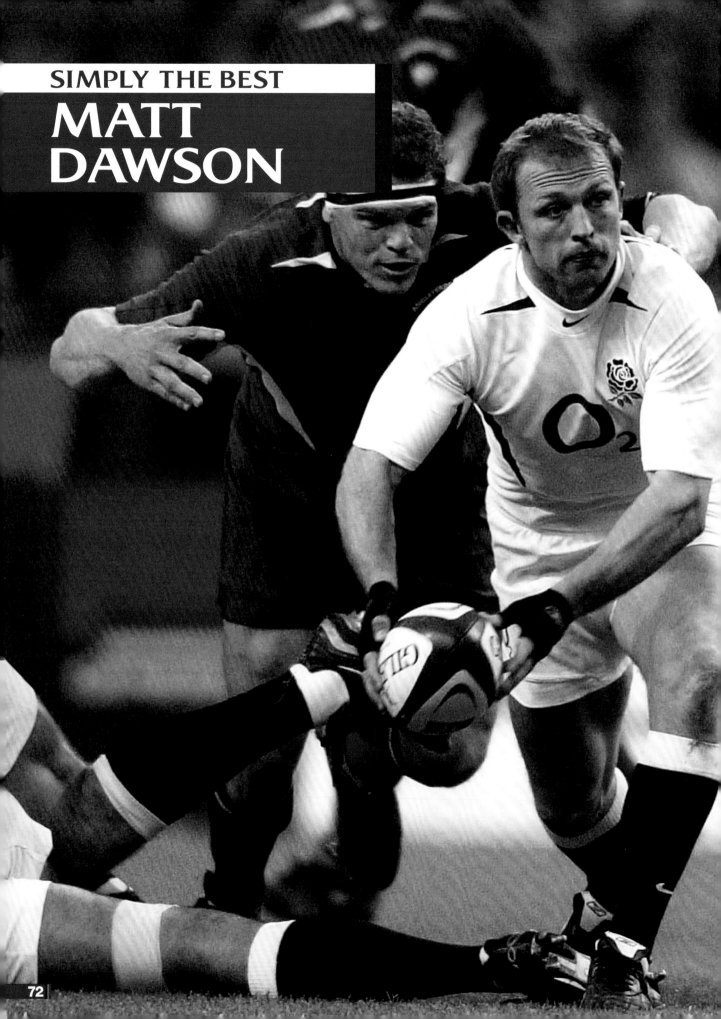

"HIS GAME UNDERSTANDING, HIS AWARENESS AND THE WAY HE PERFORMED IN THE BIG MATCHES GIVES HIM THE EDGE OVER ALL THE OTHER GREAT ENGLAND SCRUM HALVES"

NEIL BACK

Rugby World Cup-winning England flanker and current Leeds Carnegie Head Coach

Scrum halves have always had the ability to infuriate both the opposition and their own forwards with their cockiness, arrogance, cheekiness and bravado. Matt Dawson would take it as an absolute compliment to be put into such a category. Always ready with a smart aleck comment, Dawson could start an argument in a room on his own. But his ability to annoy opponents and put them off their game, then exploit that lapse of concentration with rugby of razor-sharp precision, made him the ultimate exponent of the art of the scrum half.

Born in Birkenhead, Dawson was quickly recognised as an all-round sporting talent. He represented Chelsea at football as a schoolboy and played cricket for Buckinghamshire Under 18s. But rugby was always his first love. "I was playing since I was knee-high," he says. "So it was always the natural choice." After playing his early club rugby with Marlow, Dawson joined Northampton in 1991 and was quickly talent-spotted as a Number 9 of outstanding potential. Just two years later he was a key member of the England team that won the first ever Sevens World Cup in Scotland alongside another player who was to become a major figure in the full 15 man game, Lawrence Dallaglio.

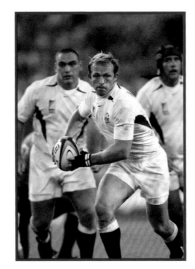

Dawson rapidly carved out a fine reputation for himself as a scrum half who was always capable of making vital yards for his team, shouldering the burden of responsibility easily enough and taking tap penalties the minute the referee signalled an infringement. His precocious style was rewarded when he made his full international debut against Western Samoa in 1995. It was two years later, though, wearing the red of the British and Irish Lions, when Dawson truly sealed his reputation as *the* emerging scrum half, throwing an outrageous dummy that shook off four Springboks and allowed him in for a try that saw the Lions to victory in the First Test and an eventual series win.

Despite facing a constant battle to make the England Number 9 shirt his own in the face of stiff competition from both Kyran Bracken and Austin Healey, both exceptional scrum halves in their own right, Dawson chalked up his 50th international cap in England's 2003 Six Nations win against Ireland in Dublin. The game sealed an England Grand Slam and teed the side up perfectly for the forthcoming Rugby World Cup in Australia.

By the time the plane touched down in Oz, England Head Coach Clive Woodward had made up his mind to install Dawson as his undisputed number one scrum half choice. It proved to be an inspired move as Dawson cajoled, controlled and just as often bullied England's pack all the way to the final against Australia. Fittingly, it was a typical Dawson moment – a darting, yard-making run from the base of a ruck in the last seconds of extra time – that set England up for victory. When the ball was recycled for skipper Martin Johnson to take on, Dawson was then quickly on his feet to fire the pass that Jonny Wilkinson dropped for World Cup glory.

After 13 years with Northampton Saints, a 2004 move to London Wasps allowed Matt to begin to develop a career in the media. A conflict of interest led to him being missing from the England squad for the 2004 autumn internationals and although Dawson returned for the 2005 RBS Six Nations it was clear that his life was moving in a new direction and he announced his retirement from all rugby at the end of the 2005/06 season.

Matt's career as a celebrity has since blossomed, with roles on *A Question Of Sport*, *Strictly Come Dancing* and *Celebrity Masterchef* making him a household name and an instantly recognisable face. But rugby fans will always remember him as the classic modern day scrum half, often irritating but always inspiring.

HOW TO PLAY AT
FLY HALF

It's the fly half who most often decides which direction the play moves in as Danny Cipriani shows

Fly half is a crucial position. The number 10 is a key decision maker, most often deciding which direction the play moves in (either left or right), the depth of the game (short or long), or whether the play is expansive and wide or narrow and close. The fly half acts as the leader of the backline, making key decisions through an astute reading of the game and then calling the necessary moves. His ideas need to be constantly varied to stop his side becoming predictable and to keep the opposition guessing. He must be able to move up a gear in the blink of an eye so he can decide how 'flat' he can take the ball – meaning how close he can get to the gain line – to threaten the opposition defence. On gaining possession of the ball the fly half must decide whether to go for a break, which requires an evasive running technique; to retain possession; or to bring centres, wings or forwards into play with a pass. There are few sights in rugby more thrilling than

seeing a fly half make a penetrative break and nothing keeps a defence on its toes more than a fly half who's capable of doing so. Increasingly in the modern game the fly half has a major defensive role to play too, first and foremost as a front line tackler, but secondly as an organiser of a side's defence, particularly at set pieces.

The top fly halves are all blessed with excellent technique. Quick hands are a must, as is the ability to kick accurately out of hand, either to gain territory or to instigate offensive moves. A first rate Number 10 will be able to kick comfortably with either foot. The game is played at such pace at the highest level that there's no time for a player to adjust their stance once a decision's been made. They will also need to be able to produce a dazzling array of kicks to be able to deal with whatever situation they find themselves in. High hanging kicks, chips, grubber and diagonal kicks are all important parts of a fly half's armoury as he

ENGLAND
RUGBY

tries to put his team in a position to retain possession. But that's not all. The number 10 must also be able to restart play effectively with a drop kick, most often 'hanging' the ball in the air for as long as possible to give the advancing forwards the best possible chance of competing for it once it's gone forward by at least 10 metres.

A fly half's passing ability is also vital as he seeks to direct the game and have a positive influence on its outcome. Reliable short passes are vital in order to bring team mates into the game, while the ability to send a long pass allows a fly half to change the pattern and direction of attack. They also need to be able to receive a pass cleanly so they have the maximum amount of time possible – for example when receiving the ball from the lineout – before deciding on the next play.

The sheer variety of skills a fly half has to master can be somewhat daunting and each and every one of them requires intense dedication to practice. But the single most important element of a fly half's game is the ability to be able to analyse any situation on the field quickly and to make the right decision about what to do next in a split second.

"YOU NEED TO BE ABLE TO HANDLE THE BALL VERY WELL, PASS ACCURATELY OFF BOTH HANDS TO PUT PEOPLE INTO SPACE AND FEEL CONFIDENT ENOUGH TO DO IT IN PRESSURE SITUATIONS"

CHARLIE HODGSON

IN A NUTSHELL

- Must threaten defences while distributing in a variety of ways
- Needs an outstanding all round kicking game, including goal kicking and restarts
- Shares in the decision making process of the team, showing very good communication skills

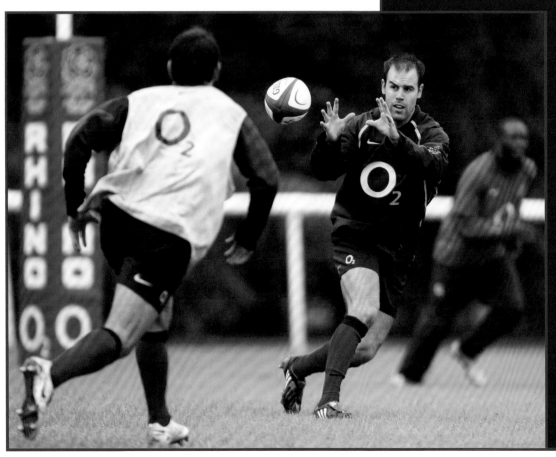

Receiving a pass cleanly – as Charlie Hodgson does here – gives a fly half more time to decide on the next play

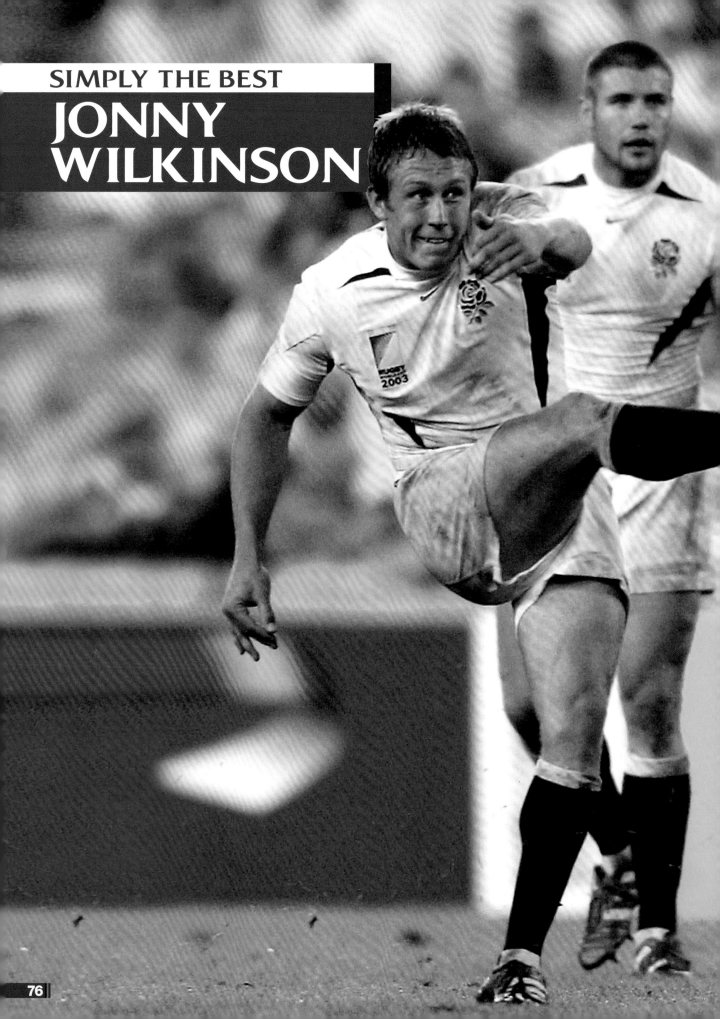

JONNY WILKINSON

ENGLAND
RUGBY

"NO ONE CAN TOUCH JONNY WILKINSON. THERE'S SIMPLY NO-ONE LIKE JONNY IN WORLD RUGBY"

DEWI MORRIS

Former England scrum half and Sky Sports rugby pundit

Jonny Wilkinson's favourite kicking foot is his left. There are many English rugby fans who will beg to differ, though. For it was with one swing of his less-favoured right that Wilko launched the ball that sent millions into ecstasy. The famous drop goal notched by the Surrey-born fly half with just 26 seconds remaining of the 2003 World Cup Final against Australia clinched the Webb Ellis trophy for England. And there was nobody more perfectly suited to sealing our greatest ever victory than the player who's come to be seen as the ultimate talisman for our national side.

Wilkinson was always marked for sporting greatness. He was an outstanding schoolboy performer at both rugby and cricket at Lord Wandsworth College in Hampshire and when he was talent-spotted by Newcastle Falcons Jonny opted to defer his studies at Durham University in 1997 to try full time professional rugby. Within a year he was a full England international after making his début from the bench against Ireland. "I'd only been involved in a couple of games for the Falcons before playing for England," he explains. "Then all of a sudden you're at Twickenham and someone has hit a high ball. You start to appreciate exactly how vulnerable and fragile you are." Vulnerable or otherwise, Wilkinson wasted no time in establishing himself as an England regular. The only blip in his upward trajectory came when he was omitted from the side for the World Cup quarter final meeting with South Africa in 1999. England lost 44-21. But Jonny came back from that disappointment to become both an England regular and one of the first names on Head Coach Clive Woodward's teamsheet. His disciplined defending, level-headed decision making and ability to instigate attacks from deep made him an instant favourite. But it was Jonny's dead ball kicking in particular that made him such an asset. His fanatical dedication to the art manifested itself in endless practice sessions,

but such attention to detail paid off in spades as a metronomic regularity saw him become one of the most consistent points scorers ever in the international game. Milestones quickly began to be marked. Wilkinson kicked all of England's 27 points in a 2000 England win over South Africa, then the following February he set an individual RBS 6 Nations points scoring record chalking up 35 against Italy. It wouldn't be the last time he would enter the record books.

After helping clinch a 2003 Six Nations Grand Slam by being named Man Of The Match in the final game against Ireland, Wilkinson headed for the World Cup in Australia as the player feared most by England's opponents. So it proved as he scored all 24 points to dispatch France in the semi-final and set up that fateful meeting with Australia in the final – and that legendary drop.

When the squad returned to England with the Webb Ellis trophy 'Jonnymania' had well and truly broken out, his good looks and modest attitude proving an irresistible draw for potential sponsors. But an incredible run of bad luck with injuries prevented Wilkinson from wearing the white of England for more than three long years. When he finally returned against Scotland in the 2007 Six Nations Wilkinson was, almost inevitably, voted Man Of The Match.

A freak ankle injury suffered in the first training session of the 2007 Rugby World Cup in France saw Wilkinson sit out the first two games of the tournament and people feared the worst. But Jonny recovered to help inspire England to the final where Brian Ashton's side came within a whisker of retaining the Webb Ellis trophy. He also became the all-time highest points scorer in the World Cup's final stages.

With such a list of achievements, Wilkinson has already cemented his reputation as a true legend of the game. But the great news for England supporters is that the man himself believes there's much, much more to come.

HOW TO PLAY AT
INSIDE CENTRE

An inside centre must be fearless in taking the ball up to the opposition defensive line and into contact himself, as Toby Flood shows here

Like the fly half who plays just inside him, the inside centre is a key decision maker, particularly when his team has possession of the ball. When his side is on the attack he is a key figure in keeping any forward movement in formation by linking the fly half with the outside backs who play outside him and provide attacking width. In the modern game there are many tacticians who believe the inside centre must be capable of slotting in as a fly half at any point in a game, particularly if the Number 10 has taken the ball into contact, been forced to commit himself to a ruck or has made a defensive tackle. But in addition, the inside centre is also expected to be fearless in taking the ball up to the opposition defensive line and into contact himself. By battering his way forward opponents are forced to commit men to the breakdown. Then if the ball can be recycled quickly there will be more space to attack. A top inside centre's physical qualities also need to be first rate in defence, as he will often be expected to make head-on tackles during the course of a game.

Good centres are strong tactically. They need to choose the right option in a split second; whether to pass, kick, head into contact or try to make a break themselves. And they must have the all-round package of skills that will allow them to execute any move soundly – especially as they operate in a crowded midfield area where they're constantly being put under pressure by the opposition. Dropping a ball simply isn't an option and the ability to burst into life with a searing burst of pace is also essential. The inside centre often has to decide whether an attack should be straightened by running straight forward with the ball, or whether it should be pushed wider to the outside centre and onwards. He needs to be able to identify the defensive organisation of the opposition and take the necessary steps to nullify it.

Inside centre passing skills must be exemplary to develop attacking moves. He must be able to pass with equal confidence off either hand, while pace and elusive running skills are also essential weapons in his armoury. They must also be able to kick with authority – either diagonally, high in the air or grubber style to beat a flat defence – and it's vital they have confidence in their own abilities, allowing them to take on and beat their opponent and play the ball safely out of the tackle. Of the two centres it's the inside centre who will most often be required to take the ball up into contact when options for 'go forward' are limited. He will often be expected to play a key role in set moves around the scrum and the lineout too.

The key to defence in this area is in the co-ordination between the inside and the outside centres. Centres should advance towards the opposition together in a flat line and on the 'inside' (nearest the breakdown) of their opponents to ensure opponents are pushed away from their main support. The inside centre often leads the defensive pattern.

The inside centre is a vital link man who helps set a team's tempo. He has to instill confidence in his team-mates so they know they have a solid and reliable midfield that will gain ascendancy in all phases of play. He needs real strength as he'll often come into contact with the opposition, but he must also be subtle in his play and skilful enough to carry out the deftest of moves. The role of inside centre demands the heart of a lion and the brain of a mathematician.

> "BEING ABLE TO KICK, PASS, BRING PEOPLE INTO THE GAME AND MAKE GOOD DECISIONS IS ALL VITAL. THE LINK BETWEEN THE FLY HALF AND THE INSIDE CENTRE IS AS IMPORTANT TO THE TEAM AS THE LINK BETWEEN SCRUM HALF AND FLY HALF"

TOBY FLOOD

IN A NUTSHELL

- Threatens defences whilst distributing in a variety of ways
- Has an outstanding all-round kicking game
- Shares in the decision-making process of the team, showing very good communication skills
- Must be technically correct and capable of making decisions under intense pressure
- Has to be one of the most complete footballers in the side

Playing at 12 requires exemplary passing skills, as Olly Barkley demonstrates

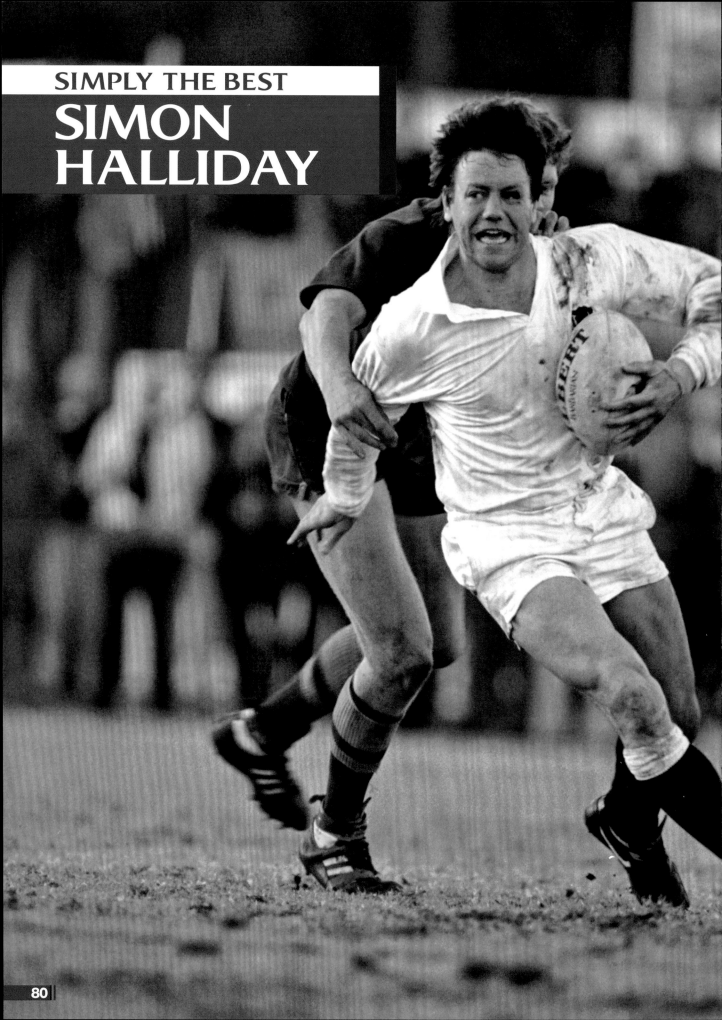

"SIMON HALLIDAY WAS UNDERRATED. SUCH A TALENTED CENTRE, A REALLY TERRIFIC PLAYER. HE HAD LOTS OF FLAIR – AND PACE TOO"

JOHN INVERDALE
BBC sports presenter and rugby nut

Modern day centres and wingers need to combine all of the finesse traditionally associated with rugby's backs together with a rugged presence that can withstand the intense physicality of today's confrontations. Despite representing his country as long ago as 1986, Simon Halliday could easily lay claim to being the very first of the new breed. After all, any back who could be called "one of the hardest men in rugby" *by a forward* – in this case England's Paul Ackford – had to be exceptionally tough. Indeed he was. Whether from his favoured position in the centre or out on the wing, Halliday always brought a certain confrontational style to any side he played in. This was perhaps all the more surprising given the fact that Simon had suffered a severe injury that kept him out of the game for a considerable period early in his career, dislocating his left ankle when playing for Somerset against Middlesex in the County Championship of 1983. Such a trauma only seemed to make him more combative and more contact-oriented, though, and his outstanding form for club side Bath saw him rewarded with a début England cap in the game against Wales on January 18, 1986. The irony was that Simon was actually born in Wales, at Haverfordwest, but this minor geographical aberration had no bearing as here was a player who was never less than 100% committed to the England cause.

Despite this full-blooded approach and hugely appreciated status at club side Bath, where Simon went on to appear in an incredible six Cup Final victories, England's selectors weren't fully convinced at first that this was a player of international class. Halliday's first two seasons of international rugby were stop-start affairs and he picked up just three caps. But 1988 proved to be a turning point as Halliday suddenly found a consistency of performance that was impossible to ignore. At both inside centre, or outside wearing the Number 13 shirt, Halliday consistently proved his worth. He attacked his opponents with a remarkable intensity when he didn't have the ball, then showed the handling skills that others could only dream of possessing. It finally looked as if Halliday's international career was about to take off, but to the astonishment of many yet again it stuttered. After narrowly failing to complete a Five Nations Grand Slam in both 1989 and 1990, England chose to select Nigel Heslop ahead of Halliday for the 1991 tournament. When England finally captured the elusive Grand Slam it looked as if Halliday's international career could already be over, especially with the World Cup just around the corner. But after a tricky quarter-final game against France in Paris, which England came through by 19–10, Halliday was brought back on the wing in place of Heslop for the semi-final against Scotland and stayed in the side for the final against Australia. Despite his best efforts, however, he was unable to inspire England to victory and he had to settle for a runner's up medal.

The disappointment was short-lived as Simon appeared on the wing in all four of the following season's Five Nations games, helping England to their first back-to-back Grand Slams since 1924 and even scoring a try in a convincing win against Ireland. Little did Halliday know that this hugely successful tournament would mark the end of his 23-cap international career. By the time the following year's tournament came around he was being increasingly troubled by his ankle and felt he had no choice but to retire, having already continued for a while against medical advice.

"I played on after people told me to stop so I knew I would have problems," he admitted since. "But most sportsmen would do the same because there's a desire to stay on the field." Proof positive, as if any more were needed, that Simon Halliday had the heart of a true rugby competitor.

HOW TO PLAY AT
OUTSIDE CENTRE

Jamie Noon shows how a good outside centre is a strong runner who can attract opposing defences

The roles performed by the centres on a rugby pitch are closely related, but as a rule the outside centre – wearing 13 – is a little quicker than the player inside him and offers more of an important attacking option. Any rugby coach will look to his outside centre to set up the players outside him, usually the wing or the full back, to make penetrative attacking breaks. That means they must be strong runners, able to attract opposing defences towards them as they make a charge, yet be blessed with soft hands and expert timing to allow them to release a pass outside at the perfect moment.

Bringing team-mates into the game when going forward isn't the outside centre's only role, though. They must also be capable of running hard and straight when they get the chance to attack the line themselves and be both strong and pacey enough to break through. Because the outside centre tends to have a little more space to work in than his

counterpart on the inside he can be a particularly dangerous attacking weapon if he's capable of using the split second of extra time he has to produce the unpredictable. As such, a powerful and effective sidestep is also very useful. Using the sidestep allows the outside centre to put his opposite number off balance and either accelerate outside him or cut back inside and maintain 'go forward'.

While an outside centre's kicking qualities aren't as important as that of the fly half – they're not even as essential as for an inside centre given that 12 and 10 will often be expected to swap roles during the course of a game – the ability to use the boot as an attacking weapon can nevertheless add significantly to a number 13's armoury. It can pay massive dividends. After breaking a defensive line a well-executed punt towards the corner can be a highly-effective option to let wingers and full backs in for a score.

ENGLAND
RUGBY

An outside centre must also have solid defensive qualities. They will often be faced with opposition players attacking from deep. This means they will have already gathered real momentum and as such the outside centre will need to have courage, strength and excellent tackling technique in order to stop his man. When engaged in defensive duties it will often be the outside centre's responsibility to make the crucial tackle that halts the opposition's quick counter attack. Therefore they need to be able to read the game well so that when they commit to the tackle they can't be easily eliminated from the game with a well-timed pass.

In order for two players to be able to operate successfully in the centre there needs to be a good understanding between them. The skill sets each player possesses must be complementary, but there also needs to be an ability to anticipate the other player's likely course of action and to be able to act on it accordingly. This level of understanding between players – and especially centres – is one of the hardest things to teach and only really develops as a result of a natural compatibility of styles and many hours spent together on the training pitch to develop that 'sixth sense' regarding what the partner will do next.

> ## "YOU NEED TO WORK HARD ON YOUR LINES OF RUNNING SO THEY'RE AS GOOD AS POSSIBLE AND ON YOUR TACKLING TECHNIQUE SO YOU CAN DEFEND REALLY WELL. BUT ABOVE ALL BE ADAPTABLE, SO YOU CAN CHANGE WHAT YOU'RE DOING IN DEFENCE OR ATTACK DEPENDING ON HOW A GAME IS UNFOLDING"
>
> **JAMIE NOON**

IN A NUTSHELL

- Offers pace, power and evasion as a strike runner
- Has creative running and handling ability
- Can read opposition defences in wider channels and respond accordingly
- Is a top class defender
- Has good ball retention skills

Dan Hipkiss knows he must run hard in order to attack his opposite defensive line

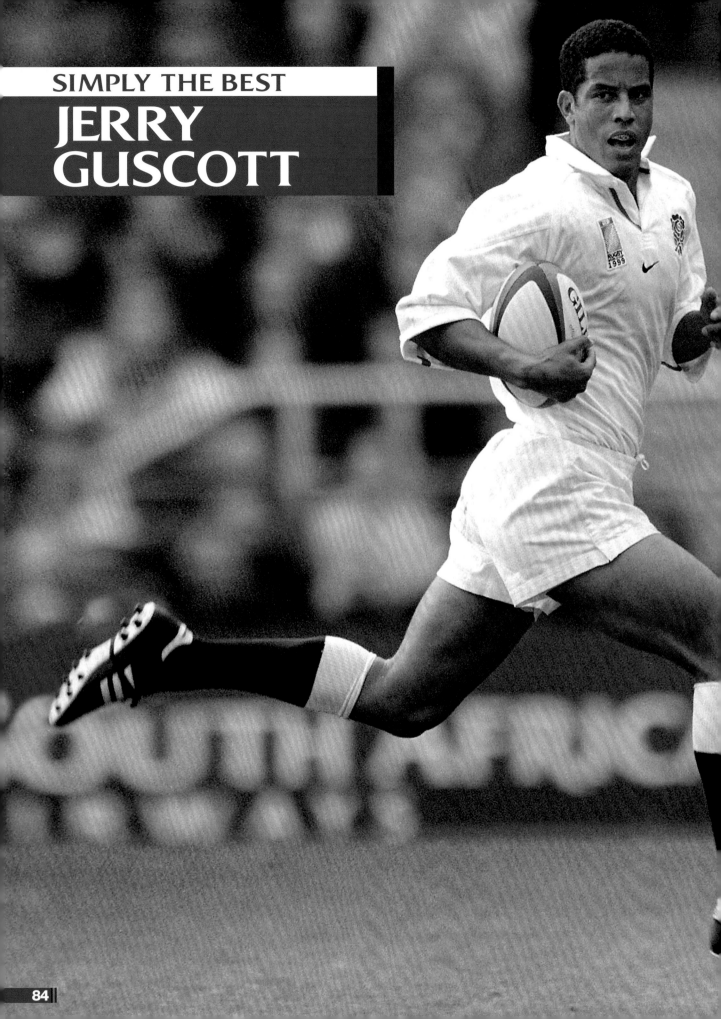

"JERRY WOULD ALWAYS BRING PLENTY OF PACE TO THE BACKLINE AND HE WAS QUITE SUBLIME WHEN HE WAS SLIDING OUTSIDE OF TACKLES"

AUSTIN HEALEY
Erstwhile England utility back

Known to one and all as 'The Prince Of Centres', Jerry Guscott announced his arrival on the international stage with a good dash of the flair that would soon become his trademark. He marked his England début by notching three tries against Romania in 1989, aged just 23. And while the opposition that day weren't about to leave anyone quaking in their boots, the former bricklayer soon served notice that this was no fluke and that his smooth as silk running style and uncanny ability to find the try line would always serve him well, even against the very best the world of rugby had to offer. Guscott's extraordinary talent quickly saw him called up to the 1989 British and Irish Lions tour of Australia and superb performances in the Second and Third Tests both established the young Bath player's reputation and earned the Lions a series victory.

But alongside that undeniable talent sat a personality that didn't always please everyone. It wasn't rugby that instilled in Guscott the propensity to rub people up the wrong way. After all, he'd already been expelled from Bath's Ralph Allen Comprehensive as a schoolboy. But Guscott never seemed to tire of letting his singular personality flirt with disaster. "It's the composed gambler in him that made Guscott such an adored, and in some circles unpopular, character," explained Bath team-mate turned journalist and broadcaster Stuart Barnes. But none of this mattered, of course, when Guscott was weaving his magic on the world's international rugby pitches. His dashing style gave the England side of the early '90s an undeniable glamour and his ability to produce extraordinary rugby moments was a decisive factor in England's back-to-back Grand Slam victories of 1991 and 1992, with a paper-thin defeat to Australia in the World Cup Final sandwiched in-between.

As much as Guscott's darts and dashes, sleights of hand, feints and luxurious breaks were synonymous

with the white shirt of England, it was perhaps in the red shirt of the British and Irish Lions that Guscott produced his single most memorable moment, slotting over a typically nonchalant drop goal to win the Second Test of the 1997 tour to South Africa and thereby clinch the series against all the odds. The sight of a clearly ecstatic Guscott with his hands raised in victory salute at the final whistle remains one of the most iconographic images in rugby. But every bit as revealing as his joy at winning was the fact that Guscott's mouthguard on that tour was emblazoned with the word 'Jack' – as in 'I'm all right Jack' – a tongue-in-cheek response to those who saw Guscott as far too self-interested an individual for the team-oriented world of rugby.

Nobody could deny that watching Guscott in full flight was one of the most mesmerising sights ever seen on a rugby pitch, so it was an undeniably sad moment when a serious and ongoing groin injury finally put paid to his career in the middle of the 1999 Rugby World Cup. Most of Guscott's season had been wrecked by a similar problem in 1993/94, which had meant that his form was patchy in the 1995 World Cup. So when trouble flared again four years later the end was swift. Guscott's last game for his country was in a Pool match against Tonga. Fittingly, he scored a memorable try after making an interception and dashing the length of the field to dot down, then received a standing ovation at the end of the game. There could have been no more appropriate way for the player to finish his international career. England coach Clive Woodward was quick to pay tribute to a player whom everyone in the world of rugby had recognised as an exceptional talent.

"Jerry Guscott epitomised the best of England rugby," said Woodward on Guscott's retirement. "He was an invaluable support to younger players and an England centre to remember."

HOW TO PLAY AT
WING

David Strettle shows the flair, speed and elusiveness that all great wingers possess

Wingers must be able to show a potent combination of flair, speed and elusiveness. They are understandably seen as crowd pleasers because they're often the players who make exciting runs and finish off team moves, which means they must be able to score effectively and precisely. But wingers – particularly in the modern game – are also a vital part of a team's defensive unit. At one time wingers were included for their pace and finishing ability alone and the idea of someone out on the flanks defending with real vigour was laughable. All that has changed. Modern wingers are now expected to be every bit as robust in their tackling as anyone else on the pitch. They have to deal with opposition kicks while being able to kick well themselves, be good at reading the game to anticipate what's going to happen next and have an excellent work ethic so they'll go looking for the ball if it isn't coming to them.

Handling skills are important as a winger attacks. He must be able to gather the ball at speed – always

judging running lines to receive the ball at pace – then use natural sprint power to pull defenders towards him, before stepping either inside or outside the defender to beat him. He must be able to vary his pace to disorientate an opponent and be strong enough to hand off a player who moves in to tackle. If stopped, a good winger will keep the ball alive by either taking a tackle and passing the ball on to a supporting player, by staying on his feet as long as possible to allow help to arrive, or by starting another attacking move, often with his full back. Understanding when it's right to kick is also vital, whether to keep play alive and give a side the chance to retain possession or to kick down the line by chipping into space and then chasing. A winger must also be able to contribute effectively to maintain attacking momentum around the mauls, rucks and tackles.

There are some important differences in left and right wing play. If a player is stronger kicking off his right foot, then he'll be more suited to playing on the right wing and using the space infield, though he will also need to be

ENGLAND
RUGBY

able to step well off the right foot to be able to come back inside. The opposite is true for a left winger. Additionally, a left wing tends to get more ball, mainly because most players are right handed and are therefore more comfortable passing to their left. Defensively a left wing may have more involvement because teams often attack that side following a scrum.

When defending at scrums and lineouts the wing on the open side may stand wide and deep to make sure that if the opposition kicks diagonally – a tactic that's becoming more and more popular – then he will be able to gather the ball more easily. Indeed, dealing with all the varieties of opposition kicks by clearing to touch or kicking long up the field is an important part of a winger's defensive game. However, once the ball has passed through the attacking fly half's hands the defending winger must move forward quickly to be in a position to tackle in conjunction with the outside centre. A winger can also operate flat with the centres from the beginning. A blind-side wing must work in harmony with his own back row and scrum half when defending inside his own 22 and always be prepared to cover across the field if the attack goes open. When defending, a winger must also be alive at all times to the possibility of launching an unexpected counter attack.

> "BELIEVE IN YOUR OWN ABILITY AND BACK YOURSELF. YOU REALLY HAVE TO THINK THAT YOU'RE GOING TO BEAT YOUR MAN. THERE'S NOTHING WORSE THAN PLAYING AGAINST A WINGER WITH CONFIDENCE"
>
> **DAVID STRETTLE**

IN A NUTSHELL

- Has genuine sprint pace and evasion skills to score tries
- Must have the ability and willingness to read the game and be effective
- Can deal with ball that's kicked at or behind him
- Is a good decision maker and communicator in defence
- Must have a high work rate

Paul Sackey demonstrates the sidestep wingers need to beat their man either inside or outside

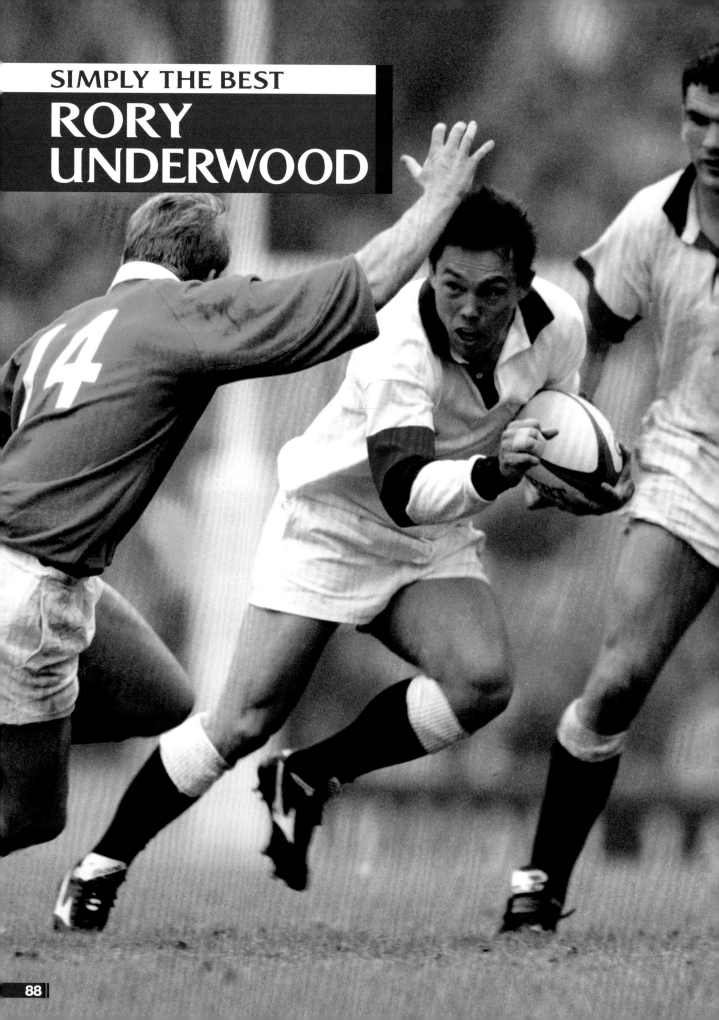

ENGLAND
RUGBY

> ## "RORY WAS THE DEADLIEST OF DEADLY FINISHERS WHO ALWAYS MADE POSSESSION COUNT. WHEN THE BALL GOT TO HIM YOU KNEW HE'D DO HIS JOB"

JON CALLARD
Former England full back and RFU National Academy Coach

They say that there are three kinds of lies: lies, damned lies, and statistics. But surely Rory Underwood's rugby statistics disprove that particular theory. The Middlesbrough-born winger made his England international début in 1984 and remained a first choice on the flanks for an astonishing 12 years. In that time he became the first Englishman ever to represent his country 50 times, reaching that particular landmark in the 1991 World Cup semi-final against Scotland. He won an impressive 85 caps, missing just nine of England's competitive matches between February of 1984 and March of 1996 and scored a staggering 49 tries along the way, a feat which makes him England's record try scorer of all time. You simply don't see statistics as exceptional as these every day. But even if you're still not about to be swayed by the figures, then maybe a few testimonials from the great and the good of the world of rugby will help you to change your mind.

"Rory scored tries that no-one else could have scored. A superb finisher," says legendary English prop Jeff Probyn. The verdict of former national team skipper Phil De Glanville? "A deadly finisher who was totally consistent." While another former England captain, Nigel Melville, insists that Rory "possessed pure speed and strength and scored tries for fun." If the praise of those who've played the game at the very top level is the highest praise of all, then Rory Underwood's status as a true legend of English rugby is without question.

Educated at Barnard Castle School alongside fellow future international Rob Andrew, Rory quickly caught the eye on a rugby pitch thanks to his devastating pace, eye for a gap and ability to finish with clinical precision. Having moved on to RAF Cranwell to prepare for a career as a pilot, Leicester Tigers were quick to invite Rory to join them and so began an inexorable rise to the top. While instantly making his mark at club level, Rory also progressed smoothly through the England international ranks, representing his country at all of Students, Colts, Under 23 and B levels before finally getting the nod to make his full international bow in the 1984 Five Nations match against Ireland at Twickenham. England won 12–9 and despite a slow start where he scored just two tries in his first 12 games, Rory quickly became an integral part of the England team.

The arrival of coach Geoff Cooke in 1988 kickstarted a golden era for English rugby and in a new and exciting line-up that was soon to sweep all in the Northern Hemisphere before it Rory was in his absolute element. With his mother often watching enthusiastically from the stands, Rory's searing turn of pace and his uncanny ability to outfox the wiliest of defenders and turn half chances into tries seemingly at will made him a darling of the Twickenham crowd. When younger brother Tony joined him in the England side in 1992, Rory graciously moved from the right to the left wing to accommodate him and the Underwoods became the first siblings to represent England at the same time since Harold and Arthur Wheatley back in 1937.

After appearing in the 1995 World Cup Finals – his third – in South Africa, Rory finally opted to bow out of international rugby at the end of the following year's Five Nations tournament. His contribution to England had been immense and his name will forever be synonymous with the kind of exciting, attacking, devil-may-care wing play no fan of the sport can ever resist. Many rugby experts believe that Rory's audacious – or even outrageous – skills would have further flourished in the professional game where speed of thought and deed are an ever more important part of the best players' armouries. Indeed it only makes the heart race faster to think what heights Rory Underwood might have risen to had he played his rugby in the open era.

HOW TO PLAY AT
FULL BACK

Full backs like Mike Brown should always look to contribute to a side's attacking potential

Full back is a unique position on the rugby pitch because it offers the player who operates there a greater opportunity than anywhere else to read the game as it unfolds in front of him, either in attack or defence. His position at the back of the field gives a full back more time and space to assess what's happening in front of him. Being able to anticipate how play will unfold and make good decisions based on that are essential attributes of the modern day full back.

Because of the space the position naturally offers, the full back should always look to contribute to a side's attacking potential. He can act as a 'strike runner' – arriving from deep into a gap he's spotted to receive the ball at pace – or as a 'decoy runner' to give the opposing defence another person to worry about. He can also act as a support runner, popping up as the extra player on the outside for example. The full back can always vary exactly where he comes into the line of attack, but he should always try to do so at pace. Timing is very important in determining whether the full back's entry into the action will be successful or not.

If he receives the ball in his own half the full back's first attacking instinct should be to link up with his team mates, often the wingers, to try to launch a counter attack.

Because he's often playing the game in an exposed area, a full back's core catching and kicking skills need to be extremely solid. He is often the last line of defence and so has to deal with a range of kicks from the opposition. Ideally the full back should be in a position to catch the ball in the air before it has a chance to bounce. But there will be plenty of occasions in a game when he will have to cope with long kicks that don't come directly to him. At that point he will either have to pick the ball up or fall on it while it's rolling on the ground to secure possession. A good full back must also be a strong tackler as he will be called on to make try-saving tackles one-on-one as the last line of defence. In these situations the full back must encourage the attacking player to try to go on the outside and use the touchline as a defensive boundary.

The full back's kicking armoury must be varied. He needs to be able to kick for touch or punt all the way back down into the opposition's half to relieve pressure on his own team. But long kicks that penetrate deep into an opposition's 22 can also set a team up to attack, especially if it has an aggressive lineout group that will put pressure on opponents at the restart. The modern full back needs a range of kicks to launch counter attacks. Up and unders can unlock an opponent's defensive structure and the arrival of the blitz defence system – the whole defensive line moving up ready to tackle as soon as the ball leaves the base of a ruck or maul – has increased the importance of the chip kick or the grubber kick to take defenders out and create space behind to exploit. Using either of these options can be seen as a high-risk strategy, but only if the execution is poor and possession is lost, exposing the full back's own side to a counter-attack.

"WORK ON YOUR ALL-ROUND SKILLS; HIGH BALL TAKES, KICKING OUT OF HAND AND ONE-ON-ONE TACKLING. ALWAYS LOOK TO SPOT GAPS IN THE OPPOSITION'S DEFENCE THAT GIVE YOU THE CHANCE TO COUNTER-ATTACK"

MIKE BROWN

IN A NUTSHELL

■ Must be a strike runner with pace and timing moving into the line or as a support runner

■ Can deal with any type of kick either at or behind him

■ Should be a panoramic decision maker who reads the opposition defence, allowing his team to attack and counter attack

■ Will be a good decision maker and communicator in defence

Iain Balshaw knows that a good full back must be a strong defensive tackler

JASON ROBINSON

ENGLAND
RUGBY

> "JASON HAD EVERYTHING YOU NEED IN THIS
> POSITION. HE WAS SAFE AS HOUSES UNDER
> THE HIGH BALL, DESPITE NOT BEING A BIG GUY,
> WAS ALWAYS PREPARED TO COUNTER ATTACK
> AND COULD RUN LIKE A SLIPPERY EEL FROM
> DEEP. AND HE WAS A SOUND TACKLER AS WELL"

MIKE BURTON

Former England and British Lions prop and sports hospitality entrepreneur

Jason Robinson is the single most successful player ever to have crossed the great divide between rugby's two codes, league and union. The ease with which he made the difficult transition, a leap that has proved too big for a number of top stars from the 13-man code, stands as a testament to his outstanding all-round footballing abilities. This isn't to say that the Leeds-born full back and winger didn't have to work hard to adapt to the XV man version of the game, though. When he left Wigan Warriors for Sale Sharks at the tail end of 2000 at the age of 26 and with a bunch of international caps under his arm he freely admitted that he didn't even know all of the rules of rugby union.

"I don't know why decisions are given or what penalties are for when I play," he said at the time, despite having already appeared in a few games of union for Bath back in 1996 at the time when league went from a winter to a summer sport. "I haven't got a clue. Sometimes I'm not able to react as quickly as I'd like because I can't anticipate the consequence of a decision." Players both as naturally gifted and as dedicated as Robinson only come along once in a blue moon, though, and soon afterwards he was so at ease in his new environment that England Head Coach Clive Woodward sent him on from the bench to win his first full international union cap against Italy in the 2001 Six Nations tournament. Quickly recognised as a 'first name on the teamsheet' type of player, Robinson flitted between full back and wing, while always maintaining that he preferred to appear at number 15. "Playing there gives me a bit of space to operate in, especially on the counter-attack, and I think I'm at my most effective in that position." It was from the wing, however, that 'Billy Whizz' – Robinson's nickname stolen from the lightning-quick *Beano* cartoon character – made his biggest impact, scorching over in the corner for England's only try of the game in the victorious World

Cup Final against Australia in 2003. Robinson's celebration after crossing the whitewash, punching the ball away with one hand while absolutely roaring with delight – remains a thrilling and enduring image for all England rugby supporters.

A quiet man with deep religious beliefs, Robinson was always quick to play down the role he played in developing his talents. But no matter where his abilities came from there was no denying the skill with which he could ally a head-spinning sidestep with jet-heeled bursts of pace to make vital yards whenever he had the ball in hand. Seeing Robinson in full flight, leaving established internationals grasping at thin air like kids playing British Bulldog in the school playground, will remain long in the memory for anyone privileged enough to have witnessed it.

After captaining his country in the wake of Martin Johnson's retirement – and scoring a hat trick of tries against Canada in his first match as skipper – Jason announced his retirement from international rugby in September of 2005, saying that he wanted to spend more time with his family. He then went on to lead Sale Sharks to their first ever Premiership title before deciding to come out of international retirement in time for England's 2007 Six Nations campaign. Unsurprisingly, Jason quickly re-established himself and became a fixture in the England side throughout an October and November World Cup campaign that saw Brian Ashton's side make it all the way to the final against considerable odds. Despite a heartbreaking loss in that final against South Africa many experts hailed Robinson as England's best player of the tournament.

Jason finally decided to hang his rugby boots up for good at the end of the World Cup, leaving behind a bucketful of memories of a player who was undoubtedly one of the most talented backs ever to wear the white of England.

THE GAME

To a novice rugby can look like a difficult sport to understand and an even trickier one to master. Don't worry. Once you're familiar with all of the different elements of rugby you'll soon feel at home with the subtlest nuances of the game and will be able to appreciate and execute all of the necessary skills to compete with confidence. Here you will find each area of the game broken down so that it's easy to comprehend – from passing, kicking and tackling, understanding when and why penalties are given, to the all-important scoring of a try. And yes, that tricky offside law is explained in full too!

PRINCIPLES OF TEAM PLAY

There are any number of philosophies on the best way to play rugby, but perhaps the single most important element of any of these is the understanding that rugby is a team game. Rugby coaches can have in mind a particular way of playing the game and can then look to develop players to execute that vision. Alternatively, they can look at the talents of the players they have at their disposal and then develop a game plan that's appropriate for those players. But without a team of players buying into a collective rugby philosophy and working together towards achieving a common goal it's highly unlikely that positive results will be consistently achieved.

The Rugby Football Union's elite coaches have developed a powerful team and game philosophy:

- **To play a mobile, dynamic, handling game and develop a style of play that is flexible, adaptable and unpredictable.**
- **To try to develop a positive attitude in our players, encourage intuitive play and emphasise try scoring.**
- **To play with speed and thought, with guile and cunning and with pride and passion.**

A rugby team must
buy into a collective
philosophy to achieve
positive results

- ■ To impose our style of play on the opposition, negate their strengths and exploit their weaknesses.
- ■ To develop winning rugby that enthuses and is appreciated.

This overall philosophy of play was then developed into the following aim:

'To Produce Total Quality Control By Multi-Skilled Rugby Athletes To Create A Winning Team'

The overall ingredients of a successful team are Fitness, Attitude, Skill and Organisation, but underpinning the Strategy and Tactics of the team is how they address the Principles of Play.

PRINCIPLES OF PLAY

Contest Possession – 'Get the ball'
Go Forward – 'Attack defenders and create space'
Support – 'In numbers, at pace, from depth'
Continuity – 'Keep the ball moving'
Pressure – 'Sustained activity creates pressure'
Points – 'Play to score'

Good communication on the field allows the team to function effectively and pulls together the qualities (game requirements) a team needs to be successful.

GAME REQUIREMENTS

- ■ **Possession and penetration in attack**
- ■ **Active, powerful scrum**
- ■ **Precise, varied lineout**
- ■ **Pressure defence**
- ■ **Effective kicking strategy**
- ■ **Organisation**

Each game requirement then breaks down into a series of key component parts that teams should try to remember and implement on the field of play. This section of your *Rugby Union Manual* will teach you about these component parts and with these elements in place any team will be in a great position to go on and win a game of rugby.

GAME REQUIREMENTS

1. POSSESSION AND PENETRATION IN ATTACK
- ■ Think attack at all times. 'Go Forward' with the ball in hand and at pace.
- ■ 'Keep it alive' – Pass before contact and out of contact (offloading).
- ■ Effective and constant support of the ball carrier.
- ■ Support strategies that provide the crucial link after the penetration.
- ■ Good management and presentation of the ball in contact.
- ■ Develop and maintain phase play with active, low body position in contact.
- ■ Provision of quick ball from breakdown areas, i.e. tackle, ruck, maul.
- ■ A varied attacking threat, but with an emphasis on back-initiated attack.
- ■ A whole team willingness to counter attack.

2. ACTIVE, POWERFUL SCRUM
- ■ Efficient, mechanical, powerful, effective unit.
- ■ Strong scrummage platform to launch attacks.
- ■ Strike moves and organise attacking game from scrums using the backs to initiate the attack.
- ■ Disruptive scrummaging in defence.

3. PRECISE, VARIED LINEOUT
- ■ An in-field kicking strategy that creates a lineout on the team's terms.
- ■ Precise, accurate, varied lineout to provide quick ball.
- ■ Strike game from lineouts that also develops phases of play.
- ■ Driving lineout game.
- ■ Organised, effective lineout defence.

4. PRESSURE DEFENCE
- ■ Think ATTACK in defence – concentration, communication, organisation, offensive defence.
- ■ 'Step up, knock back, knock down' attitude.
- ■ Selective involvement at ruck and maul situations until turnover time.
- ■ Discipline, mental hardness and belief in the defence.
- ■ No silly penalties and improved discipline.

5. EFFECTIVE KICKING STRATEGY
- ■ An infield kicking strategy with precision, length and accuracy.
- ■ An effective pressure game to make the kicking strategy effective.
- ■ A varied kick-off game.
- ■ A kick-off reception game that gives the team control – catch the ball!
- ■ A penalty/free kick policy to increase tempo and initiate a running and handling game.

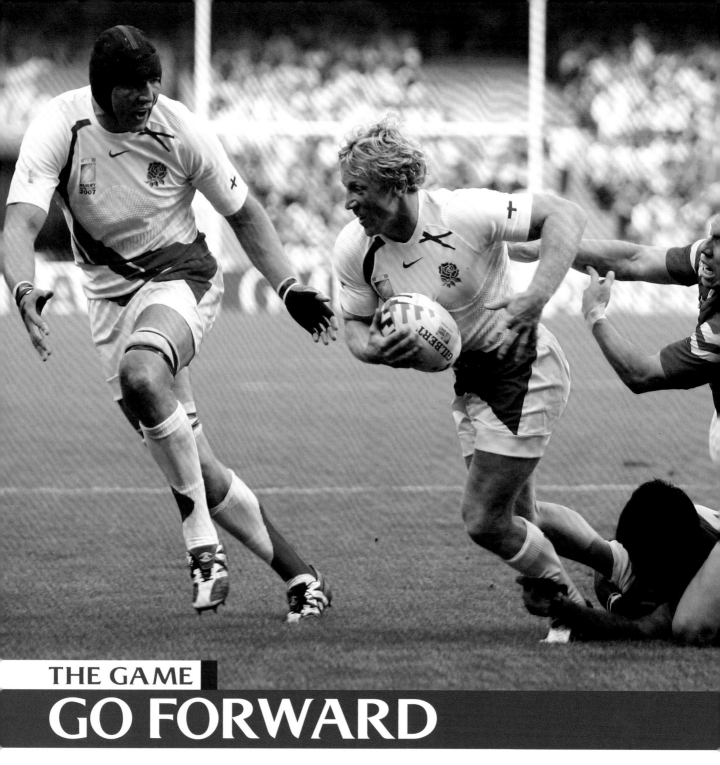

THE GAME
GO FORWARD

In order to gain an advantage over the opposition a rugby team must always be looking to 'go forward' on the field of play. In doing so there are a number of things a team is looking to achieve…

- **To score a try**
- **To get a ball carrier beyond the tackle line and so over the gain line. This allows a team to make the opposition both lose their shape and be turned, so that the attackers are running at a disorientated defence that's on the retreat**
- **To make opposing defenders concentrate their**

attention and their energies on one particular area, so that attacking space is created in other parts of the pitch

Both forwards and backs can contribute to providing 'go forward'. Forwards retain possession and drive forward, either individually or collectively. When the drive is stopped by the opposition, or if possible even before, the forwards must look to deliver the ball to the backs with the intention of allowing them to run hard against the retreating defenders.

Backs allow forward momentum to be maintained by using their natural athletic and rugby skills. This can be via

Ben Kay picks the perfect running line to provide support for ball carrier Peter Richards

ruck or maul. To reach the gain line attackers have to break the tackle line, the position where tackles are made. This is dependent on the alignment and reaction of the defending team. It's critical for defenders to move forward into contact.

The glue that sticks all of these 'go forward' skills together is communication. Every player in the team must know his role and have the necessary skills to perform that role effectively. But without the ability to communicate with team mates and work in harmony with them to unlock opposition defences it's unlikely that a team will be able to achieve consistent success.

PROVIDE SUPPORT

It's rare in rugby that a single ball carrier can beat an entire defence and it's for this reason that support and continuity skills are so important. Players will spend most time during a game running lines of support and as such require an appetite for hard work and selfless dedication to the overall good of the team. Support runners must offer support on both sides of the ball carrier and keep some depth behind them. The most effective support comes from directly behind the ball carrier, because this gives the runner the most time possible to decide which side of the ball carrier he'll run to. A worthwhile attack is sustained by the efforts of all the support runners as they provide different options to the ball carrier, make use of space, provide continuity, secure the ball when the carrier is tackled and provide more lateral support for outflanking plays.

Support players need to be good at communicating direction and distance with the ball carrier to let them know where they are, to explain exactly where they want the ball and even what type of pass they're looking to receive. They also need to be good in contact so that there are other options available besides simply going to ground.

The running lines that support players pick are extremely important. If running lines are good then support can arrive quickly. Arriving from depth allows runners to react either to the left or to the right and at pace.

Fitness will also play a major part in support play, as the fitter players are, the easier it will be for them to get into good supporting positions and the more players there are supporting the ball carrier the more attacking options there will be. Achieving the right balance between a sufficient number of supporting runners and a good distribution of players so the ball can be moved out into space is key. It's also important for the ball carrier to remember that once the ball has been passed he in turn must become a support player.

accurate passing, clever running either with the ball in hand or acting as a decoy runner, using speed or agility to evade opposition tacklers and accurate kicking over or through a defence to regain possession. All of these skills help to keep a team moving forward.

While the attacking side attempts to move forward, opposing defenders will be trying to disrupt the attacking side's attempts to take the ball upfield. They too will be trying to provide their own 'go forward' by making tackles beyond the 'gain line' to stop their opponents from making ground. The gain line is an imaginary line that runs parallel to the goal line and through the centre of the restart,

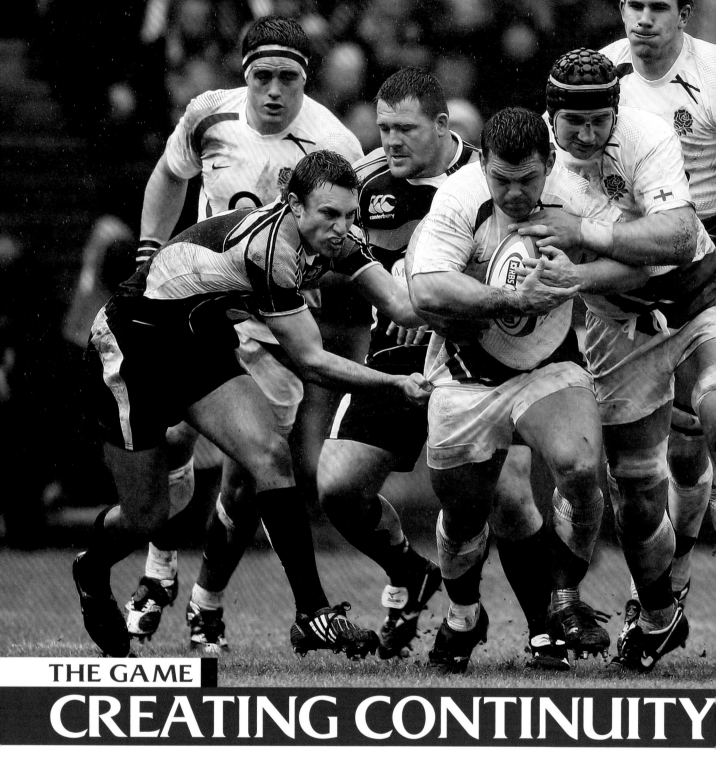

CREATING CONTINUITY

The term 'continuity' is simply a team's ability to sustain an attack. Many attacking sides find that the ball dies after the first attempt to score. Players win possession and develop an attack leading into contact, but they often lose possession at this point while trying to sustain the attack. This means they then have to win the ball back again, thereby starting the cycle all over again.

If a team has fit and mobile players who can run at the space between defenders and then recycle and retain possession of the ball after being tackled, then the cycle of continuity can be developed. The result of

greater continuity is more pressure exerted on the opposition defence. Each play should be developed with a view to scoring a try, but if this proves impossible then the object is to recycle the ball, maintain continuity and try again until an attacking move finally succeeds.

Good continuity needs good support running and high quality second, third and fourth phase ball when play breaks down in situations such as the ruck and the maul. It also requires excellent decision making each time that play comes to a temporary stop.

When the ball is in open play carriers should

Lee Mears remembers
that the first option of
the ball carrier is always
to try to run at space

- ■ Hit the opposition defender and spin out of the tackle
- ■ Stand in the tackle and play the ball
- ■ Wait for the first support hit, allowing them to rip the ball and feed it
- ■ Wrap the ball up, then drive, maul and recycle

In controlling the ball after contact a player can choose to go to ground and...

- ■ Pass on contact
- ■ Place the ball
- ■ Wait for a supporting team mate to play the ball or to drive defenders away
- ■ Wait for supporting team mates who can drive, ruck and recycle

■ TECHNIQUES FOR CONTINUITY

HIT AND SPIN

The ball carrier must focus on the contact area with his chin off his chest and his eyes open. Maintaining a low body position he should keep the ball in two hands and away from the contact, using small steps leading up to the point of impact, which should be onto the side of the defender. On contact the carrier should step wide with power, putting the front foot close to the defender's feet and setting his body in front of the ball. The target area is the defender's shoulder and contact should be side on, allowing a spin to the outside of the shoulder while maintaining contact, followed by a forward-facing burst away from contact.

STAND IN THE TACKLE

Focus on the area of contact to the side of the defender with the chin off the chest, the eyes open and body position low. The ball should be kept in two hands away from the contact area using small steps on the approach. Use quick footwork to hit onto one side of the defender, planting the front foot close to the defender's feet and keeping the body before the ball. Contact should be engaged side on with the hard part of the body – the shoulder, hip or leg – where the player must drive from low to high, aiming to get his shoulder past the defender's own shoulder. It's

always be looking to make a pass sooner rather than later because a late pass is more likely to put the receiver in difficulty. Precise passing will allow a team to maintain continuity.

The first option for the ball carrier is always to try to run at space. The next option is to pass before contact. But when these two options are impossible the ball carrier should then look to take the ball into contact and either move the ball onwards or control the ball ready to set up the next play.

In moving the ball on contact the player has a number of options. He can stay on his feet and...

Topsy Ojo prepares
for contact with the
primary objective of
retaining the ball and
maintaining continuity

important to keep a low and stable base, holding the
ball close in to the body at hip height. After bracing and
taking the impact the player should transfer the ball
backwards after the initial forward momentum.

POP PASS

The technique leading into contact is identical to that
of standing in the tackle, up to the point of planting the
feet and getting the body before the ball. At this point
the player should get his shoulder both to the side and
beyond the defender's body before making contact
side on with the hard parts of his body. Now the player
should maintain a low and stable base, with chin up
and eyes open, then turn his head to look for support
while screening the ball with his body. The ball is then
popped up as a short pass to a supporting player. The
player making the pass shouldn't forget his own role to
support the player receiving the ball.

BALL CARRIER ON THE GROUND

Using the same technique as before going into contact
the ball carrier should use strong and powerful steps
on impact to keep momentum going, then use a
strong leg drive forward before going to ground. The
ball must then be placed to the side of the body in
the direction of the support players, then released or
passed to a runner. The body should be at right angles
to the touchline and the player should get to his feet as
quickly as possible afterwards.

FIRST SUPPORT PLAYER WHEN THE BALL IS ON THE GROUND

The first support player should approach the ball from
depth and parallel to the touchline and call for the
pass if he believes it's the best option. If it isn't, then
he should take up a low driving position, then secure
position by straddling over and in front of the ball. The
player must then either drive forward, binding into the
opposition and past the ball, or pick up the ball himself,
drive forward and set or pass.

RUCK AND MAUL

Of course the ruck and maul (see pages 118-121) are
major ways of building continuity, but they do slow
down the production of the ball following contact.

PRESSURE POINT

There's a saying in rugby that pressure
brings points. In defence a team
pressurises the opposition by making
aggressive tackles as far behind the gain
line as possible, putting in strong tackles
that will drive opponents backwards and
potentially secure turnover ball, disrupting
the attack's ability to retain the ball at the
contact area and working hard to organise
quick and comprehensive cover.

An attacking team must produce
pressure to unsettle a defence by
attacking their weak areas, producing and
using good ball, following up kicks and
challenging positively, forcing a defence
to overcommit to one area of the pitch,
so freeing up space to attack elsewhere,
recycling the ball quickly in contact and
running both incisively and evasively.

EFFECTIVE CONTINUITY RELIES ON...

- The ball carrier dominating the contact area
- Effective decision making
- Good ball handling and retention skills to maintain control of the ball
- Support players running both close and wide arriving at pace and from deep
- Making the ball available
- Good rucking and mauling ability

THE GAME
DEFENDING AS A TEAM

There are a number of ways for a rugby team to defend, but the ultimate aim is always the same – to stop the opposition scoring a try. To do so all the defending team's individuals must be skilled in the art of defending and focused above all on making tackles in front of the gain line. But no matter how good an individual player may be defensively, a collective team effort is essential if a team is to defend successfully. Players must work together and concentrate on their collective shape, organisation and communication. There has to be a defensive plan in place that all players understand and can implement together.

The basic systems of defence at set pieces are…

- **Man for man, where each player is responsible for marking his immediate opposite number**
- **Drift defence, where players move outwards as the ball is passed. Inside centre, for example, moves to mark outside centre and so on**
- **One out. The defending fly half lines up immediately opposite the attacking inside centre, leaving his opposite number to be covered by the defending scrum half and forwards**
- **Out to in. When there are equal numbers of attackers and defenders, or when a tram is defending close to its own try line. Defenders align flat and as the ball is played they rush straight up in a line and curve back inside to stop the ball going wide, and force the ball carrier to run into the vacuum created**
- **Blitz defence. The defenders deny attackers time and space by sprinting forward as a line**

At the breakdown the standard defensive pattern is a flat line on either side of the ruck or maul. In this situation players need to communicate with each other constantly to make sure they have the right numbers on either side of the ruck. The defenders who are closest to the ruck take the role of guards. Some teams put two guards on either side of the breakdown to defend this crucial area. They should move straight forward when the ball emerges. A player (often the scrum half) organises the defence to avoid being outnumbered, especially on the blind side. Then the defenders must work out who is the right player to tackle when the attacking team moves the ball, while constantly encouraging their own team mates

to work together. It's important for a defending team not to commit too many players to the ruck or maul as this will leave the attacking team with extra men available out wide. The widest defenders need to be just inside the attacking side's end men at each side of the ruck and maul and the gaps between players need to be as small as possible, most importantly around the area of attack. It's also crucial that the defensive line moves forward together, which means defenders must always play with their heads up, watching what the opposition is doing and reacting accordingly.

COMMON DEFENSIVE MISTAKES

- **The defensive line is too short**
  If the attacking team moves the ball out wide quickly then the defence will be outflanked.

- **One player moves up too fast, often referred to as a 'dogleg' defence**
  A player who advances ahead of the defensive line will leave a gap that allows an offensive player to attack the space, then offload to a support runner.

- **One player moves up too slowly**
  Again, if a defending player is out of step with the rest of his line a gap will emerge. The attacking player will target the slow defender directly, carrying the ball through the first line of defence before offloading to a support runner on either side.

- **Guards at the breakdown do not defend with discipline**
  Guards go across the field (either player or ball watching) and leave space for the opposition to come forward and cross the 'gain line'.

Without good organisation and good communication – as shown by England here – defending as a team is impossible

GOOD DEFENSIVE TEAMS HAVE...

- **Good organisation**
- **Good communication**
- **Players who make their one-on-one tackles**
- **Attitude**

ATTACKING AS A TEAM

The primary objective in a rugby match is to win the game. Scoring tries gives a side the most points for one single action and so creating opportunities to score tries is at the root of a team's attacking strategy.

There are a number of ways to work try-scoring opportunities and the options chosen by a coach and a team will depend on the strengths of the players involved. Certain sides will base their strategy on a core of 10 players, the eight forwards, the scrum half and the fly half, if they feel they have a particularly dominant pack. The forwards tend to keep the ball, gaining territory by using good rucking and mauling techniques. If the attacking

moves stall the ball is then fed to the fly half who kicks for territory or for touch if he feels his forwards are a strong lineout unit and will be able to win the ball, even on the opposition's throw, and use strength to drive for the line.

A forward-oriented attacking strategy can reap rewards, but modern thinking insists that the most effective way to attack is from all over the field, utilising fast and creative backs to penetrate the defensive line or to create the space and numbers to outflank the defence. Another method to beat a defence is to kick the ball either over or through them. Backs can also be used in attack to gain ground and provide attacking targets for the forwards to

ENGLAND
RUGBY

The principles behind all
attacking team play are:
i) **Gain Possession**
ii) **Go Forward**
iii) **Support**
iv) **Create Continuity**
v) **Apply Pressure**

RUNNING AND PASSING AT SPEED

Players stand on the outside of the channel and run in towards the ball which is passed from left to right, but pass the ball out along the line. Each player runs in and passes out, then continues to the next line after making the pass, then runs along that line until the ball carrier on the far right starts another move.

Running at speed is vital if a player wants to attack effectively, because a burst of true speed is very difficult to defend against. But speed needs to be controlled so that skills such as effective, accurate passing can be performed efficiently. Good passing is dependent on taking the ball early and on the pass being made *for* the receiver rather than *at* the receiver.

PENETRATION

To break through a well-organised defence a team needs both individual and collective skill and for all the players to be dedicated to practice. In order to be able to penetrate a defence effectively it's important for the attacking side to organise the alignment of the back line. Younger players will need to stand further away and at a more pronounced angle from the opposition to give them the necessary time and space to carry out their set moves. This is known as a 'steep alignment'. More experienced players can line up closer to their opponents in what is known as a 'flat alignment' to give them more chance of breaking the tackle line, though this requires a higher level of skill given the fact that there is automatically less room to work in. There are a number of attacking advantages that come from playing with a flat alignment. Players take on defenders more quickly, giving the opposition less time to react. It's easier for anyone passing the ball to provide support for the receiver as a ball that has been passed flat means the receiver is more likely to be in front of the passer when they receive the ball. Players make it to the gain line more quickly and are encouraged to run straight onto a pass rather than drifting away from it.

Correct player alignment helps players to cross the tackle line – the point where attacking and defending players first engage and progress towards the gain line. This is the imaginary line that runs through the middle of the set piece of the breakdown denoting attacking and defensive territory. Once a player gets over the gain line he has his support players behind him, while a good number of defenders will be out of position and unable to contribute to defending, thus making attacking easier.

support, generating further phases of play.

In order to break through a defensive line it's vitally important for backs to be able to create space and recognise it when it appears on the field. This is done by being able to handle the ball quickly and by being able to execute running lines effectively. The best way to understand the importance of space in which to work is through the creation of channels. Channels encourage back line members to run straight in attack in order to maintain space on the outside. In training the width of these channels should be around five metres for adults and three to four metres for children.

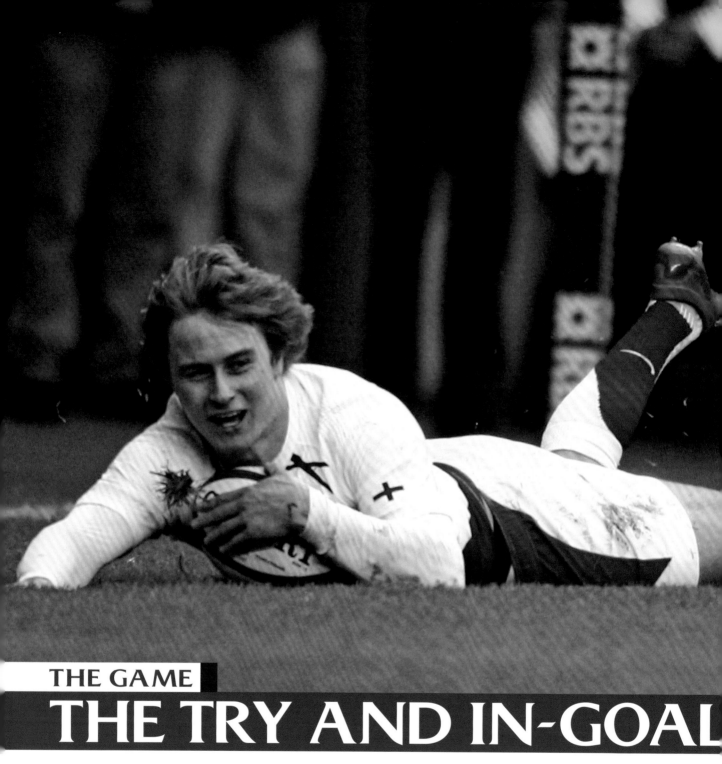

THE TRY AND IN-GOAL

Touching down for a try is the manner of scoring that yields the most points – five – in rugby. An attacking player scores a try by being the first person to ground the ball in his opponent's in-goal area, either on or behind the goal line. In order for a try to be awarded neither the player holding the ball nor the ball itself can be in touch. The touchline, the dead ball line and anywhere beyond either are out of play. The Experimental Law Variations introduced in August of 2008 state that a player may now touch the corner flag, yet still score a try. Any part of the body that is airborne above the lines or outside the field of play is

not in touch. The goal posts and any padding surrounding them are considered as part of the goal line and so a try is permitted if the ball is grounded against either of these areas.

Grounding the ball means either holding or touching the ball on the ground, or putting the hand, the arm or the front torso on top of a ball that is on the ground in-goal. This action only needs to happen for a split second for a try to be awarded; the only criteria that need to be fulfilled are that the player was intending to ground the ball and they had control of it when they did so. It is also permissible for the

ENGLAND
RUGBY

Mathew Tait enjoys the
best feeling in rugby –
going over for a try!

AREA

THE PENALTY TRY

The referee has the authority to award a
penalty try if he believes the defending
team has deliberately (or persistently)
infringed in order to prevent the
attacking team from scoring a try. The
official only needs to believe in the
probability of a try being scored in order
to award the penalty try, which is always
awarded beneath the posts regardless of
where the transgression took place.

THE ROLE OF
THE TELEVISION
MATCH OFFICIAL

At the professional end of the game
the referee can ask for advice from a
television match official who has access
to slow motion images to help decide if a
try can be awarded.

attacking player to score a try even if he falls to the
ground before reaching the goal line as long as his
momentum carries him forward so that the ball
touches either the goal line or the in-goal area. If a
player can stretch out and touch down in the in-goal
area even after being tackled short of the try line, then
a try can be awarded.

A player who is in touch, but who isn't carrying the
ball may still score a try by grounding the ball in goal.

If the ball is dropped in-goal the referee considers
this action as a knock on and will not award a try.

If there is a doubt in the referee's mind about

whether it was an attacking player or a defending
player who grounded the ball first, then the attacking
team is a awarded a scrum at the five metre line. A
player in a scrum is permitted to down the ball within
that scrum as soon as it either reaches or crosses the
try line.

Once a try has been awarded the team that has
scored is also awarded a conversion, a kick at goal
worth two points. The kick can be taken anywhere on
the field in line with where the try was scored and
parallel to the touch line. The ball must pass over the
crossbar and between the posts to be successful.

THE GAME

THE LINEOUT

There are more lineouts in the modern game than ever before, so this is an area of rugby where success is crucial. A lineout is called when the ball is kicked over or simply goes over the sideline, when a player runs over the sideline while carrying the ball or when a tackle forces the player carrying the ball over the sideline. The team that hasn't taken the ball out of play wins the right to restart the game with a throw-in.

When the ball is kicked directly into touch by a player standing in his own 22 or in the goal area behind his try line, the lineout is formed where the ball went out and the opposition is awarded the throw-in. If the kicker is outside his own 22 and the ball goes directly into touch the lineout is awarded to the opposition where the kick was made. However, new Experimental Law Variations state that if the defending team either takes or passes the ball back into their own 22 metre area, then they cannot kick directly into touch.

The throwing team's objective in a lineout is to gain control of the ball and the opposition must try to disrupt this and gain control of the ball themselves. When the ball is won it must be delivered from the lineout to the backs to set up attacking options.

There must be at least two players in any lineout. There's no maximum number of players allowed, and under the new Experimental Law Variations either team can put any number of players into a lineout. The two lines must stand against each other, with around a metre gap between. The front of the lineout can't be less than five metres from the sidelines and the back must be no more than 15 metres away.

Successful lineout play needs quality throwing, players in the lineout who can jump well and control their bodies in the air, speedy footwork to manoeuvre on the ground and help create aerial dominance over the opposition, effective support for the jumper from the rest of the lineout from the time he starts his leap until the time he returns to the ground and good communication between all players.

Lifting in the lineout is only permitted for players aged 16 or over.

THE THROW

A lineout won't function properly without an accurate thrower to deliver the ball. This role is usually fulfilled by the hooker and in order to achieve these aims he must have excellent technique, especially the ability to throw the ball straight as the laws of rugby stipulate. A right-handed player needs to hold the ball in both hands, with feet astride, shoulder-width apart and the knees bent. The left foot should be slightly forward, yet still be outside of the field of play. The right hand goes on the rear right of the ball and the left hand is placed on the centre of the left-hand side to maintain stability.

To produce throwing power the player must take the ball back directly over his head. Putting the ball in this position also allows the thrower to hide his intentions from the opposition jumpers, because that way it's hard to work out exactly when the ball will be thrown in. The thrower then transfers his weight to the back foot before transferring the weight again, this time to the front foot. The elbow leads and the forearm and wrist should be whipped through towards the target. The wrist should snap as the ball is rolled off the fingers and into play, then the arms follow through with the player's body weight moving forward over the front foot. The pattern needs to be switched for a left-handed player.

THE JUMPERS

Once the ball is in play the target generally has three choices for his jump.

i) Take the ball coming forward
ii) Take the ball straight up
iii) Take the ball going backwards

A jumper must be explosive when he leaps in order to have the best chance of winning the ball. He can then secure possession either with a clean catch or by stretching higher than normal and deflecting the ball toward a team mate outside of the lineout using the inside hand, the one nearer the opposition.

The jumper must jump with equal power from each foot. Hips, head, shoulders, arms and hands should be over the feet and the leg should be bent at 120 degrees with the torso always upright. If the jumper needs to move before jumping he should do so with a series of quick steps, then gather himself for a split second to help with balance before leaping. The feet

Once the jumper is airborne he must keep his head still and focused on the ball, as Simon Shaw demonstrates

Perfect lifting from his support players allows Steve Borthwick to make a clean lineout catch. The French lift is perhaps not quite as impressive

A stable lifting platform will give a lineout jumper like Ben Kay the best chance of winning the ball

ball over the defending jumper. In this situation there is a greater margin for error. Understanding which areas of the opposition's lineout are weak will allow a defending jumper to jump in such a way as to force the hooker to throw to those weak areas.

THE SUPPORT

The two lineout players who normally support the jumper need raw strength to perform their task effectively. They must also have fast feet and hands to provide a stable lifting platform, with the feet shoulder width apart and knees bent to 120 degrees. The hands need to be up and the arms flexed at the elbow with the elbows tucked in. The support players must always have their eyes on the point where they intend to grip the jumper on the shorts as the jumper leaves the ground.

To be able to put power into the lift support players should drive the knees forward, lower the backside and then drive upward with the legs. Then just before the legs become fully extended the support players should drive the arms upwards with real dynamism to the point where they're fully extended and locked at the elbow. To maintain stability the body must be completely straight, leaning in and as close as possible to the jumper. Support players must continue their role until the jumper returns to ground.

In order to maximise the potential of a lineout it's vital that all the players involved know which jumper the ball will be thrown to and what the ensuing attacking play will be if it's successful. A designated lineout leader has the task of making lineout calls. These are always in code so that the opposition won't know what's about to happen.

should remain closely together with the inside foot slightly ahead, while elbows should be kept in and arms bent to help speed up movement and maintain better balance during the jump.

Once the jumper is airborne – making sure to direct the power of the jump both upwards and inwards – the hands should be up and relaxed with the head kept still and focused on the ball. The jumper should keep his legs straight, so that the supporting players can hold him in the air. The angle of take-off allows the catcher to turn in the air while making the catch, so that he can then come down with knees bent, back to the opposition and facing his own scrum half.

When defending a lineout the jumper should always look to get up in front of the attacking jumper to win the ball. Early jumping will put pressure on the opposing hooker and make him attempt to throw the

REMEMBER!

Contest – When the ball is in flight
Protect – When the ball is caught
Tidy Up – When the ball is fumbled or bobbling

THE GAME
THE SCRUM

The scrum is one way of restarting the game after an infringement. Because there is serious contact and impact between the two sides in this area of rugby safety is paramount when teaching the scrum. Laws governing the scrum develop through the various age levels to help ensure this safety and all rugby coaches and players should be familiar with all of these law variations. The scrum can be an effective tool in launching attacks either through the back row or through the backs themselves, or as an attacking weapon in itself to drive the opposition backwards. It can even be used defensively in order to disrupt an opponent's possession. Each front five player must be a specialist in his position – again because of safety concerns – and every player must stay bound in the scrum until the ball has left.

THE BASICS OF SCRUMMAGING
- Heads must be up with the chin off the chest with the player looking through the eyebrows.
- Eyes must be focused on the target area and players should under no circumstances look away.
- The feet, the hips and the shoulders must all be square.

The scrum is not only used as an attacking weapon but can also be an effective tool in disrupting the opponent's possession

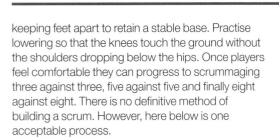

keeping feet apart to retain a stable base. Practise lowering so that the knees touch the ground without the shoulders dropping below the hips. Once players feel comfortable they can progress to scrummaging three against three, five against five and finally eight against eight. There is no definitive method of building a scrum. However, here below is one acceptable process.

THE FRONT ROW

The hooker stands just off the mark on the ground that has been made to show where the scrum should engage. He must be bent at the knees and hips with his weight on the balls of his feet. The loose-head prop should approach the hooker from the rear, reach behind the hooker and bind on his hip area at the top of his shorts. The tight-head prop should also approach from behind and bind in the same way, in a manner that allows for his shoulders to remain square. Grips need to be with the full hand and be both tight and comfortable. The shoulders, feet and hips need to be square, the spine in line with the touchline and the feet parallel.

Engagement of the scrum should initially be practised with the front row only. Players should focus on the target area where their heads and shoulders will make contact with their opponents. Heads go to the left of the opposition player.

The engagement sequence – Crouch-Touch-Pause-Engage – should always be managed by the match referee (*see over*).

THE SECOND ROW

There are a number of methods for locks to join a scrum and this is one such method. Once the front row is confident in its binding and engagement, then the second row can be introduced, with the aim of binding the front five together and transmitting power through the front row. During the formation stage second rows have their inside knee touching the ground, with hips together and both knees flexed. They then bind strongly around each other with the inside arm and around the hips of the prop in a five-man scrum at midi level. In an eight-man scrum, however, they may choose to go into formation

■ The knees and hips must be bent, feet parallel to the touchline and weight on the balls of the feet.
■ Stomach and chest must be pushed out and the back must be straight.
■ The shoulders must be above the hips at all times.

In order to scrummage positively and effectively players must actively enjoy the process. This can initially be encouraged by scrummaging one against one. This way players get comfortable and experience both flexibility and stability while moving around. The two players can move round in a circle,

crouched and with both knees off the ground, bind with the inside arm and then up through the props' legs. The binding should be as close to their own ear as possible, with the elbow up and gripping the props' shorts.

The two locks should bind together strongly, place their heads between the hooker's and props' hips with their shoulders below the props' buttocks, look up into the scrum with chins off chests, flatten out the back and shoulders and aim to get the point of their outside shoulder in line with the props' tailbones.

THE BACK ROW

Again, once the front five are confident in the process of binding and engagement the Number 8 and the two flankers can be introduced to create the full eight-man scrum. The Number 8 binds around the second rows' hips, looks up into the scrum with chin off chest and flattens out the back and shoulders. The flankers, meanwhile, bind over the backs of the second rows, then push at a slight angle with the inside shoulder moving onto the props' buttocks.

THE ENGAGEMENT SEQUENCE

■ Crouch

The knees bend slightly with the upper body inclined from the hip, the shoulders above the hips and with weight on the balls of the feet. Props visualise the area they're going to hit while all players keep their chins off their chests. The shoulders should hunch and brace, though no pressure should be applied to the front row from behind. Players should then balance and hold, waiting for the referee's next instructions.

■ Touch

The contact point – the space on the opponent's left – is visualised. This is called 'sighting the target'. The props touch their opponent's shoulder or upper arm with the outside arm or hand. This position is held for two to three seconds, again without pressure coming from behind. The props then pull their arms back.

■ Pause

A vital part of the process, allowing players to balance and sight their contact area.

■ Engage

With chin off chest and looking through the eyebrows the engagement happens without charging. The loose-head props bind on to the back of the opposition tight-head as high as possible, keeping the elbow up. The tight-head prop binds onto the opposition loose-head in the same way. Pressure must be applied horizontally only, though a slight upward movement may help this. Engagement must only happen on the referee's instruction and movement forward must only be with very short steps.

THE PUT IN

The scrum half must stand with his own forwards to the right and introduce the ball into the scrum as soon as the respective front rows have engaged. The scrum half should hold the ball in two hands with its major axis parallel to the ground and the touchline over the middle line between the front rows, midway between

knee and ankle. The hooker is allowed to strike as soon as the ball leaves the scrum half's hands. The ball must be put in straight. If the scrum half tries to put the ball in directly to the hooker's feet this is a 'crooked feed' and the opposition will be awarded a free kick. If the scrum collapses the referee must stop play immediately and it is vital that players stop pushing. Players must not move or twist their bodies or pull down on an opponent to make the scrum collapse.

If the scrum is turned – or wheeled – through 90 degrees another scrum must be set, with possession being awarded to the team that had not thrown the ball in during the previous scrum.

At Under 19 level the scrum can only wheel 45 degrees before it is reset and the ball is thrown in by the same team. In addition, the scrum can only be pushed 1.5 metres at Under 19 level. For other limitations on the scrum refer to the continuum for mini/midi levels.

AFTER THE PUT IN

Once the ball is introduced into the scrum both attacking and defending packs will try to shunt the other backwards. It's usually the team throwing the ball in that wins the ball, but when the other team's hooker does manage to win possession this is known as a strike against the head.

Once the ball has been won it is channelled to the back of the scrum, usually between the two locks and back to the right-hand side of the Number 8 so it's given maximum protection from the opposing scrum half. No-one must touch the ball with their hands until the ball has been cleared away.

A scrum that is either stable or moving forward makes for more interesting attacking possibilities, and if the scrum is angled slightly towards the side the team plans to attack then so much the better as this will help to take opposition defenders out of play.

THE RUCK

The ruck is a phase of play in which one or more players from each team are in physical contact while still on their feet and close around the ball on the ground. Open play has ended. A ruck often takes place after a tackle has been made and players are rucking when they are using their feet to try to win or keep possession of the ball. In this situation the player who has been tackled can place the ball on the ground to the advantage of his own team mates if he does so immediately.

The first forwards to arrive at a ruck often bind together, grabbing their opponent around the shoulders or waist, then attempt to drive their opposite number backwards and step over the ball. Then any other players who arrive at the ruck must be bound with at least one arm around a team mate. This bind must be executed properly using the whole arm. The ball can't be touched with the hands, but players are allowed to rake the ball backwards to a team mate. Alternatively an attacking group can drive ahead and step over the ball so it emerges on their side of the ruck where an awaiting player – usually the scrum half – can distribute. There is obviously an advantage to the side that wins the ball

It's usually the scrum half – in this case Richard Wigglesworth – who distributes the ball away from the ruck

'BRIDGING'

The team in possession of the ball at a ruck often tries to retain it by 'bridging' players over the tackled player and ball. In 'bridging' the player takes his weight on his feet and his arms, which are on the tackled player. Often his shoulders are lower than his hips as he virtually covers his team mate with his body. This is against the letter of the law, but is now accepted in the higher levels of the game.

in doing this quickly so that the ball can be worked into the next attacking position before the opposition defence has time to organise itself properly.

The key elements to remember when competing at the ruck are to bind to another player and drive over the ball with short steps, going from a low body position to a high one. The chin must be off the chest with the head up and the eyes open, with the head and the shoulders above the hips. It's imperative for the player to be on his feet in a ruck and to try to remain on his feet. It is illegal for a player to deliberately fall or kneel in a ruck,

to jump on top of a ruck or to collapse a ruck.

In the ruck players aren't allowed to block access to the ball if they've fallen to the ground. They must roll away. A player rucking for the ball must not ruck players on the ground. The referee should penalise players who are preventing the ball from emerging.

The ruck is a crucial area of engagement and because it's so fiercely contested with so many players committed to winning the ball the referee needs to exert strict control over proceedings. When joining a ruck players must join from behind the back foot of the last player by going through 'The Gate'. The gate is the width of the ruck, which is determined by the bodies of the players involved in the ruck. Players must not use their legs to pick the ball up or use their hands at any time except if the ball is over the try line and a player is able to score a try from the move.

Once the ball has left a ruck it must leave the area, which means that it isn't permitted for a player to kick the ball back into a ruck. Nor is it permitted for a player to fall on the ball or even over it once it has left a ruck. If at any point a ruck becomes unplayable due to the number of bodies competing for the ball then the referee will blow his whistle and call a scrum. The team which was advancing most at the ruck will be awarded the put-in.

THE MAUL

A maul happens when a player carrying the ball is held by one or more opponents and one or more of his own team mates bind onto the ball carrier. All the players involved must be on their feet and moving towards the goal line. The maul is created most often when an attacking player takes the ball into the tackle area and then turns backwards to face his supporting team mates to offer more protection to the ball and to prevent the defending team from ripping it from his hands. The supporting players grab the ball carrier by the waist and shoulders to protect the ball as effectively as possible.

Players joining a maul must do so from behind the foot of the last team mate in the maul by going through the 'gate'. The player may join alongside this last player.

Once a maul has formed it must always move forward. If a defending team manages to stop forward motion then the attacking team must either use the ball at once or get the maul moving again. If this doesn't happen then the referee will award a scrum to the team that did not initiate the maul. If the maul collapses while it's moving forward and the ball isn't retrieved immediately the defending side will be awarded the scrum. If at any point the maul becomes unplayable then play is stopped and a scrum is awarded to the team that did not initiate the maul.

Once a maul has formed it must always move forward

should attempt to stay upright and keep driving forward with legs pumping, while arriving team mates should go for a lower body position to give them a better platform to push the maul forward. If the ball carrier loses the initial contact and needs support straight away, the first support player should drive in and over the ball. If the ball carrier has led with the left shoulder, the first support should drive onto the ball with the right shoulder, and vice versa. With one arm on the ball and one arm bound onto the ball carrier both players should drive together, the support player keeping his spine in line with the touchline on the initial drive. The second wave of support players should bind over the first player and try to keep a balanced shape with one supporting player on either side. Again, the spine should be in line with the touchline while the outside arm should be bound onto the opposition with the shoulders above hips at all times. The rule is that one player looks after the ball, while everyone else looks after the ball carrier.

THE ROLLING MAUL

A rolling maul is used to attack where the opposition appears weakest defensively. The ball is transferred to a player on the side of the maul, then the other players roll around to the same side and in doing so push the player with the ball forward. By repeating this move the ball is moved from one player to the next and the maul advances. The rolling maul is one of the most effective attacking moves as it's hard for the defending team to work out where the ball is as the attacking team changes direction and it's even more difficult to try to win the ball themselves.

You will often see the scrum half standing at the back of a maul to direct the attacking effort and decide at what point – if any – to move to another point of attack.

There are some important laws to remember in relation to the maul. Players can only join from an onside position and once involved in a maul players must do everything they can to stay on their feet. Players are not allowed to drag opponents out of a maul but under an Experimental Law Variation introduced by the IRB for season 2008/09 it is possible to take a maul down in a strictly prescribed manner. Any other method to collapse a maul will be penalised. If the ball carrier goes to ground he must make the ball available at once. If the ball is dropped, then the maul becomes a ruck and the players must act accordingly, using only feet and not hands.

THE DRIVING MAUL

As the name suggests a driving maul occurs when the attacking team tries to drive forward through the defence. The ball is often passed back from the player who initially takes the ball into contact to a team mate in either the second or third line of the maul to give it greater security and protection. The lead attacker should head into contact with eyes open and chin off his chest, taking a long stride before contact and turning at the last moment to make contact with both his hip and shoulder. The ball should be kept away from the contact area as the player drives from low to high. Once in contact the lead player

KICKING

K icking is a vitally important part of the game of rugby, both in attack and defence. Besides being the means of restarting the game and scoring points, kicks can be used to gain ground, to relieve pressure on a defence or to get behind an advancing defensive line and regain possession in an advanced offensive position.

There are a wide variety of kicks that can be used depending on what situation a player finds himself in. But all kicks should be made accurately and with a view to achieving an end result that will benefit the team. Poor kicking gives away hard-earned possession.

■ THE MAIN KICKS

THE PUNT

The punt can put pressure on the opposition by gaining field position or relieve pressure on a defence by sending the ball into touch. To perform a punt effectively requires control as well as technique and power. The head and shoulders must be kept still and the ball should be held with both hands in the direction in which it will be kicked. With eyes on the ball the player should point the toe of his kicking foot, then make contact by dropping the ball onto the bootlaces

Jonny Wilkinson knows
that accuracy in kicking
is hugely important

THE GRUBBER KICK

The grubber kick is used to put pressure on the opposition by putting the ball through and behind the defence for the attacking side to chase and then regain possession, or to find touch outside the 22 metre line.

The kick is performed by holding the ball in two hands, with the long axis of the ball in line with the kicking foot. The top of the ball should be pointed slightly backwards and towards the body, while the kicker must keep his eyes on the ball and his head over it. To execute the grubber drop the ball onto the foot, point the toe and make contact, keeping the knee slightly ahead of the ball. The side of the foot can also be used to attempt a more controlled kick that will most likely produce less distance. Then with a short stabbing motion punch the ball along the ground. The aim is to make the ball roll end over end, which will allow the chasing players to pick the ball up easily. The key to successful grubber kicking is to perform the kick with enough finesse that it allows support players to reach it before the opposition can gather it and so gain possession.

THE DROP KICK

The drop kick allows a team to score points direct from the field of play or to restart the game in a way that will apply pressure on the opposition and ensure possession is regained. With the non-kicking foot facing the target the player should hold the ball in two hands with the fingers pointing downwards and the top of the ball angled slightly backwards towards the kicker. With the head and shoulders still and over the ball and eyes focusing on it, the player should then drop the ball directly onto its point to the side of the non-kicking foot and slightly ahead of the kicking foot so that it bounces back to the kicker. The kicker must then swing through the line of the ball, making contact with it on the half volley, and follow through using the opposite arm to the kicking foot for balance.

THE PLACE KICK

The place kick is used when teams have the chance to kick for goal for points, either as the result of a penalty for three points or as a conversion for two points. This

(the ball should not be thrown into the air) while keeping his head over the ball and his knee bent for power. It's important to kick the widest part of the ball for the best contact, so it must be dropped onto the boot with the long axis of the ball in line with the foot. Swing the kicking leg straight through while maintaining balance on the non-kicking foot. Then follow through along the line of the ball rather than across it, keeping the head down and using the opposite arm to the kicking foot for balance. If the toe of the kicking foot is angled upwards on contact then the ball will give the punt extra height.

Olly Barkley's follow-through takes his leg directly through the tee to the middle of the posts

Danny Cipriani plants his supporting foot as close as possible to the ball to give himself maximum stability while kicking

makes the place kick hugely important because penalties often settle the outcome of a match. Because the ball is kicked off the ground the set-up is crucial. Use a kicking tee to stand the ball up straight (a mound of sand or a divot in the ground can also be used), line the seam of the ball up direct with the target, going right through the posts. The kicker should then take three or four steps back in line with the ball and the goal, then move either to the right of the ball for a left-footed kicker or to the left for a right-footed kicker in order to create a 45 degree angle between the player, the ball and the posts. It's at this point that concentration becomes crucial. The kicker needs to block everything else out and focus on the exact piece of stitching on the ball that he intends to make contact with, always visualising a positive outcome for the kick. The area of the ball to strike should be about a third of the way up from the bottom of the ball. Some players find that leaning the ball slightly in the direction of the foot they kick with helps them to find what's known as 'the sweet spot'.

The run-up to the ball should be in an arc with the body turned at 45 degrees. The non-kicking shoulder must be turned side on to the target, with the supporting foot landing as near as possible to the ball to help with stability, with body weight forward and over the ball.

Contact should be made with the ball across the top of the foot, between the big toe and the instep, the foot hitting hard and up through the ball, heading towards the top of the posts. This action of swinging the leg high will take the kicker through the middle of the ball where the 'sweet spot' is. Once the ball has been struck the kicker's follow through should take the leg directly through the tee to the middle of the posts and the chest should end up facing the target.

■ ADDITIONAL KICKS

THE CHIP KICK
The chip is a short kick from the hands of the attacking player that aims to land just over the heads of the opposition so the ball can be gathered again behind the defensive line. Many coaches view the chip as a high-risk kick that is only used because the player concerned fails to beat his man. However, there's no doubt that if the ball bounces favourably for the advancing player then the chip offers some great attacking possibilities.

THE UP AND UNDER
The idea is to hang the ball in the air for as long as possible, giving the attacking team the maximum amount of time to get under the ball and pressure the opposition. Team mates in front of the kicker when the ball is punted will be offside, so the kicker must chase his own kick in order to play his team mates onside.

THE BOX KICK
Mostly used by scrum halves, the box kick is usually used after a scrum or a lineout on the blindside (or short side) of the pitch. The idea is to put the ball behind the opposition forwards and chase effectively to isolate the defender who is about to catch the ball.

THE CROSS KICK
The cross kick is a diagonal punt, usually to the openside and beyond the last defender. It's a simple way of catching a defence out of position and has become a very effective means of try-scoring in the modern game.

ENGLAND
RUGBY

THE GAME
PASSING

To play effective rugby a player must be confident at handling the ball and be able to pass as a reflex, which will require good basic technique. This will allow a player to send and receive the ball to and from different heights and at differing speeds. It's vital to remember that passing needs to be accurate, rather than merely sending the ball in the general direction of a team mate.

■ THE MAIN PASSES

THE LATERAL PASS

The lateral pass is used to maintain continuity of play by releasing the ball to a team mate in a better position. While carrying the ball spread the fingers around its centre, keeping the arms relaxed, the elbows slightly bent and close to the sides and with the ball held in front in both hands. When moving into the pass the chest should be kept facing the opponent, with eyes looking at the receiver's target area. Swing the hands across the body, keeping the elbows close, and pass to the receiver's hands, then let the hands and arms follow through towards the target.

It's vital that the ball arrives at chest height. If it arrives below the chest the receiver will have to look down to take the ball, meaning he'll take his eyes off the opposing defence and will most likely miss an attacking opportunity. It's also crucial that the ball arrives at a speed that the receiver can deal with comfortably. It's very difficult, for example, to take a hard pass at close range. Once the pass has been made the passer should support the receiver.

THE MISS PASS

The miss pass – an extension of the lateral pass – is designed to move the ball wide as quickly as possible, passing across the front of another player to the intended receiver.

The principles of the miss pass are the same as those of the lateral pass, but the pass must be delivered strongly and the middle player must hold back so as not to obstruct the pass, run towards the ball carrier to offer the short pass option and call as normal for the pass in order to deceive the opposition defence. Of course this is a more difficult skill to

master, especially for younger players, as it calls for accuracy over a greater distance.

THE SWITCH PASS

The switch pass is mainly used to change the direction of the ball and therefore of the attack.

The ball carrier runs straight, then at an angle or a gentle curve towards the intended receiver. What is called a soft pass is made by use of the wrists and fingers just in front of the receiver, allowing the ball to hang in the air for the receiving player to run on to. The weight of the pass is crucial for effective delivery. The receiver must change the running line to come behind the ball carrier, make themselves a target and call for the ball. Then they either take the pass and change the running line or act as the decoy runner for a dummy pass.

Left: **Toby Flood makes a lateral pass – the mainstay of any player's passing game**

Below: **When making a pass from the ground scrum half Danny Care must sink into a crouch through the hips**

THE LOOP PASS

The loop pass allows players to create an extra pair of hands in attack, to make an overlap or to put another player into space. It's also possible to use the looping player as a decoy runner.

To perform the loop pass the ball carrier passes the ball, then runs behind the receiver and into the next gap to receive a return pass – or to act as a decoy runner. The receiver moves into the pass to create space for the runner, then holds the ball in front of the body and passes into the next space for the runner. The runner coming into the loop space must take his new running line first, then go into the gap, while communicating his arrival in the gap to the new ball carrier.

THE SCRUM HALF PASS FROM THE GROUND

This is the basic scrum half pass that's delivered from the base of a scrum or a ruck. The pass is normally delivered from a wide base with the feet apart.

The scrum half's back foot must be positioned beside the ball with his front foot pointing towards the receiver. With the body low, the player should sink into a crouch through the hips, with his weight resting on the rear foot. Once hands are on the ball the player must sweep the pass off the ground with his head over the ball. There should be no back lift and the weight should be transferred onto the front foot. Once the ball has been passed it's important to follow through by extending the arms along the line of the trajectory, keeping the body low and the head down, looking along the line of the pass.

THE SCRUM HALF DIVE PASS

The dive pass is used when the scrum half is under real pressure from the opposition. When opting for the dive pass the feet must be together and behind the ball, with the body between the ball and the opponent. The scrum half must crouch down with both hands on the ball and use power to drive from the legs, then extend the body into a dive, with the arms extending to deliver the ball along the line of the pass. It's important to keep the head up and the chin off the chest. As soon as the pass has been delivered it's vital that the player gets back on his feet as quickly as possible.

ENGLAND
RUGBY

THE GAME
CATCHING AND THE MARK

It's simple. If you can't catch a rugby ball you won't ever be a good rugby player and practising such a basic part of the game should never be underestimated. In order to catch effectively it helps to have a good feel for the ball and that comes through familiarity. Young players could do worse than simply carry a ball around with them so that they get used to what it feels like to hold one and so that it eventually becomes totally natural to work with the ball.

When taking a basic catch it's important to use the hands to make a target for the ball. They should be at chest height, with the thumbs up and the fingers spread. The hands should be extended towards the ball, but shouldn't be overstretched as this could lead to a loss of balance. Eyes should be kept on the ball all the way into the hands.

CATCHING A HIGH BALL
The high ball is a tactic that is often used in rugby, either at the kick off, in open play or as a set move. It's designed to gain ground both quickly and effectively and to put the opposition defence – and especially the full back – under pressure. This means that backs are more likely to be required to catch a high ball, but all players should be able to deal with this particular catch effectively.

The player attempting to make the catch should call for the ball, then turn his body side on to the onrushing attackers and establish a wide base to ensure good balance and to reduce the chance of the ball bouncing off the chest. With eyes constantly on the incoming ball, arms raised, fingers spread and relaxed and palms pointing upwards, the player should then reach for the ball and catch it in his spread fingers. The ball should then be pulled down into the arms and chest with the elbows tucked in, before the player sinks into a stable position. It's important that team mates support the catcher and offer protection so that he has the best possible chance of making a clean catch. It is possible to catch a high ball without jumping off the ground, but when under pressure from the opposition it's likely that a jump will be needed to try to ensure the defender can get to the ball first.

THE LINEOUT JUMP
In the lineout there are usually two main target jumpers for the hooker to aim at. When the pre-organised set move has been called by the hooker or the scrum half the jumpers must prepare to make their move. As the ball is released the legs must be coiled and the arms thrust upwards to help with providing extra power for the jump. The eyes must be on the ball on at all times. Despite the one metre gap between the two teams competing at the lineout and the fact that pushing, charging or holding an opponent isn't allowed there will still be plenty of competitive behaviour around the ball, so getting a clean hold on it is very important. If this isn't possible then the palm and fingers can be used to deviate the ball to a waiting player.

CALLING THE MARK
A player who catches a high ball cleanly inside the 22 metre line can shout 'mark' and the referee will award a free kick on the spot where the catch has been taken. However, a mark can't be called when the ball is caught directly from the kick off.

Left: **Note how Iain Balshaw's eyes are on the ball and his fingers are spread and relaxed**

Below: **To catch the ball effectively at the lineout you have to be competitive, as Chris Jones shows here**

THE GAME
TACKLING

Tackling is one of the absolute fundamentals of rugby and as such needs to be learnt safely and thoroughly. A tackle occurs when a ball carrier is held by one or more opponents and is brought to the ground or the ball touches the ground. The ball carrier is the tackled player and opponents who go to ground are the tacklers.

There are a number of different styles of tackle to explain. These are...

■ **The side tackle**
■ **The rear tackle**
■ **The passive front tackle**

■ **The active front tackle**
■ **The smother tackle**

There are recommended tackling progressions that should be used when teaching the skill in order to develop confident and effective defenders. Firstly, however, the ball carrier must understand what happens when contact occurs. His goal is to pass the ball – or offload – to a support player to keep play moving forward. If he can't do this then he should go to ground with the ball close to the body and held with both hands, then pass to a team mate immediately or make a second

If a side can't tackle
effectively it won't win
games. But tackling
must be done safely at
all times

vi) **Ball carrier jogging, tackler walking**
vii) **Ball carrier jogging, tackler jogging**
viii) **Ball carrier running, tackler running**

These progressions should be practised little and often, depending on conditions. Soft ground will help build confidence, though players should avoid getting too wet at the beginning of a training session. The pace of the activity should be adjusted to increase complexity, as should the width of the grid in which the activities are practised. The wider the grid, the easier it will be for the ball carrier. Tackles should be practised on both the left and right side and should be taught in order, beginning with the side tackle, which is generally considered the easiest.

■ THE SIDE TACKLE

The Tackler Should...
- Imagine a target on the bottom of the ball carrier's shorts
- Keep his head up with his chin off his chest
- Brace his shoulders
- Make initial contact with his shoulders on the ball carrier's thigh
- Wrap his arms around the carrier's legs
- Keep his head up and his eyes open behind the ball carrier's backside
- Drive with his legs, gripping with his arms and hands, to bring the ball carrier to the ground
- Get up immediately after the tackle to compete for the ball

The Ball Carrier Should...
- Go with the impact of the tackle
- Turn his outside hip and land with his body braced and on a rounded shoulder
- Present the ball

■ THE REAR TACKLE

The Tackler Should...
- Imagine a target on the bottom of the ball carrier's shorts
- Keep his head up with his chin off his chest
- Brace his shoulders
- Make initial contact with his shoulders on the ball carrier's thigh

movement to present the ball in a convenient place for support players to pick up.

RECOMMENDED TACKLING PROGRESSIONS FOR THE SIDE TACKLE

i) **Ball carrier kneeling, tackler kneeling**
ii) **Ball carrier standing, tackler kneeling**
iii) **Ball carrier standing, tackler squatting**
iv) **Ball carrier walking, tackler squatting**
v) **Ball carrier walking, tackler walking**

- Wrap his arms around the carrier's legs
- Keep his head up and his eyes open to one side of the ball carrier's legs
- Drive with his legs, gripping with his arms and hands, to bring the ball carrier to the ground
- Land on top of the tackled player
- Get up immediately after the tackle to compete for the ball

The Ball Carrier Should...
- Go with the impact of the tackle
- Turn away from the tackler's head and land with his body braced and on a rounded shoulder
- Present the ball

THE PASSIVE FRONT TACKLE

The Tackler Should...
- Imagine a target on the bottom of the ball carrier's shorts
- Keep his head up with his chin off his chest
- Brace his shoulders
- Make initial contact with his shoulders on the ball carrier's thigh
- Wrap his arms around the carrier's legs
- Keep his head up and his eyes open to one side of the ball carrier's legs
- Use momentum to take the ball carrier over the shoulder
- Twist around and land on top of the tackled player
- Get up immediately after the tackle to compete for the ball

The Ball Carrier Should...
- Try to make contact with the side (the arms) of the defender
- Go with the impact of the tackle
- Turn away from the tackler's head and land with his body braced and on a rounded shoulder
- Present the ball

THE ACTIVE FRONT TACKLE

The object here is to drive the ball carrier behind the advantage line. This tackle should only be practised with older players and with the aid of a soft landing mat.

The Tackler Should...
- Get his lead foot as close to the ball carrier as possible
- Keep his eyes on the point of impact
- Keep his head to the side
- Drop his hips to lower his centre of gravity
- Drive his shoulder up to the centre of the target area, either the stomach or the chest
- Power should come from an explosive drive upwards through his legs and backside
- Keep his back straight
- Wrap the ball carrier with his right arm if tackling with the right shoulder
- Use his left arm to pick up the attacker's right leg
- Drive upwards and then back with the aim of finishing on top
- Roll away, get up and contest possession

The Ball Carrier Should...
- Go with the impact of the tackle
- Turn away from the tackler's head and land with his body braced and on a rounded shoulder
- Present the ball

THE SMOTHER TACKLE

The idea of the smother tackle is to wrap the ball carrier up so he can neither pass nor release the ball. This tackle should be taught to players who are already comfortable tackling.

The Tackler Should...
- Get his lead foot as close to the ball carrier as possible
- Keep his eyes on the point of impact
- Wrap his arms around the upper part of the ball carrier's body
- Try to trap the ball and the player's arms
- Add his own weight to the ball carrier to bring the player to the ground
- Land on top of the tackled player
- Roll away, then get up and contest possession

The Ball Carrier Should...
- Go with the impact of the tackle
- Present the ball

AGILITY, BALANCE AND

While there are many game-specific skills that a player needs if he is to progress at rugby, it's also important not to ignore the key athletic components of agility, balance and speed. Agility is the ability to change direction or body position quickly and precisely and rugby demands that all players change direction while running. This can happen at any point and after any distance, but most directional changes take place between five and 10 metres after the start of a run.

True agility is achieved through a combination of acceleration, deceleration and directional change. To achieve good agility a player needs to work on foot

speed, balance and reaction. Foot speed ladders are useful in educating the legs and feet to work at pace and to develop fast footwork patterns. Good balance relies on strength and stability so it's important to develop these qualities, while being able to react to what unfolds on the pitch quicker than an opponent helps a player to make the necessary body movements to progress. This can be improved through handling drills. A simple obstacle course with markers placed at regular four to five metre intervals can help to develop agility. Simply passing through the markers, pushing off first the left foot, then the right foot, helps to develop the skills needed

True agility as displayed by Topsy Ojo is achieved through a combination of acceleration, deceleration and directional change

SPEED

by the side and allow the feet to tap the hands each time. It's important to keep the body upright.

■ High Hops
Using a skipping action lift into high hops, raising the knee as high as possible.

■ Driving Practice
Work on this drill over a distance of 30 metres. With both feet pointing forward and from a standing start drive outwards, trying to keep contact with the ground for as long as possible with each drive.

■ Skips
Aim for long and low skips using an easy and rhythmical action.

■ Leg Speed
Run flat out for 50 to 60 metres concentrating primarily on leg speed. Then run for 20 to 30 metres at full pace with a normal stride range, then turn on the leg speed for the next 30 metres. This means quickening the leg cadence slightly.

■ Running On The Spot
Face a partner, lift the knees high, exaggerate the arm movements with the shoulder square and with eyes to the front. Then run as follows...

i) Running at half speed. Two repetitions of 30 seconds with a 30-second walking recovery.
ii) Running at three quarter speed. Two repetitions of 15 seconds with a 30-second walking recovery.
iii) Running at seven eighths speed. Two repetitions of 10 seconds with a 30-second walking recovery.

■ Sprinting
Because rugby is such an explosive sport players need to be able to move from a standing start to top speed in a matter of a second or two. This makes sprinting an important part of a player's armoury and sprint training an essential component of their preparation. In order to improve sprinting capacity do intervals of ten 30-metre sprints with a 10-second recovery, then five 50-metre sprints with a 20-second recovery and finishing with two 100-metre sprints with a one-minute recovery.

to sidestep away from a potential tackler in a game.

In order to increase overall speed it's useful for players to break down the running action into its constituent parts, and practise drills such as...

■ High Knees
Bring the knees up higher than parallel to the ground, then pick up the speed of movement. Try to maintain the knee lift while staying relaxed.

■ Heel Flicks
Flick the heels up quickly to the backside, leave the arms

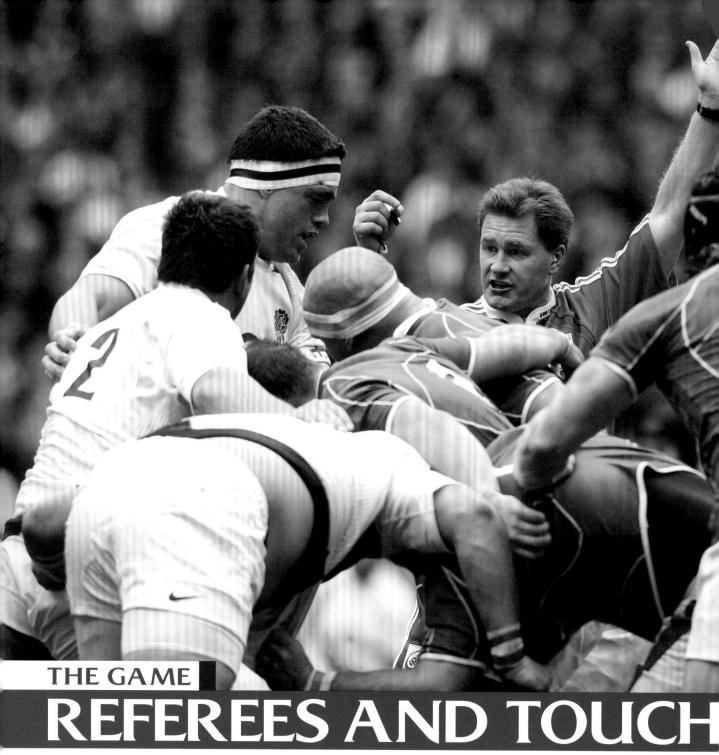

REFEREES AND TOUCH

Rugby union is a marvellous sport to play, but there is an old rugby adage that says "without a referee there will be no game." Rugby's unique mixture of free-flowing play, together with intense competition for the ball at the breakdown, requires a strong and decisive referee to ensure that the game is a pleasurable experience for both players and spectators. The referee's job is first and foremost to provide a safe environment for all the players, to implement the laws of the game and to punish foul play for the benefit of the sport. This is not always easy, especially since rugby has many nuances in its laws, is often played at pace and

with a great number of bodies coming together at the action point. It's a difficult job that requires immense knowledge of the laws of the game, a high level of physical fitness and an ability not only to impose discipline on proceedings, but also to win the confidence of all the participants. Rugby has an excellent reputation for the authority that the referee is able to bring to the sport. Players do not question the referee's decisions and treat the official with respect, in turn enabling the referee to concentrate on implementing the laws in a calm and unbiased manner.

The referee is assisted by two flag-carrying touch

ENGLAND RUGBY

The referee's job is first and foremost to provide a safe environment for all the players, to implement the laws of the game and to punish foul play

JUDGES

the laws correctly. In major matches there is also now a Television Match Official (TMO) who has access to television images in order to adjudicate whether a ball has been successfully grounded for a score and whether there is any reason why a try cannot be awarded. This is the only area of the game where the referee can call for the intervention of the TMO. Trials using the TMO in incidents relating to foul play were not adopted.

People often decide to take up refereeing to remain active in the sport after injury or retirement, to enjoy a sense of achievement in a job well done and to provide an invaluable service. There are 40 Referees' Societies in England and, after joining, anyone wishing to progress as a referee will have their development properly managed via regular appointments at a variety of matches. By meeting other referees this will also allow people who are interested in refereeing to share experiences and knowledge.

The RFU has introduced the Entry Level Referee Award (ELRA) which is a three-stage award specifically designed to provide new referees with all of the core skills they need to referee the sport of rugby union. If a potential official joins a Referees' Society he will be required to complete all three stages. However, if he wishes to remain within his own school, club or university he needs only complete stages one and two. These stages look at a variety of elements of the game from a refereeing perspective, including:

- **Materiality and contextual judgement**
- **Management and control**
- **Problem solving**
- **Refereeing the key phases of the game**
- **Positioning and communication**

Many referees are happy to remain active at the lower levels of the sport, but for those who would like to progress – like top English referee Wayne Barnes – there is an RFU-approved Refereeing Pathway that is designed to take the best referees all the way up to National League fixtures as one of the best 60 referees in the country.

For more information on refereeing and details of your local Referees Society log on at *www.rfu.com/referee*

judges, who are sometimes referees themselves. The touch judges have a number of very important roles to play; deciding who last touched the ball before going out of play and hence who is awarded the throw in, exactly where a lineout should be formed and confirming whether penalty kicks have been successful. At the higher levels of the game touch judges are able to alert the referee to forward passes and knock ons and bring incidents of foul play to the attention of a referee, who might not have been able to see an offence taking place.

At the top level of the sport the referee and touch judges communicate via radio contact to implement

ENGLAND
RUGBY

THE GAME
PENALTIES AND FREE KICKS

One of the key roles of the rugby referee is to ensure that any match is played within the laws of the game. If a player on the field acts in such a way as to be against either the letter or the spirit of these laws this is called foul play and the referee can penalise the player concerned and award an advantage to the opposition. This advantage can be either the award of a penalty kick, a free kick, or a sanction of the player concerned depending on the nature of the foul play. The most common instances of foul play in a match that lead to players being penalised are as follows...

OBSTRUCTION
There are a number of ways in which a player can be guilty of obstruction. Charging or pushing an opposing player other than by going shoulder to shoulder is not allowed, nor is running in front of the ball carrier to prevent the opposition making a tackle. Blocking an opponent who is trying to make a tackle, deliberately preventing an opponent from playing the ball, and running into a team mate who is ahead of you at a set piece are all examples of obstruction and are punishable by the awarding of a penalty. In addition, a flanker in the scrum must not stop the opposition scrum half from moving around the scrum. Again, the punishment for this form of obstruction is a free kick.

UNFAIR PLAY
A player is not allowed to infringe any of the game's laws deliberately. A player who does so intentionally can be warned about his behaviour, cautioned that committing another offence will result in a sending off at the same time as being expelled from the game for 10 minutes, or he can be sent off. In these circumstances a penalty is awarded to the opposition. A penalty try must be awarded if an offence is committed that prevents a try being scored. The player committing the offence must be cautioned and temporarily suspended or he must be sent off.

Timewasting is punishable by the awarding of a free kick to the opposition.

A player must not knock, throw, push or place the ball into touch or touch-in-goal or over the dead ball line with his arm or hand. In this case the referee must award a penalty kick on the 15 metre line if the offence has been committed between the 15 metre line and the touchline or wherever the offence was committed if it happens anywhere else on the pitch. If the infringement occurs in goal then the penalty kick is awarded five metres from the goal line and at least 15 metres from the touchline.

REPEATED INFRINGEMENTS
Repeated infringement results in a penalty kick and the player being temporarily suspended regardless of whether the infringement was intentional or not. If a player then commits another cautionable offence he must be sent off. If a team is repeatedly infringing then the referee must give a general warning to the offending team. If the team repeats the offence then the offending player must be expelled for 10 minutes. If the infringement occurs again that player must be sent off.

DANGEROUS PLAY AND MISCONDUCT
Striking an opponent results in a penalty kick to the opposition. Stamping, trampling, kicking and tripping are equally sanctioned by a penalty. A player must not tackle an opponent early, late or dangerously (above the line of the shoulders). A stiff arm tackle is dangerous play and a penalty kick is awarded. Playing a player without the ball – except in a scrum, ruck or maul – and tackling a player whose feet are off the ground will also result in a penalty being given.

It is against the laws to charge or knock down an opponent who is carrying the ball without trying to grasp them. Tackling a jumper in the air either in a lineout or in open play is illegal and results in a penalty being awarded, while a front row of a scrum rushing against its opponent will be punished in the same way. Nor must front row players lift opponents off their feet or force them upwards out of the scrum intentionally. Again, a penalty is awarded.

Players are not permitted to enter a ruck or maul without binding onto a player in that ruck or maul, nor must players deliberately collapse a ruck or scrum. In both of these cases the sanction is a penalty kick. Retaliation of any kind is considered as misconduct, as is any gesture or action that is against the spirit of

If a player on the field acts against the letter or the spirit of the laws of the game, a referee will penalise him

ENGLAND
RUGBY

As well as penalising
players for their
misdemeanours
the referee can also
award advantages to
the opposing team in
the form of a penalty
kick or free kick

good sportsmanship. No player should commit any act of misconduct while the ball is out of play. The offender will be penalised with a penalty kick being awarded to the opposition.

If a player is late in charging down a player who has just kicked the ball the opposition may choose to take a penalty either where the infringement took place, where the ball landed or where it was played next.

THE FLYING WEDGE

A flying wedge usually happens near the goal line when the attacking side has just been awarded a free kick or a penalty. Once the kicker taps the ball he may drive for the line himself or pass to a team mate who then drives. Players bind on to the ball carrier in a wedge formation, but if any team mate is in front of the ball carrier this is an illegal formation and is penalised by a penalty kick where the infringement originally took place.

THE CAVALRY CHARGE

Again, the cavalry charge usually takes place near the goal line following the award of a penalty or a free kick to the attacking side. Attacking players form a line across the field behind the kicker at a distance of a metre or two apart. The kicker signals for all the players to charge forward and once they're near the kicker taps and passes. This charge is illegal and a penalty kick must be awarded to the opposing team.

YELLOW AND RED CARDS

When a player has been cautioned and temporarily suspended during a match the referee will show the player a yellow card and the player must leave the field for 10 minutes' playing time. This is known as the 'sin bin'. When a player has been sent off in a match he will be shown a red card by the referee. Once a player has been sent off he is not allowed to take any further part in the match and the referee will submit a report to his constituent body, who will organise a disciplinary hearing and subsequent punishment.

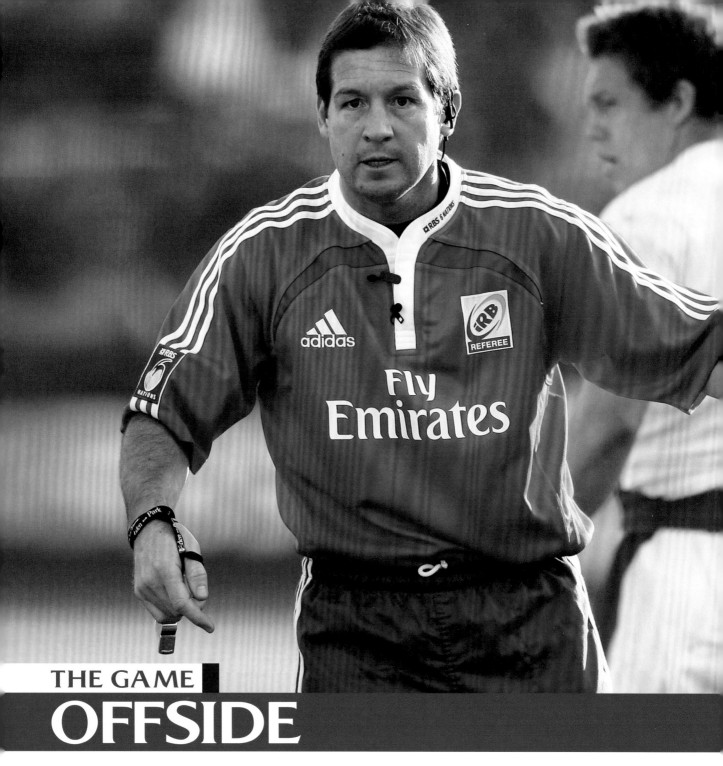

OFFSIDE

The offside laws have often confused rugby players and supporters alike, but the principles of offside are relatively straightforward. In general play a player is offside when he is in front of a team mate who has the ball or the team mate who last played it. This will happen to all players during a game, but they will not be penalised unless they try to take part in the game. If a player is penalised for being offside the referee will award a penalty to the opposition.

Once a player is offside he isn't allowed to participate in the game in any way until he's onside again. This includes moving towards any opponents who are waiting to play the ball. A player can become onside again after...

■ **A team mate who kicked the ball when behind now runs in front of the player**
■ **Any other team mate who was onside when the ball was kicked now runs in front of him**
■ **A team mate with the ball runs in front of him**
■ **The player runs behind any of these onside team mates**

Many people think
the offside rules are
confusing but in fact
they are relatively
straightforward

THE REF'S VIEW

"The most confusing part of offside for
spectators tends to be in a ruck situation.
To stay onside opposing players have to
stay behind the hindmost foot of their team
mates in the ruck until the ball is in play.
But 'in play' actually means as soon as the
player initiating the next move – often the
scrum half – has both hands on the ball, not
just when he's picked it up and played it"

TONY SPREADBURY
Elite Referee Development Manager

At scrums, rucks, mauls and lineouts different
offside laws apply. The offside line at a ruck or maul
runs from the hindmost foot of the last player from
either side. In effect, there are two offside lines, one
for each team. If a player isn't part of the ruck or maul
then he must either join it at once or get back behind
the offside line. Likewise at a scrum the offside line
is dictated by the back foot of the hindmost player of
each side. Backs must stay behind this line until the
scrum is over. However, the new Experimental Law
Variations that began being trialled in August of 2008
dictated that the offside line at a scrum will be five
metres back from the hindmost foot.

At the lineout the players taking part – those in the
lineout itself, plus the scrum half, the player throwing
in and their opposite numbers – have an offside line
that's known as the 'line of touch'. This line is the
imaginary line that runs at right angles to the touch
line and through the point from where the ball will be
thrown in. This offside line is operational until a ball has
touched either a player or the ground. The offside line
for the players not participating in the lineout runs at a
distance of 10 metres from the line of touch and lasts
until the lineout is over. A lineout is over when the ball
or a player carrying it leaves the lineout.

In addition players must consider the 10 metre law
in relation to offside. If a team mate standing behind an
offside player kicks ahead, the offside player must not
move forward or go within 10 metres of an opponent
waiting to play the ball. If the offside player is nearer
than 10 metres to this opponent then he must move
back until he is at least 10 metres away, otherwise
he'll be penalised. A player who's offside under the 10
metre law can't be put onside by an opponent. Any
other offside player is put onside if an opponent runs
five metres with the ball, kicks or passes the ball or
intentionally touches the ball but doesn't hold it.

REFEREE SIGNALS

There are over 46 different arm signals a rugby referee can use during a game to indicate the decisions he has made. Here are some of the important ones you will see and the times when the referee will use them.

TRY

The referee stands with his back facing towards the dead ball line, and raises one arm above his head. The other points to the spot where the ball was grounded.

PENALTY KICK

The referee raises his arm in the air and then clearly points to the side that has been awarded the penalty.

FREE KICK

The referee raises his arm and bends it at the elbow to make a right angle. The arm will be directed towards the team that has been awarded the free kick.

OBSTRUCTION

The referee crosses his arms across his chest.

THROW FORWARD/ FORWARD PASS

The referee moves his hands in front of his body and pretends to pass an imaginary ball forwards.

KNOCK ON

The referee raises his arm above his head and keeps the palm open, then moves it backwards and forwards.

ENGLAND
RUGBY

HIGH TACKLE (FOUL PLAY)

The referee raises his arm and brings it in front of his neck, with the palm of the hand open.

NOT RELEASING BALL IMMEDIATELY IN THE TACKLE

The referee brings both arms close to his chest in imitation of holding an imaginary ball.

HANDLING BALL IN RUCK OR SCRUM

The referee bends forwards, lowers his arm down towards the ground and moves his arms as if handling an imaginary ball.

THROW IN AT LINEOUT NOT STRAIGHT

The referee puts one hand above his head and keeps his shoulders in line with the touchline. He then moves his arm backwards and forwards.

STAMPING (FOUL PLAY. ILLEGAL USE OF BOOT)

The referee raises one leg and bends it at the knee. He then moves it up and down as if stamping.

BLEEDING WOUND

The referee crosses his arms above his head to indicate that a player is to leave the field and that a temporary replacement may come on.

ADVANTAGE

The referee stretches his arms out at the waist in the direction of the team that hasn't committed an offence for about five seconds.

FORMING A SCRUM

The referee has his elbows bent, with his hands above his head and fingers touching.

IMPROVING YOUR GAME 4

So you've got all the basics of rugby sorted. Now's the time to develop your ability even further through specific and stimulating training drills as developed by the England rugby coaches and used by the England team. This section first explains the crucial role of the coach as players strive to improve, then shows you the exact exercises to practise – complete with clear explanations, diagrams and photographs – in order to fully hone your rapidly-advancing rugby skills. We'll also show you that there are different forms of rugby for you to choose from, take a look at how the Rugby Football Union is seeking to improve elite player performance through the use of top class facilities and innovative coaching and training programmes, as well as letting you know how you can get involved in rugby yourself.

THE ROLE OF THE COACH

Great players require great coaches. Natural talent, drive and determination will get a talented athlete a long way, but if they don't have knowledgeable, enthusiastic and dedicated mentors throughout their career it's highly unlikely they will ever reach their full potential. But not only does a good coach have to bring out the very best in the individuals in his care, he also has to be able to mould a set of individuals into an effective and winning unit. No matter how talented a bunch of individuals may be, outstanding teams are always greater than the sum of their parts.

In order to coach successfully a coach first needs an in-depth knowledge of rugby. But coaches also need to emanate a positive, player-centred attitude, have access to a varied collection of game-related drills to improve skills, a good eye for identifying where players are going wrong and a number of methods for correcting those faults. To do all of this, a coach needs to be able to perform a number of functions well. They need to fill the roles of leader, organiser, manager, friend, counsellor, teacher, motivator, innovator, hero, fall guy, decision maker, bearer of bad tidings, role model and planner. All of

England Team Manager
Martin Johnson. A
wide range of human
attributes give a
coach the tools to
improve players

A GOOD COACH

...sees what's right and praises it.

...sees what's wrong.

...understands why it's wrong.

...knows how to put it right.

priorities. That way it's more likely that the players will retain a real enjoyment of the game – and enjoyment is paramount in player development.

In order to achieve all of these many and varied aims coaches should ensure that their coaching sessions adhere to the principles of what is known as '**APES**'.

- **Activity –** All players should be involved at all times.
- **Purpose –** Make sure that there is always a clear objective.
- **Enjoyment –** The sessions must always be varied and fun.
- **Safety –** The activities and the environment in which they're carried out must always be appropriate and safe.

Working off these fundamentals, then, a coach needs to plan, do and review. Effectively this means working out what goals need to be achieved, then delivering the activities that will enable this to happen before finally reviewing how well things went.

It's essential for coaches to have the ability to communicate. This includes being able to receive as well as to give information. Many coaches understand that giving instructions and explanations is an essential part of their work, but it's vital that they also have equally good listening skills. Good communication is a two-way process.

Research has shown that fewer than 10% of any message is conveyed by the actual words that are spoken, that almost 40% is conveyed by the *way* in which the words are spoken and that the remaining parts of the message are conveyed by body

these human attributes will give a coach the tools with which to improve their players and get the best out of them all the time, to develop their techniques to turn them into real skills and also to build up a player's 'game sense', which in short is the ability to assess what's happening in a match and make the best tactical choice on how to react.

It's important for coaches to remember, however, that putting more emphasis on winning individual matches than on long-term player development will achieve only short-term gains. A coach must always keep the needs of players at the top of the list of

language such as gestures and expressions.

Verbal communication is particularly useful when time is short or when a coach is dealing with a large group of players. The words used should be clear and precise, spoken at an even pace and with emphasis on vital words. Simply telling, however, can lead to the message being misunderstood or interpreted as criticism and this can end up stopping players from taking responsibility for decision making.

Non-verbal communication using gestures and body language can help to indicate such things as size, shape and direction. Making eye contact also helps to emphasise the message.

Interestingly, however, a good coach will watch and listen more than they speak. Coaches can learn a huge amount about their players from watching their expressions, gestures and body language. Then by listening properly, with full concentration, they will be able to make sound judgements on what their coaching requires next. Asking questions is also an excellent way of understanding players better.

England coaches
Mike Ford and John
Wells, together with
Team Manager Martin
Johnson, know that
to do the job well they
must listen as well as
communicate

PLANNING AND EXECUTING SESSIONS

A coaching philosophy is a reflection of an individual's personal values
and beliefs, but it's always important for a coach to mould his
aspirations to the reality of the players he works with, their capabilities
and desires. Realism is important in coaching.

SET GOALS
Planning starts by establishing a set of targets together
with the players, then identifying areas to concentrate on in
order to achieve those goals. Each session should deliver
technical, tactical and physical elements and the following
session should always build on what was learnt in the
previous one.

KEEP THINGS MOVING
It's essential to keep everybody active throughout the
session by providing activities that are specific to the sport
and which allow for maximum participation. If players are
kept standing around they'll soon get bored.

VARY THE TASKS
It often takes many repetitions to master a skill, but small
changes in the process of practising can stop boredom
setting in. It's also important to apply the activities to a
game situation.

SHOW AND TELL
It's important for a coach to demonstrate to his players, but
demonstrations and explanations should be kept short and
simple. Players learn better and more quickly by doing.

PRACTICE MAKES PERFECT
A coach should always stop players when they're not
performing a practice correctly, otherwise an incorrect
technique will stick and will be difficult to correct later.

TAKE SMALL STEPS
Simple skills must be mastered correctly before moving
on to more complex activities. Progressions must be small
enough to be achievable, yet big enough to be challenging.

TREAT PLAYERS AS INDIVIDUALS AND INVOLVE THEM IN PLANNING
A coach must provide all players with the best possible
chance of improving, whatever their rate of learning. This
should also allow for players to have some input into the
planning process to reinforce their own commitment.

BE FLEXIBLE
Being organised is important, but being open to change is
also essential if circumstances dictate it.

EVALUATE THE SESSION
Assessing how well a session went will include getting
feedback from participants and keeping a diary on what
worked and what didn't for reference in the future.

THE BEST COACHES ARE ENABLERS RATHER THAN DICTATORS. THEY WILL...

i) ...recognise and try to meet the needs of
each player, encouraging them to explore
their own potential.

ii) ...strive to help the player to learn to
lead rather than simply passing on
technical knowledge.

iii) ...encourage players to reflect on what
they do and to take responsibility for their
own future development.

IMPROVING YOUR GAME
SKILLS AND DRILLS

THE FOLLOWING EXERCISES DEMONSTRATE HOW TECHNIQUES CAN BE DEVELOPED INTO SKILLS

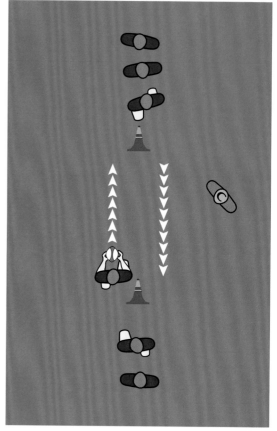

COACHING TIPS

- The ball must be carried in two hands, with the fingers spread wide across the middle of the ball.
- The thumbs and forefingers should be spread by more than 90 degrees.
- Players should feel a five-finger pressure on the ball.
- The ball needs to be carried close to and in front of the sternum.
- The elbows should be pointing outwards.

This simple warm-up exercise aims to help players develop good habits that will ensure a strong grip on the ball and a secure carry. These two elements provide the basis of effective handling. Core skills such as this should be practised and revisited often.

Two groups of players are lined up facing each other. The first player picks the ball up, runs to the opposite cone and places it down, concentrating on a good grip and carry of the ball at all times. The exercise continues as a simple relay.

2 DEVELOPING A STRONG GRIP AND CARRY WITH A RUNNING DISTRACTION

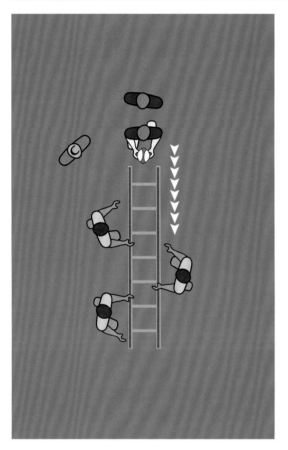

COACHING TIPS

■ The attacking players must concentrate on the carry and on retaining a strong ball grip.

■ The ball must be kept in two hands whenever it is not under threat.

■ The player should hold the ball close to the sternum with the elbows out.

An exercise that is designed to develop a player's grip and carry by adding a running distraction to the practice.

Any number of players must run through a ladder that is laid out on the ground, keeping the ball in two hands while three defenders try to knock the ball out of the hands and down. As the defenders try to dislodge the ball the attackers move it out of danger by transferring the ball to a one-handed carry, then back to two hands once the ball has been secured. This manoeuvre is only possible if the player retains a strong grip on the ball.

①

②

③

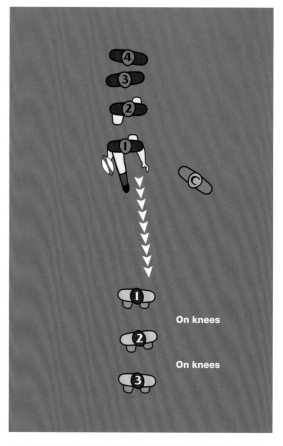

COACHING TIPS

■ Attacking players must ensure that their grip and carry is accurate.

■ The attackers can offload out of the tackle with a lift pass or a pass off the chest.

■ The exercise can be made more challenging in time by inviting attacking players to offload with a one-handed pass, while still maintaining a tight grip on the ball at all times up to the point of the offload.

As with the first two drills this is designed to underline the vital importance of a strong ball grip and carry, but this routine adds the complication of a tackle and pass.

Four attackers line up one behind the other. Ahead of them lie three defenders, all of whom are on their knees. Attacker 1 runs at the shoulder of Defender 1, who needs to make a passive tackle (no force should be exerted). The ball must then be offloaded to Attacker 2, who in turn repeats the exercise with the third attacker and so on and so forth.

4 EARLY CATCHING WITH CORRECT FEET POSITIONING

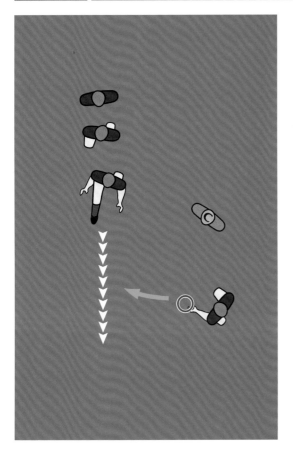

COACHING TIPS

■ The catcher must have his thumbs together with the hands and arms up in anticipation of the early catch.

■ The quoit needs to be received with the outside foot pointing forwards to make sure that the body stays square.

■ After taking the quoit the catcher needs to bring it in towards the chest without grasping it too tightly to the body.

After mastering the grip and carry, the next stage of handling is to develop a basic catching technique. The early catch is a fundamental aspect that must be learned so that it becomes a reflex, while the correct feet positioning when receiving is also vital.

The early catch can be introduced by using quoits or rubber rings instead of rugby balls. A feeder passes the quoit to a catcher who catches the quoit, grips it and then continues at walking pace.

5 DEVELOPING THE MECHANICS OF THE PUSH PASS

①

②

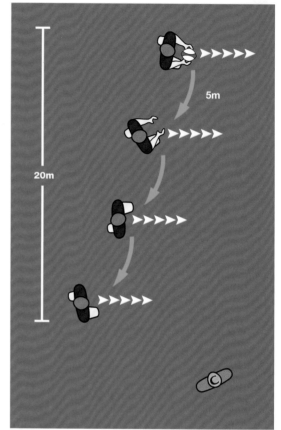

20m

5m

③

The push pass is one of the most effective means of passing the ball. Again this is a core rugby technique that needs to be assimilated to the point of becoming a natural reflex.

This drill involves players walking up the pitch in groups of four. Players should be angled at a slight backward curve at a distance of five metres apart and must pass the ball using the push pass technique. The drill can be made more difficult by increasing the pace at which it's carried out and by widening the gap between the players.

COACHING TIPS

■ Players should be ready for the early catch with the hands raised and the outside foot pointing forwards.

■ Players should carry the ball at the height of their sternum.

■ The flight of the ball should be flat and hard and must reach its target just in front of the catcher.

■ The receiving player should catch the ball with the outside foot raised.

■ The pass should be made as the player steps onto the inside leg.

■ Players should not forget to keep moving forward both during and after the pass to make sure that they commit a defender.

6 DEVELOPING OFF THE BALL RUNNING TO MANIPULATE DEFENDERS USING THE IN TO OUT BALL

This particular drill has been devised to help develop 'off the ball' running and movement, which is vitally important in order to create and manipulate space for the ball carrier and support runner. Good running lines and effective decision making by attackers occur when they keep their heads up and analyse the defensive line. It's vital that the ball carrier is supported by players who execute their running and passing techniques effectively. The exercise can be progressed by incorporating different running lines such as 'out to in' or 'under'.

In this instance the objective is to manipulate space off the ball using a running line which is either 'in to out' or 'over'. A grid 15m x 15m should be used for this drill. Players should be set up two against two with another player feeding the ball. The first receiver, Attacker 1, runs and 'fixes' Defender 1 by maintaining a straight running line and heading for the inside shoulder. This obliges the defender to maintain his position. Then the first receiver must concentrate on making an accurate pass to the outside runner, Attacker 2, who runs an 'in to out' line and takes the ball at pace, beating Defender 2 on the outside.

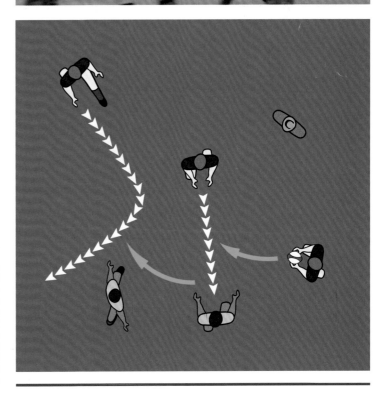

COACHING TIPS

- The attackers should run a line that will take the defenders in.

- The gap on the outside then needs to be opened by curving the run and changing the angle to 'out'.

- The gap must always be hit at pace, using a sidestep outwards to find the gap and take the pass.

- The attack should be mounted on the outside shoulder of the defender.

- The attackers must learn to recognise clues as to what the defender is shaping to do by understanding head, body and feet positions.

- There must be no compromise on good passing technique.

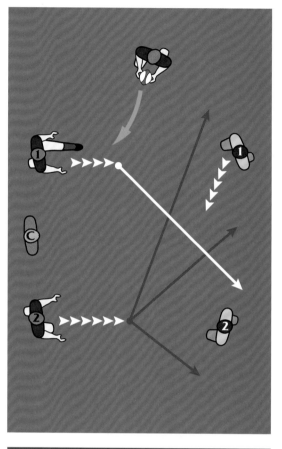

Being able to execute a cut, switch or scissors while running off the ball helps to create uncertainty and disruption in the opposition defence. This drill helps develop these moves two against two.

A grid 15m x 15m should be used for this drill. Using two attackers and two defenders, Attacker 1 receives the ball and runs straight at Defender 1 before changing his angle at speed and heading directly towards Defender 2. Attacker 2 must hold his line and assess the options open to him depending on what Defender 2 does. He can decide to take an 'out' line and receive a short push pass (cut), switch inside Attacker 2 and accelerate through the gap (switch) or take a more shallow switch and run inside Defender 1 (scissors).

COACHING TIPS

- The ball carrier must learn to look for clues as to what the defenders are intending to do and how they should proceed. Understanding the positioning of the defender's head, eyes, hips, shoulders and feet, as well as how the body is balanced, will allow the attacker to make good decisions and identify where gaps can be exploited.

- The ball carrier must always have a good grip and carry.

- They must also show the ball to their own support player, make a good decision on what they intend to do and execute an accurately weighted pass.

- The support player must run a good line with excellent timing and react to what the ball carrier is doing.

8 PRACTISING SPIN PASSING IN A CONDITIONED GAME OF RUGBY NETBALL

The spin pass forms an important part of a player's core handling skills, especially since all players will need to clear the ball effectively from a ruck with an accurate spin pass at some time. This drill puts some fun into the learning process. Technical practices are all extremely important, but incorporating skills training into a conditioned game can make the process more enjoyable and productive.

Two teams of seven players each play across half the pitch. A try is scored if a player catches the ball in the five-metre area. Only a spin pass is allowed and the first pass in any move must be backwards, after which the spin pass can be in any direction. Players are allowed to run with the ball, but a turnover is awarded if a player in possession is touched with two hands by an opposition player or if the ball is dropped. After a try has been scored the same team continues to attack, but in the opposite direction.

COACHING TIPS

- Players must hold the ball with fingers spread and hand positions level, or with a split grip, and remember the early catch technique when receiving the ball.

- The top hand provides the spin and power for the pass.

- The bottom hand gives direction.

- Elbows must be bent with the arms moving to full extension.

- The follow-through must be with long arms in the direction of the pass without crossing the hands.

- Players must stay balanced over their feet with head and upper body over the ball.

- The flight of the ball should be flat and hard arriving at chest height in front of the target.

- Players must look to create and manipulate space by running hard off the ball.

- Supporting the ball carrier effectively is key.

- Good decisions must be made as to whom to pass to and when.

- There must be accurate, hard and flat spin passes to players in space.

- There should be constant emphasis placed on good passing and catching technique.

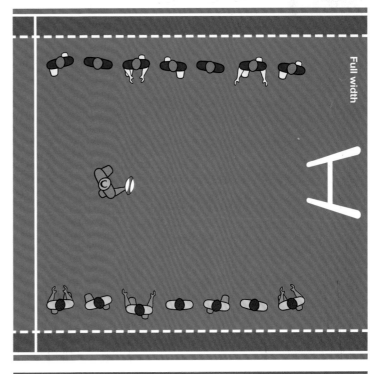

Full width

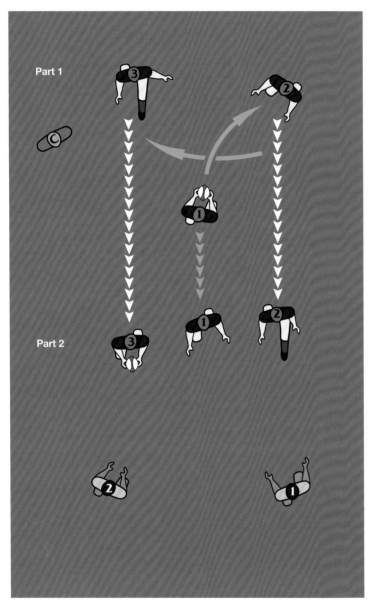

Part 1

Part 2

COACHING TIPS

- Attacking players must always keep their heads up and look at what is unfolding in front of them.
- Cues should be picked up from the defender's head, eyes, hips, shoulders and feet positions.
- Ball carriers need to be aware of the positioning of defenders and of their support players.
- Attackers must keep scanning their options and then be prepared to make a decision.
- Accurate execution is, as always, a must.
- The catcher must run at speed to attract, then hold the defender.
- Support runners must keep their depth to give them time to react to the ball carrier and read the body language of defenders.

This drill helps develop players' understanding of when and why a pass should be made.

A grid 15m x 15m should be used for this drill. This is a two-phase practice that requires three attackers and two defenders. In the first part of the exercise Attacker 1 starts with the ball and passes it either to Attacker 2 or Attacker 3. Both Attacker 2 and Attacker 3 then try to beat Attacker 1 using a simple 'two on one' move. When he has been beaten Attacker 1 then joins the attack against the two defenders, creating a 'three against two'. The attacking players must work a try-scoring opportunity through simple and accurate passes and by running good lines both inside and outside.

10 DEVELOPING EFFECTIVE SUPPORT AFTER THE LINE BREAK

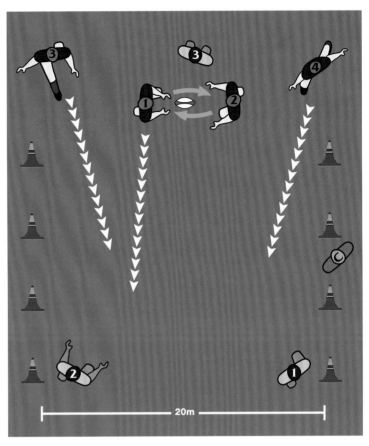

20m

COACHING TIPS

■ The ball carrier must work out where space is available to exploit, identify where the defenders are coming from and where the support is.

■ They must also be able to make a good decision based on what they see in front of them, then be able to attack at speed and execute the chosen move accurately.

■ The support carrier must be able to identify the same solution to the problem as the ball carrier, while understanding what the other support runners are doing.

■ Support carriers must react appropriately and communicate their intentions while attacking the available space.

While it's vitally important to develop attacking practices that can create an opportunity for breaking a defensive line, there also needs to be effective support after the line break has been made.

This practice requires four attackers and three defenders. A 20-metre grid is marked out on the pitch using cones. Defender 1 and Defender 2 start at the back of the grid and one of the two players is nominated as 'active'. Attacker 3 and Attacker 4 start wide at the top of the grid while Attacker 1 and Attacker 2 start at the top of the grid and in the middle. Attacker 1 and Attacker 2 throw the ball to each other until the coach starts the exercise. Whoever has the ball begins the attack, supported by Attackers 3 and 4. The remaining attacker isn't involved. The object of the drill is to beat the defenders and score.

Defender 3 begins on his knees behind Attackers 1 and 2. When play begins he must chase back at the same time as the active defender runs up to engage. This way the attackers have to deal with pressure from both in front and behind.

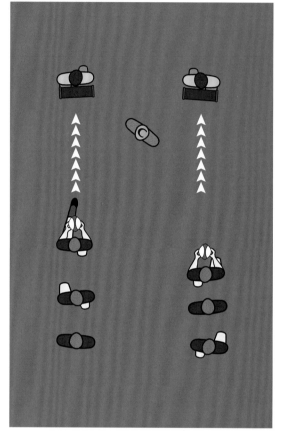

This straightforward exercise is designed to teach players how to present the ball under control when tackled to the floor in order to maintain momentum.

Two defenders are positioned alongside each other holding tackle shields. The shields represent a space in the defence that the ball carriers must attack and drive at. Ball carriers line up in single file and attack the shields alternately.

COACHING TIPS

■ The bag must represent space that's being attacked.

■ Players must drive their legs through the tackle to stay on their feet for as long as possible, to make ground and to buy time.

■ The ball must be kept secure and away from the opposition.

■ Body management is important. The ball must be under the chest, the player must then fight his shoulder down to the floor, while still making sure that this doesn't result in him ending up on his back making it easy for an opponent to rip the ball.

■ The player should keep the top shoulder over the ball and decide whether to place or roll the ball if under pressure.

2 THE ART OF LATCHING

COACHING TIPS

■ The first attacker must show strong leg drive and low body height.

■ There must be good communication between the two attacking players to facilitate the initial drive forward.

■ It's important for the latch to happen early and from the rear with a strong inside arm to hold the ball carrier up, close hips and an effective slide past the ball.

■ The primary aim is to hold the ball carrier up and drag him through the tackle.

■ The defender should be cleared out of the way if possible.

The aim of this drill is to introduce the concept of latching. Latching is gripping onto and assisting the ball carrier through the tackle to maintain forward momentum and allow good ball presentation.

A single defender holds a tackle bag, while Attacker 1 takes the ball into the shield. Attacker 2 arrives early from the rear as a support player, making sure that the hips are close and that his inside arm is supporting the ball carrier strongly. The support player aims to hold the ball carrier up using his free arm and drag him through the tackle, then slide past the ball to drive the defending tackler away allowing Attacker 1 to present the ball cleanly.

❶

❷

❸

❹

Dynamic and effective clearout techniques are vital for players in all positions to remove opponents from the tackle area. Competition for the ball is becoming fiercer in this area and good clearout allows for quick ball and the maintenance of continuity. This drill helps develop those skills.

Defender 1 is equipped with a tackle shield and stands over the ball carrier, Attacker 1, who is on the ground. Attacker 2 acts as a support player and hits the tackle shield from a distance of two metres, clearing the tackler away from both Attacker 1 and the ball.

COACHING TIPS

■ It's important for the supporting attacker to look for the ball and know exactly where it is.

■ The player who is about to clear defenders out must get his body into the correct position early with his head up and his spine in line.

■ The support player must get lower than the defensive threat, with hips sunk lower than the shoulders.

■ It's important to step strongly over the ball as the hit is made, staying on the feet.

■ The drive must be from low to high, forcing the tackler up and back.

4 IDENTIFYING THREATS FROM DIFFERENT ANGLES

COACHING TIPS

- Early identification of defending threats to retaining possession is crucial.

- Attacking players must communicate to let each other know of these threats and to offer potential solutions.

- The ball carrier must always be encouraged to stay on his feet.

- All attackers should work their leg drives while latching whenever it's possible.

- Good clearout technique is a must.

- Players should use their arms to grab defenders and gain as much ground as possible without compromising the security of the ball.

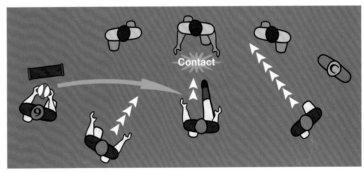

Attacking support players must have good decision-making capacities at the contact area when they have more than one defender facing them. By simulating a match situation players can learn to make good decisions.

Four attackers and three defenders are all wearing tackle suits. A tackle bag is used to indicate a ruck situation. Attacker 1 passes to the first receiver, Attacker 2, from the base of the ruck. Attacker 2 either attacks the spaces between the defenders or passes to the second receiver, Attacker 3. Support players then encourage the ball carrier to stay on their feet, latch on if possible and clear the defenders away from the contact area.

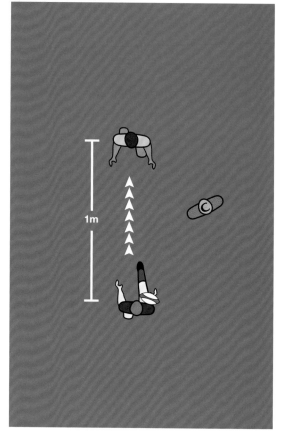

COACHING TIPS

- The attacker must keep the ball away from the defender, holding it tight and low under the chest.

- The attacker should take a big step into the defender, staying low and keeping a strong, wide base.

- The attacker must use a strong leading arm to both grab and control the tackler and keep him at bay.

- They must fight to stay on their feet at all times, making use of a wide, low base.

Going to ground in contact is often the only attacking option, but it's important to recognise alternatives when they present themselves. Staying on your feet and buying time for supporting players to arrive and initiate a maul is one such option.

One attacker steps into the tackle with a single defender about a metre apart. He must then fight to stay on his feet. The tackler must attempt to put the ball carrier on the floor in a controlled manner.

6 SUPPORTING AND DRIVING AT THE MAUL

COACHING TIPS

■ Players must communicate with each other to help the move work efficiently.

■ The ball carrier must execute a strong rip technique with a low body height and a wide base, with the elbow high and driving the shoulder down.

■ The support players must work past the ball with a strong inside arm and leg, creating an 'arrowhead' shape.

■ Support players should be 'head to head', working on the inside of the defenders.

■ The third support player must both take and secure the ball, stay in line and behind, as well as take control of the communication between players.

■ Once the maul is properly organised there should be controlled movement forwards.

The maul and drive is a fundamental part of any side's attempt to maintain 'go forward'. Two defenders face four attackers in a diamond shape with Attacker 1 at the front of the diamond. Attacker 1 rips the ball from the defender. Attackers 2 and 3 act as support players and drive past the ball, leaving Attacker 4 to take it. The group drives for five metres with the two defenders opposing them before repeating the exercise.

❶

❷

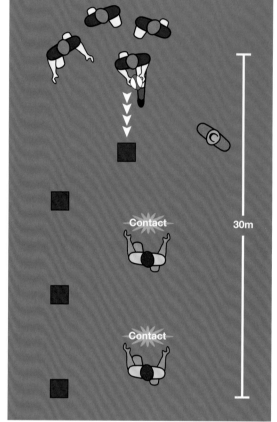

30m

Contact

Contact

All of the skills developed through the drills in the Contact & Continuity section are vital in order to retain possession in contact and to keep moving forward. But the best way to maintain momentum in attack is usually to offload the ball either before or on contact. This drill is designed to create several offload situations in one single exercise.

A number of tackle bags are placed in a narrow channel over a distance of 30 metres. Two defenders in tackle suits also stand in the channel. The ball carrier, Attacker 1, runs at the first bag and offloads to Attacker 2 acting as a support runner. Attacker 2 takes the ball towards the next bag before offloading again to Attacker 3. Attacker 3 is then tackled by Defender 1 and he must pass out of this tackle. All of the attacking players carry on through offloading and supporting, with Defender 2 also making a tackle. The exercise can be varied and made more difficult by moving the defenders to different points in the channel and by replacing the tackle bags with live defenders.

COACHING TIPS

- ■ **Communication between players about options and intentions is again vital.**

- ■ **Support runners must concentrate on coming from depth and using good footwork to change the angles of their runs.**

- ■ **The ball carrier must keep the ball in two hands and move it away from the tackler to one hand as he approaches.**

- ■ **The ball should be moved back to two hands in order to offload. The tackle bags encourage ball carriers to pass prior to contact.**

- ■ **Players must be precise in the weight and accuracy of their passes so that the support players can run onto the ball easily.**

- ■ **Whenever possible players should consider passing the ball before contact.**

8 DEVELOPING DECISION MAKING BEFORE, DURING AND AFTER CONTACT

❶

❷

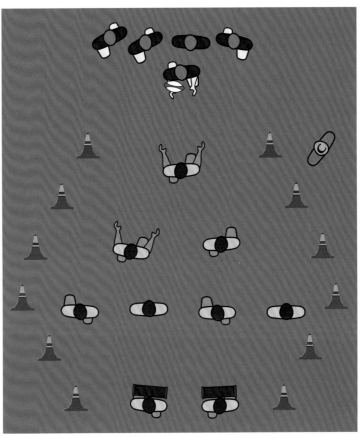

COACHING TIPS

■ **Decisions need to be made early and attacking players must be positive in their forward play, attacking the space and then looking to draw defenders and pass wherever possible.**

■ **Staying up and mauling is an option, but going to ground is a last resort.**

■ **Maintaining possession of the ball is key. Players must work on ball retention even if a wrong decision has been made.**

■ **Support players must always look to communicate, keep their depth and use good footwork to change their running angles. All actions must be looking for the end result of supporting the ball carrier.**

■ **All aspects of technique must be correct and precise.**

By working on each of the different areas of contact play, players should have developed offloading skills, support for the ball carrier, setting up and driving the maul, ball presentation and clearout techniques when the ball goes to ground. This practice aims to bring all of these techniques together in one decision-making exercise.

An area of the pitch big enough to allow attackers to run into space and offload is coned off with a narrow channel at the start. The area then widens out in the centre and narrows towards the end. The group of players is divided into two teams of equal numbers and lines of tackle-suited defenders are positioned as shown, with the final two defenders holding tackle shields. The attacking group runs at the spaces and must make good decisions about which contact techniques they use at each stage – pass early, offload, stand up and maul or as a last resort go to ground, place the ball and clearout. The defenders should start at 50% intensity, using enough physicality to stop the attackers making unrealistic yards up the pitch, then build up to full intensity.

❶

❷

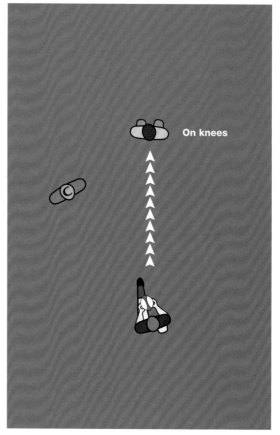

On knees

The drills in the Contact & Continuity section so far have looked at contact from an attacking team's perspective. But when a team is defending it's important to contest hard for the ball, work to turn opponents over and then play quickly so that the opposition defence will be disorganised and therefore easier to attack.

This is a simple one-on one exercise that focuses on a defending player who is on his knees. The ball carrier runs either side of the defender who makes a good, controlled tackle. He then gets back on his feet quickly to compete for the ball. The ball carrier, meanwhile, concentrates on his ball presentation technique. This is a low-intensity drill that aims to work on the technique of both players in competing and presenting. The exercise can be progressed by adding two support players.

COACHING TIPS

■ The defender must focus on making a positive tackle and controlling the ball carrier to the floor.

■ The defender should then spin round onto his feet as quickly as possible, with his chest on the tackled player and staying as low to the ground as he can to stay strong.

■ Body weight must be kept on the tackled player through the arms.

■ The defender must then get his hands on the ball with his leg and chest over and past the tackled player.

10 | USING ALL DECISION-MAKING AND CONTACT SKILLS UNDER PRESSURE

This exercise is a full eight versus eight game with the defending team in tackle suits, where all of the techniques learnt in the previous exercises come into play. The playing area is designated as the area between the 22 and the halfway line, with try-lines at the full width of the pitch. The attacking side has a two-minute time limit in which to break down the defence and score using passing, offloads, mauls or going to ground and clearing out as a last resort. Any turnover by the defence leads to the ball being thrown back to the attackers' goal line for a quick restart. The width of the pitch can be changed to encourage different decision-making processes.

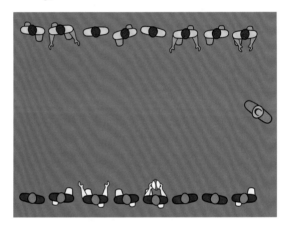

COACHING TIPS

- Players should try to use all options; pass, offload or maul, with a ruck as the last resort.

- Good ball retention is key to the exercise.

- All the techniques learned must be applied.

- Players should be encouraged to play with the ball in hand and to attack space, always going forward with the leg drive.

- Players should make good decisions, support the ball carrier quickly, be direct and achieve quick ball in contact.

- The target is always to keep the ball and move forward.

①

This one-on-one exercise is designed to establish basic tackling technique. In order to make a good tackle a player must develop a strong base and body position. The attacker wears a tackle suit and holds a tackle shield. The defender keeps his hands behind his back, then drives into the tackle shield from two metres away and between two cones. Players should start the exercise at walking pace, then progress to jogging pace and introducing three small steps at the point where the shoulder is in contact with the tackle shield.

②

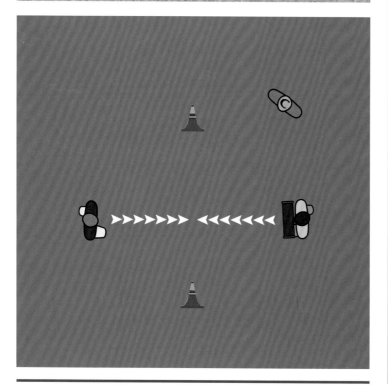

COACHING TIPS

■ Steps should be shortened as the tackler moves near to the target.

■ The tackler must stride or step into the split between the attacker's legs to get close to provide a strong base and avoid jumping and planting both feet.

■ Defenders must stay big for as long as possible, then sink at the hips and knees once they step into the split.

■ The contact must be initiated with the same side shoulder as the leading leg.

■ The head should be up and the eyes open at all times and in line with the spine to ensure a safe tackle.

■ Hips must be kept square on to the attacker. Imagine wearing a belt buckle facing directly at the target.

■ The defender should place his head close to the side of the target. Then the shoulders will automatically follow close.

■ The defender must drive through the tackle with three small steps to keep the feet on the ground and make sure there is no diving into the tackle.

■ The attacker should offer the split on different sides to vary the tackle.

2 INTRODUCING BOXER HANDS AND PRACTISING THE TACKLING SEQUENCE

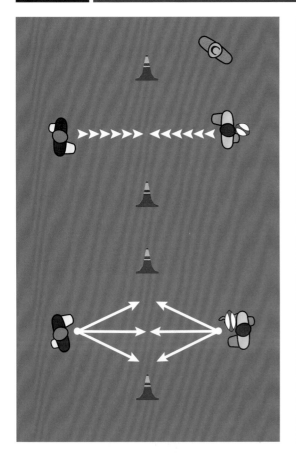

COACHING TIPS

■ The defender's hands must be up and in front of the body like a boxer's hands.

■ The arms and hands shoot forward quickly on contact with the shoulder and only then grip strongly around the attacker, making contact beneath the ball.

■ The tackler must not go for the ball immediately, but must concentrate on grip and squeezing the arms as they drive through the tackle.

■ The practice sequence of the tackle is foot position, body position with hips square, shoulder contact, drive, hands and arms gripping tightly.

This drill progresses the learning of tackling technique to introduce the hands and the arms. One defender faces one attacker in a tackle suit. The attacker holds a ball behind his back. The tackler walks towards the attacker and executes a tackle to knock the ball to the ground. It's vital to concentrate on all the points from the first tackling drill in addition to adding the hands and arms. The attacker must approach from different directions so the defender has to alternate the tackling shoulder.

EMPHASISING THE USE OF ARMS, THE LEG LIFT AND THE DRIVE

THIS DRILL SHOULD ONLY BE USED WITH ADULT PLAYERS

①

②

③

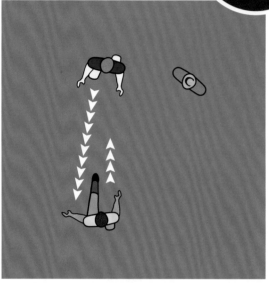

This exercise is developed for one defender and one attacker. Concentrating on basic tackle technique, the defender practises this front-on tackle, involving a leg lift, that is one of the basic defensive tools. The exercise is progressed by adding a ball, then with the defender putting the attacker to the ground and getting up to compete after the tackle has been made.

COACHING TIPS

- ■ The head and leg lift must be on the same side.

- ■ The defender hooks the attacker just above the knee at the short base of the hamstring to put him off balance.

- ■ Tacklers must drive through, lifting the leg with an action that mimics pulling the starter cord on a lawnmower.

- ■ It's important to maintain a strong grip with both arms.

- ■ Once progressions have been added the shoulder must be targeted just below the ball.

- ■ The defender must drive the feet through the tackle, lifting the attacker's leg and putting him on his back.

- ■ Tacklers should follow through to land on top of the attacker.

- ■ The principle of 'reloading' – defender getting back on his feet quickly to compete for the ball – is encouraged.

- ■ Make sure defenders understand that it is their responsibility to place the attacker on the ground rather than launch them in the air to avoid dangerous play.

4 INTRODUCING THE SIDE TACKLE

COACHING TIPS

■ Defenders must stay tall and get their feet in close to the attacker before making the tackle.

■ Head position is very important. The head must go behind the attacker.

■ The tackler's grip must be strong and he should hit with his shoulder aiming for the attacker's thigh, between the knees and the hips.

■ The defender should drive through with the legs, avoiding diving into the tackle, and tackle the attacker to the ground, landing on top of the tackled player.

■ The defender should 'reload' onto his feet quickly to compete for the ball.

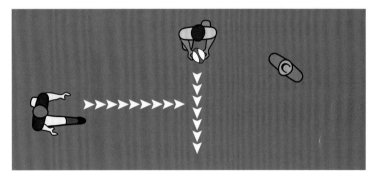

This practice teaches players how to chase down an opponent and make a tackle, which can often be a technique that saves tries in game situations. In this one-on-one exercise both players wear tackle suits. The attacker holds the ball in the hand that is furthest from the oncoming defender, then starts off at walking pace as the defender comes in from the side to execute the tackle. The attacker must always attempt to keep moving forward and must not stop when being tackled. Tackles must be executed from both sides and off both shoulders. As the exercise progresses the attacker builds up to around 75% pace and adds in a fend off or a hand off to increase the difficulty for the defender.

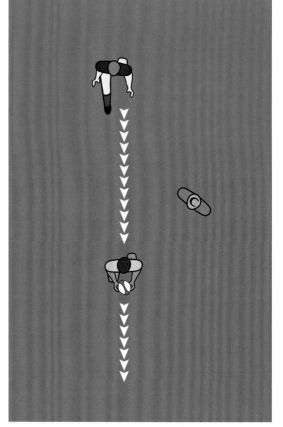

If an attacking player makes a line break straight through the middle, the rear tackle is the most effective means of stopping him. Again, this is a one-on-one drill with the attacker wearing a tackle suit. The ball is held in two hands by the attacker, who should start moving in a straight line at walking pace, but with a head start on the defender. The defender must chase the attacker down and make the tackle. The attacker must try to keep moving forward and must not stop in the tackle. To progress this drill the attacking player must build up to 75% speed.

COACHING TIPS

■ The defender must chase down the attacker and get his feet close before making the tackle.

■ The defender's grip on the attacker must be strong and tight with both the arms and hands.

■ He must start the tackle at the waist and slide down the attacker's body to the ankles, with his head to the side and tight to the legs.

■ The tackle must be fully completed before the defender reloads onto his feet to compete for the ball.

6 DEVELOPING TECHNIQUE FOR A PASSIVE GUARD TACKLE IN A STATIC SITUATION

COACHING TIPS

- The defender must start low by adopting a three point stance, with his legs spread a little and the fingers of one hand resting on the ground in front.

- There must be no indication given to the attacker of the defender's intentions.

- The defender then explodes upwards into a higher position with the spine in line, leaning forward with a wide base, with feet offset and split for stability.

- The defender must then attack the back of the attacker's shoulders and pull him down with a strong grip.

- In conceding a metre the defender is able to attack the ball quickly with two hands, clamping the ball under the attacker's chest with his head low and close to the attacker's body.

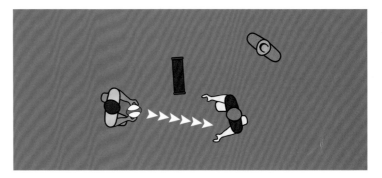

The exercise has been created to develop strong tackle technique in static game situations. Learning the correct way in which to make a guard tackle is crucial in stopping opponents from making ground at the ruck. This is a one-on-one drill with both players wearing tackle suits. Using a tackle bag as a ruck indicator and with the attacker starting behind the bag, the attacker picks up the ball as if in a ruck situation and drives forward. The defender must engage. This technique for the passive guard tackle is generally used outside the defender's 22-metre area where the defence should be prepared to concede a metre in contact in order to isolate the ball carrier and be able to contest for the ball.

①

②

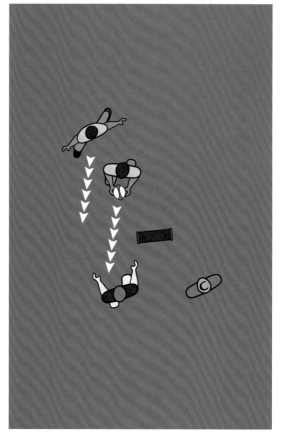

③

In the event of a ruck close to the tryline then the defender's primary objective must be to stop the attacker moving forwards. This exercise helps players to do so by introducing the concept of the impact guard tackle.

A tackle bag represents the ruck area as two attackers line up a single defender. All players are wearing tackle suits. Attacker 1 picks up the ball and drives, with Attacker 2 latching on in support. The defender must aim to drive the attackers back into the ruck.

COACHING TIPS

■ The defender must first stay low in the three point stance.

■ The defender should then explode into the space early, ensuring that he stays on his feet without either diving or lunging forward.

■ With the spine in line, eyes open and head to the side, the tackler must use short fast steps to drive the opponent backwards and into the ruck.

■ Defenders must sink at the knees and bend at the waist to stay lower than the attacker and aim to hit just underneath the ball.

■ It's important to stay low and use the leg lift to unbalance the attacker and drive him back on his own side of the ruck, thereby conceding no ground.

8 INTRODUCING THE DRIFT DEFENSIVE SYSTEM

Tackling is a fundamental individual rugby skill, but it's usually most effective when used in conjunction with other team mates and within the context of a defensive system. This drill works on tackling teamwork within the Drift Defence system. This system is usually used when there are more attackers than defenders.

Four attackers in tackle suits run out against three defenders, forming an attacking line and a defensive line. A feeder passes the ball to the attackers, who can only pass. The defenders must be slightly staggered and must move up together. As the attackers pass the ball each defender pushes across from in to out, each covering the next attacking opponent.

COACHING TIPS

■ The aim is to develop a 'heads up' defence, where each defender must scan between the ball and the attacking alignment to make sure they are numbered off against an opponent.

■ Defenders must make sure they are staggered slightly behind the defender inside.

■ Defenders align with the outside foot forward and opposite the inside shoulder of the attacker.

■ Spacing is important. Defenders must mark as much space as possible, with the end defender setting the width of the line.

■ The defensive line must start from an onside position.

■ Individual defenders should point at the attacker they are lining up and communicate with their fellow defenders.

■ Line speed is also important and is set by the inside defender.

■ All defenders must take the space first, heading up and then out. The first two steps must be forward.

■ The first defender initiates the drift only when his man has passed the ball.

■ For the drift defence to work, defenders must trust their support defender on the inside, keeping the shape of the line at all times.

■ Defenders can make a tackle if it's appropriate while thinking of using the touchline as another defender effectively.

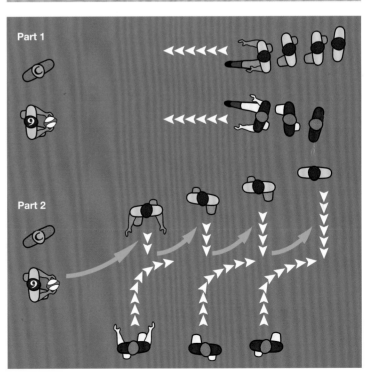

9 INTRODUCING THE MAN ON MAN DEFENSIVE SYSTEM

①

②

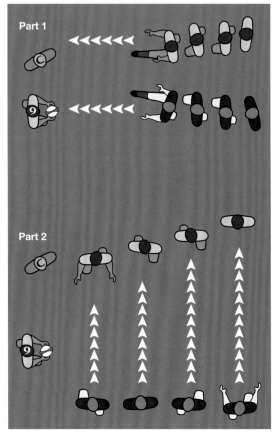

Part 1

Part 2

③

The man on man defensive system is normally used when there are equal numbers of attackers and defenders, or more numbers in defence.

Four attackers in suits run out against four defenders, forming an attacking line and a defensive line. The attackers can only pass the ball. The defenders align in a 'flat four' shape. As the attackers pass the ball the defenders race forward as a line with each player marking the attacker opposite.

COACHING TIPS

■ The key to man on man defence is for each player to align opposite the same shoulder of their opponent with the outside foot forward. It can be inside or outside shoulder, but each defender must do the same thing.

■ Defenders must point out the man they are marking and communicate their intentions to each other.

■ The defenders must move up together in a flat defensive line, keeping the shape at all times.

■ Line speed is important. Players should move straight up as fast as possible, staying in a flat defensive line and putting the attack under pressure.

10 | INTRODUCING THE OUT TO IN DEFENSIVE SYSTEM

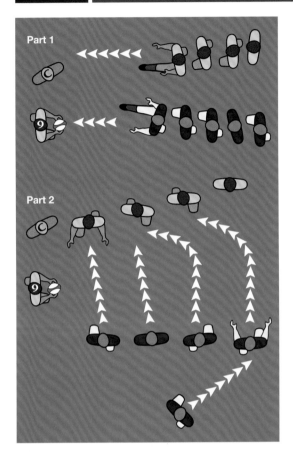

Part 1

Part 2

❶

❷

COACHING TIPS

- The aim of 'out to in' defence is to force the ball back inside and stop it getting to the wide men.

- Defenders align with the outside foot forward and opposite the outside shoulder of the attackers.

- The outside defender sets the line speed and leads the defence.

- A fast line speed is very important for the outside defenders.

- If the ball gets to the outside attackers the covering full back must make the tackle.

❸

This exercise introduces a third defensive system, which is normally used when there are equal numbers of attackers and defenders, more defenders than attackers, or when a team is defending close to its own try line.

Four attackers in suits run out against five defenders, forming an attacking line and a defensive line with a covering full back. The defenders align in a 'flat four' shape. As the ball is played they rush straight up in a line, then curve back inside to stop the ball going wide and force the ball carrier to run into the vacuum they've created.

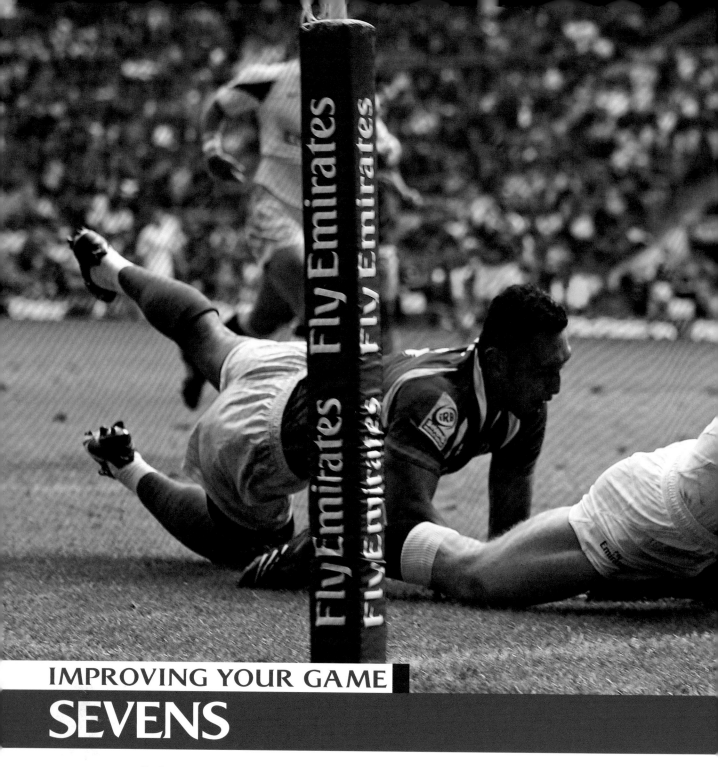

IMPROVING YOUR GAME
SEVENS

While the 15-man game of rugby still dominates, the introduction of a seven-man version of the sport has both thrilled fans and allowed players to develop their all-round skills in a fast-paced and demanding environment.

The concept of sevens began back in 1883 when Ned Haig, a Scottish butcher from Melrose, was looking for ways to raise money for his local rugby club. His idea was to create a form of fast-flowing and exciting rugby where each team would field just seven players on a full-size pitch. From such humble beginnings sevens has now grown into a form of

rugby with a genuine worldwide audience.

The first ever officially-sanctioned international sevens tournament took place at Murrayfield in 1973 as part of the Scottish Rugby Union's centenary celebrations and because fans voted the experiment a success the Hong Kong Sevens series – still a much-loved and highly-anticipated event – was launched three years later. Hong Kong is now just one of the individual tournaments which go to comprise the officially-sanctioned IRB Sevens World Series, a yearly tour event which is held all across the world and where the team that has

ENGLAND
RUGBY

section, but the key differences in comparison with the 15-man game are as follows…

- **There are seven players on the field instead of 15.**
- **There are five substitutes rather than seven and only three substitutions per game are allowed.**
- **Halves run to just seven minutes each rather than 40 minutes, except competition finals where halves run to 10 minutes each.**
- **Half time lasts just one minute, except in competition finals where it lasts two minutes.**
- **Matches that are drawn after regulation time are continued into five-minute sudden death periods.**
- **Conversion attempts must be drop kicked.**
- **Scrums are contested with three players instead of eight.**
- **The scoring team kicks off rather than the non-scoring team.**
- **A yellow card results in a two-minute suspension rather than 10 minutes.**

THE ROLE OF SEVENS

The Rugby Football Union views the sport of sevens as an important means of aiding player development and providing a pathway for the 15-man game. In effect, while it's the aim for any team representing England to win its matches, sevens acts as a learning ground and a stepping stone towards the elite end of 15-man rugby for our most talented players. The success of this policy can be seen in the number of established internationals who have passed through the Sevens system over the years, including Mathew Tait, Josh Lewsey, Mark Cueto, David Strettle and Tom Croft.

This development policy can, of course, cause difficulties in terms of England's sevens continuity. When promising players start to fulfil their potential the system often sees them moving into a higher level of 15-man game than they had previously experienced. However, there is usually a core of four players in the England Sevens squad of 12 who are viewed as sevens specialists and who help to cement some of that all-important continuity. But as Ben Ryan, England Sevens squad coach for the 2007/08 campaign commented, "The proof that we provide a great tool for developing players is that they don't stay in the system for a huge amount of time."

gathered the most points awarded according to success across all the tournaments becomes IRB Sevens Champion. There is even a Sevens World Cup, first introduced in 1993 and held every four years, with the next tournament scheduled for 2009 in Dubai.

Sevens demands speed, skill and fitness and because of the pace of the game a team usually features only backs. There are a number of variations on the laws of the traditional game to help speed up Sevens and take into account the reduced number of players. These laws are laid out in full in our Rules

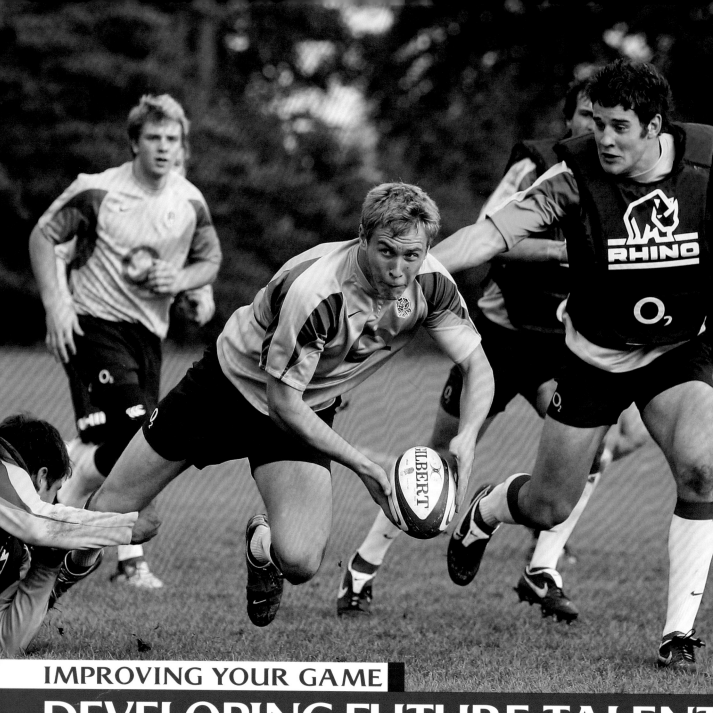

IMPROVING YOUR GAME
DEVELOPING FUTURE TALENT

England's rugby ambitions aren't just about the present national team's performances. They're also very much about developing and improving the standards of the country's *future* international players. And the England Rugby Academy is the structure that the Rugby Football Union has put in place to achieve that goal.

Former Irish international full back Conor O'Shea was the man charged with delivering better England players to the senior squad in his three years as National Academy Director. Now with the English Institute Of Sport, O'Shea is still immensely proud of creating a pathway and a structure that allows talented English-qualified players to fulfil their potential.

Young players who are in the Under 13 age group and who are involved with the game at their local club or school can now be selected for one of 28 Constituent Body Schools Of Rugby development squads. These schools deliver a core rugby curriculum – not seven days a week, but about once a month – with a view to improving basic skills such as handling, defence, contact and continuity, together with organised matches. The

The England Rugby Academy system is designed with the specific purpose of "making each generation of players better than the previous one"

CBs will also advise young players on issues like diet and conditioning.

From there the Academy works like a pyramid, starting with a broad base and then narrowing down at a further two levels. The first of these levels is a network of 14 Regional Academies – in general affiliated to and working in conjunction with the major professional clubs. These serve all areas of the country and support up to 300 players in the Under 16 to Under 21 age group. The second is the National Academy that works with a select group of 64 players, mainly from the age of 16 through to 20. National Academy coaches also work with older players in the England Saxons set-up.

According to O'Shea the system is designed with the specific purpose of "making each generation of players better than the previous one," though he accepts that the system isn't 100 per cent scientific. "It's 80 per cent science and 20 per cent gut feeling when we look to develop a player. But what we're trying to do is make sure that by the time an athlete makes it to the England Saxons then he really is the very best he can be."

This is achieved at Regional Academy level by specialist RFU coaches working together with the Academy's regular staff in whatever area they can add value once somebody has been signed as a professional. If, for example, a player has been identified as a kicker of real potential, but his club doesn't employ a specialist kicking coach, the RFU can send in one of their Academy specialists to work one-on-one with the player. It benefits everybody – and above all it benefits the individual concerned. Academy input can also help focus on more long-term development goals, where with Premiership clubs it's understandably always about the next week and the next game.

Naturally, the Academy structure is a brutal environment in terms of the selection process. Of the young hopefuls who attend Academy screening sessions hoping to be given the chance to take the first steps on the ladder towards success, very few will make it all the way through to senior international status. If each Regional Academy had just one success from a screening it would be a remarkable achievement. For the best of the best, though, the National Academy set-up is in place as the next step up the ladder. It's there where the most outstanding players can train and learn together in an elite environment, creating the top of the 'pyramid' of the Academy structure and offering the best opportunity for players to maximise their potential.

The benefits of the Academy system have already been seen, with a number of senior internationals – among them Danny Cipriani, Tom Rees and James Haskell – having progressed through it. O'Shea believes the system is working because in his opinion the latest crop of Under 18 talent is the best group to date. The goal of the Academy structure is always resolutely about player development rather than actual results at age group levels, but the management team are also wary of hiding too much behind a system that isn't results-oriented. It's a balance that they monitor constantly.

With a budget of £2.4 million per year invested in the Regional Academies since 2001 some might think excellent results in terms of bringing talent through is to be expected. But it's the last step of the journey that's always the great unknown. How will a player react in front of 80,000 fans at Twickenham? No matter how much promise they show, some will sink and some will swim. It's what provides the ultimate measurement of the Academy's success. And yet the whole process is about something else too. O'Shea defines that other underlying ethos.

"Any player who's been part of the system should be able to look in the mirror regardless of whether they made the grade or not and be able to say, 'I know that every opportunity was given to me and I gave it everything I had.'"

The success of the Academy structure was further highlighted by the England Under 20s, who reached the final of the inaugural age group World Championships in Wales in June 2008.

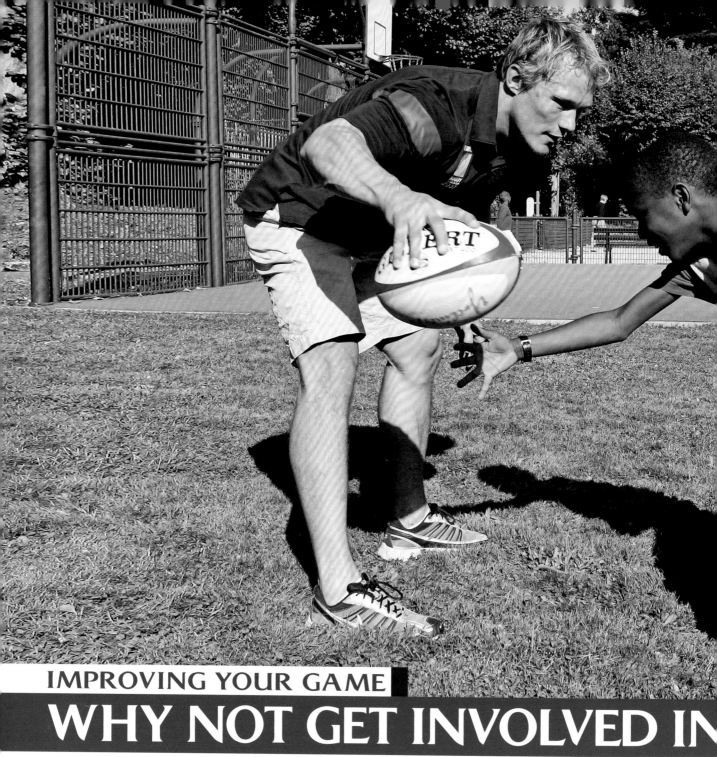

WHY NOT GET INVOLVED IN

One of the reasons why rugby is such an attractive sport to play is because there is a position on the field for everybody, no matter what their size. From bruising front rows to rangy locks to nippy scrum halves, rugby offers a chance for everyone to shine. The sport's legendary camaraderie between team mates, respect for the rules and authority, together with a high regard for opponents, has also instilled many basic life values in participants, as well as allowing players to build lifelong friendships. Rugby is about so much more than simply competing and keeping fit.

Rugby clubs have always had a reputation for being friendly and welcoming environments for anyone interested in playing the sport. So it's no surprise that the Go Play Rugby Campaign, launched in 2007 with a budget of £1 million contributed by the Sports Foundation, the RFU and sponsors O2 and The Chelsea Building Society, has been a huge success in bringing new players to the sport, as well as encouraging people who'd drifted away to come back and lace up their boots again. More than 9,500 adults were enticed back in season 2007/08 and inspired by such a success a new initiative – entitled Play On – has

RUGBY?

ENGLAND
RUGBY

You don't have to be a professional to get involved in rugby in some way. Try it for yourself and see how much you enjoy it

who would like to experience rugby's famous spirit of conviviality. Organisations are always on the lookout for new volunteers to help with the running of their club, from organising competitions and tournaments, to registering players or even helping keep the pitch and club equipment in good order. Coaching is also another good way to get involved, as is helping to run a club website or contributing to the matchday programme. In fact, the possibilities for experiencing the magic of rugby are almost endless and can offer considerable personal benefits. Volunteers can use and develop their skills, gain qualifications, add to their CV and improve their job prospects, build confidence and learn to be part of a team, feel a sense of achievement, be recognised by others for their efforts and last but not least have a lot of fun along the way.

To make those important first steps towards getting involved all you need to do is ask. You could contact your local Rugby Development Officer (RDO) or Community Rugby Coach (CRC). They'll be delighted to help you.

There is also a Community Leaders Award scheme run by the RFU that offers young volunteers the perfect place to start. The course lasts approximately five hours, with two hours spent on the community delivery of a rugby-based project. There are no course pre-entry requirements and the scheme is aimed at the 16+ age group, covering seven topic areas. These are…

- **Leadership**
- **Planning and preparation**
- **Coaching**
- **Community delivery**
- **Refereeing**
- **The ethos of rugby**
- **Networking**

To find out more about the RFU Community Leaders Award contact your local Rugby Development Officer.

been developed by the RFU together with sponsors O2. Play On will create a support network of Pathfinders to guide young players along their rugby journey as they make the transition from school to higher education and into employment, while directly promoting rugby to sixth formers and young people in higher education. Play On will also engage and expand the rugby community with summer rugby festivals, like the O2 Scrum On The Beach event, which promote different forms of the game.

But even if playing the sport isn't for you, there are still plenty of other opportunities available for people

USEFUL WEBSITES

Go Play Rugby website: *www.rfu.com/goplayrugby*
Play On website: *www.playonrugby.com*
Rugby Development Officers: *www.rfu.com/volunteer*

5 THE LAWS

The laws of rugby are many and varied and in order to truly appreciate this marvellous sport it's vital that players understand the laws of the game they're involved in. This section gives you every one of the official IRB laws of the game, including variations that occur at Under 19 level and in Sevens, together with the new Experimental Law Variations that are being trialled throughout the world. Now you need never scratch your head in bemusement again when the referee makes a decision.

Following a decision by the IRB council in 2004 to review the Laws of the Game, the council approved a global trial of certian Experimantal Law Variations (ELVs). The Laws Project group will monitor the trial for 12 months and the council will review the ELVs at the end of this period before deciding if they should be accepted into full law.

The following Laws of The Game are printed with permission of the International Rugby Board.
Visit **www.irb.com** to get more information on Laws & Regulations, tournaments and IRB World Rankings

Law 1 The Ground

DEFINITIONS

The Ground is the total area shown on the plan. The Ground includes:

The Field of play is the area (as shown on the plan) between the goal lines and the touchlines. These lines are not part of the field of play.

The Playing Area is the field of play and the in-goal areas (as shown on the plan). The touchlines, touch-in-goal lines and dead ball lines are not part of the playing area.

The Playing Enclosure is the playing area and a space around it, not less than 5 metres where practicable, which is known as the perimeter area.

In-goal is the area between the goal line and the dead ball line, and between the touch-in-goal lines. It includes the goal line but it does not include the dead ball line or the touch-in-goal lines.

'The 22' is the area between the goal line and the 22-metre line, including the 22-metre line but excluding the goal line.

The Plan, including all the words and figures on it, is part of the Laws.

1.1 SURFACE OF THE PLAYING ENCLOSURE
(a) Requirement. The surface must be safe to play on at all times.
(b) Type of surface. The surface should be grass but may also be sand, clay, snow or artificial grass. The game may be played on snow, provided the snow and underlying surface are safe to play on. It shall not be a permanently hard surface such as concrete or asphalt. In the case of artificial grass surfaces, they must conform to IRB Regulation 22.

1.2 REQUIRED DIMENSIONS FOR THE PLAYING ENCLOSURE
(a) Dimensions. The field of play does not exceed 100 metres in length and 70 metres in width. Each in-goal does not exceed 22 metres in length and 70 metres in width.
(b) The length and breadth of the playing area are to be as near as possible to the dimensions indicated. All the areas are rectangular.
(c) The distance from the goal line to the dead ball line should be not less than 10 metres where practicable.

1.3 LINES ON THE PLAYING ENCLOSURE
(a) Solid Lines. The dead ball lines and touch-in-goal lines, both of which are outside the in-goal areas; The goal lines, which are within the in-goal areas but outside the field of play; The 22-metre lines, which are parallel to the goal lines; The half-way line which is parallel to the goal lines; and The touchlines which are outside the field of play.
(b) Broken Lines. The 10-metre lines, which run from one touchline to the other, are 10 metres from each side of the half-way line and parallel to it; and The 5-metre lines, which run from one 5-metre dash line to the other, are 5 metres from and parallel to the touchlines. The 15-metre lines, which link the 5-metre dash lines, are 15 metres from and parallel to the touchlines.
(c) Dash Lines (i) Six dash lines, each being I metre long, 5 metres from and parallel to each goal line positioned 5 metres and 15 metres from each touchline

and in front of each goal post. (ii) Two dash lines, 5 metres long, 15 metres from each of the touchlines, which start at the goal line and end at the 5-metre dash line. (iii) One dash line of 0.5 metre long intersects the centre of the half-way line. All the lines must be suitably marked out according to the Plan.

1.4 DIMENSIONS FOR GOAL POSTS AND CROSSBAR
(a) The distance between the two goal posts is 5.6 metres.
(b) The crossbar is placed between the two goal posts so that its top edge is 3.0 metres from the ground.
(c) The minimum height of the goal posts is 3.4 metres.
(d) When padding is attached to the goal posts the distance from the goal line to the external edge of the padding must not exceed 300mm.

1.5 FLAG POSTS
(a) There are 14 flag posts with flags, each with a minimum height of 1.2 metres above the ground.
(b) Flag posts must be positioned at the intersection of touch-in-goal lines and the goal lines and at the intersection of the touch-in-goal lines and the dead ball lines. These eight flag posts are outside the in-goal area and do not form part of the playing area.
(c) Flag posts must be positioned in line with the 22-metre lines and the half-way line, 2 metres outside the touchlines and within the playing enclosure.

1.6 OBJECTIONS TO THE GROUND
(a) If either team has objections about the ground or the way it is marked out they must tell the referee before the match starts.
(b) The referee will attempt to resolve the issues but must not start a match if any part of the ground is considered to be dangerous.

Law 2 The Ball

2.1 SHAPE
The ball must be oval and made of four panels.

2.2 DIMENSIONS
Length in line 280–300 millimetres; Circumference (end to end) 740–770 millimetres; Circumference (in width) 580–620 millimetres.

2.3 MATERIALS
Leather or suitable synthetic material. It may be treated to make it water resistant and easier to grip.

2.4 WEIGHT
410–460 grams

2.5 AIR PRESSURE AT THE START OF PLAY
65.71–68.75 kilopascals, or 0.67–0.70 kilograms per square centimetre, or 9.5–10.0lbs per square inch.

2.6 SPARE BALLS
Spare balls may be available during a match, but a team must not gain or attempt to gain an unfair advantage by using them or changing them.

2.7 SMALLER BALLS
Balls of different sizes may be used for matches between young players.

Law 3 Number of Players – The Team

DEFINITIONS

A Team A team consists of fifteen players who start the match plus any authorised replacements and/or substitutes.
Replacement A player who replaces an injured team mate.
Substitute A player who replaces a team mate for tactical reasons.

3.1 MAXIMUM NUMBER OF PLAYERS ON THE PLAYING AREA
Maximum: each team must have no more than fifteen players on the playing area.

3.2 TEAM WITH MORE THAN THE PERMITTED NUMBER OF PLAYERS
Objection: at any time before or during a match a team may make an objection to the referee about the number of players in their opponents' team. As soon as the referee knows that a team has too many players, the referee must order the captain of that team to reduce the number appropriately. The score at the time of the objection remains unaltered.
Penalty: Penalty at the place where the game would restart.

3.3 WHEN THERE ARE FEWER THAN FIFTEEN PLAYERS
A Union may authorise matches to be played with fewer than fifteen players in each team. When that happens, all the Laws of the Game apply except that each team must have at least five players in the scrum at all times. Exception: matches between teams of seven-a-side are an exception. These matches are covered by the seven-a-side variations to the Laws of the Game.

3.4 PLAYERS NOMINATED AS SUBSTITUTES
For international matches a Union may nominate up to seven replacements/substitutes. For other matches, the Union with jurisdiction over the match decides how many replacements/substitutes may be nominated. A team can substitute up to two front row players and up to five other players. Substitutions may only be made when the ball is dead and with the permission of the referee.

3.5 SUITABLY TRAINED AND EXPERIENCED PLAYERS IN THE FRONT ROW
(a) The table below indicates the numbers of suitably trained and experienced players for the front row when nominating different numbers of players.

Number of Players	Number of Suitably Trained and Experienced Players
15 or less	**3** players who can play in the front row
16, 17 or **18**	**4** players who can play in the front row
19, 20, 21 or **22**	**5** players who can play in the front row

(b) Each player in the front row and any potential

replacement(s) must be suitably trained and experienced.

(c) When 19, 20, 21 or 22 players are nominated in a team there must be five players who can play in the front row to ensure that on the first occasion that a replacement hooker is required and, on the first occasion that a replacement prop forward is required, the team can continue to play safely with contested scrums.

(d) The replacement of a front row forward must come from suitably trained and experienced players who started the match or from the nominated replacements.

3.6 SENT OFF FOR FOUL PLAY
A player sent off for foul play must not be replaced or substituted. For an exception to this Law, refer to Law 3.13.

3.7 PERMANENT REPLACEMENT
A player may be replaced if injured. If the player is permanently replaced, that player must not return and play in that match. The replacement of the injured player must be made when the ball is dead and with the permission of the referee.

3.8 THE DECISION FOR PERMANENT REPLACEMENT
(a) When a national representative team is playing in a match, a player may be replaced only when, in the opinion of a doctor, the player is so injured that it would be unwise for that player to continue playing in that match.

(b) In other matches, where a Union has given explicit permission, an injured player may be replaced on the advice of a medically trained person. If none is present, that player may be replaced if the referee agrees.

3.9 THE REFEREE'S POWER TO STOP AN INJURED PLAYER FROM CONTINUING
If the referee decides – with or without the advice of a doctor or other medically qualified person – that a player is so injured that the player should stop playing, the referee may order that player to leave the playing area. The referee may also order an injured player to leave the field in order to be medically examined.

3.10 TEMPORARY REPLACEMENT
(a) When a player leaves the field to have bleeding controlled and/or have an open wound covered, that player may be temporarily replaced. If the player who has been temporarily replaced does not return to the field of play within 15 minutes (actual time) of leaving the playing area, the replacement becomes permanent and the replaced player must not return to the field of play.

(b) If the temporary replacement is injured, that player may also be replaced.

(c) If the temporary replacement is sent off for foul play, the replaced player may not return to the field of play.

(d) If a temporary replacement is cautioned and temporarily suspended, the replaced player may not return to the field of play until after the period of suspension.

3.11 PLAYER WISHING TO REJOIN THE MATCH
(a) A player who has an open or bleeding wound must leave the playing area. The player must not return until the bleeding is controlled and the wound has been covered.

(b) A player who leaves a match because of injury or any other reason must not rejoin the match until the referee permits the player to return. The referee must not let a player rejoin a match until the ball is dead.

(c) If the player rejoins the match without the referee's permission, and the referee believes the player did so to help that player's team or obstruct the opposing team, the referee penalises the player for misconduct.

Penalty: A penalty kick is awarded at the place where play would restart.

3.12 SUBSTITUTED PLAYERS REJOINING THE MATCH
If a player is substituted, that player must not return and play in that match even to replace an injured player.

Exception 1: a substituted player may replace a player with a bleeding or open wound.

Exception 2: a substituted player may replace a front row player when injured, temporarily suspended or sent off.

3.13 FRONT ROW FORWARD SENT OFF OR TEMPORARILY SUSPENDED OR INJURED
(a) If after a front row player has been sent off or during the time a front row player is temporarily suspended, and there are no further front row players available from the nominated team, then uncontested scrums will be ordered. It is not the responsibility of the referee to determine the suitability of trained front row replacements nor their availability, as this is a team responsibility.

(b) After a front row player is sent off or during the time a front row player is temporarily suspended the referee, upon awarding the next scrum, will ask that player's captain whether or not the team has another player on the field of play who is suitably trained to play in the front row. If not, the captain chooses any player from that team who then must leave the field of play and be replaced by a suitably trained front row player from the team's replacements. The captain may do this immediately prior to the next scrum or after another player has been tried in the front row.

(c) When a period of temporary suspension ends and a front row player returns to the field of play, the replacement front row player leaves the field of play and the nominated player who left the field of play for the period of the suspension may resume playing in the match.

(d) Furthermore, if, because of sending off or injury, a team cannot provide enough suitably trained front row players, the match continues with uncontested scrums.

(e) An uncontested scrum is the same as a normal scrum, except that the teams do not compete for the ball, the team throwing in the ball must win it, and neither team is allowed to push.

Law 4 Players' Clothing

DEFINITIONS

Players' clothing is anything players wear. A player wears a jersey, shorts and underwear, socks and boots. Detailed information relating to the permitted specifications for clothing and studs maybe found in IRB Specifications (Regulation 12).

4.1 ADDITIONAL ITEMS OF CLOTHING
(a) A player may wear supports made of elasticated or compressible materials which must be washable.

(b) A player may wear shin guards which conform with IRB Specifications (Regulation 12).

(c) A player may wear ankle supports worn under socks, not extending higher than one third of the length of the shin and, if rigid, from material other than metal.

(d) A player may wear mitts (fingerless gloves) which must conform to IRB Specifications (Regulation 12).

(e) A player may wear shoulder pads which must bear the IRB Approval Mark (Regulation 12).

(f) A player may wear a mouth guard or dental protector.

(g) A player may wear headgear which must bear the IRB Approval Mark (Regulation 12).

(h) A player may wear bandages and/or dressings to cover or protect any injury.

(i) A player may wear thin tape or other similar material as support and/or to prevent injury.

4.2 SPECIAL ADDITIONAL ITEMS FOR WOMEN
Besides the previous items, women may wear chest pads which must bear the IRB Approval Mark (Regulation 12).

4.3 STUDS
(a) Studs of players' boots must conform with the IRB Specifications (Regulation 12).

(b) Moulded rubber multi-studded soles are acceptable provided they have no sharp edges or ridges.

4.4 BANNED ITEMS OF CLOTHING
(a) A player must not wear any item that is contaminated by blood.

(b) A player must not wear any item that is sharp or abrasive.

(c) A player must not wear any items containing buckles, clips, rings, hinges, zippers, screws, bolts or rigid material or projection not otherwise permitted under this Law.

(d) A player must not wear jewellery such as rings or earrings.

(e) A player must not wear gloves.

(f) A player must not wear shorts with padding sewn into them.

(g) A player must not wear any other item which does not conform with the IRB Specifications for such clothing (Regulation 12).

(h) A player must not wear any item that is normally permitted by Law, but, in the referee's opinion that is liable to cause injury to a player.

(i) A player must not wear a single stud at the toe of the boot.

(j) A player must not wear communication devices within that player's clothing or attached to the body.

(k) A player must not wear any additional item of clothing that does not conform to IRB Regulation 12.

4.5 INSPECTION OF PLAYERS' CLOTHING
(a) The referee or the touch judges appointed by or under the authority of the match organiser must inspect the players' clothing and studs for conformity to this Law.

(b) The referee has power to decide at any time, before or during the match, that part of a player's clothing is dangerous or illegal. If the referee decides that clothing is dangerous or illegal the referee must order the player to remove it. The player must not take part in the match until the items of clothing are removed.

(c) If, at an inspection before the match, the referee or a touch judge tells a player that an item banned under this Law is being worn, and the player is subsequently found to be wearing that item on the playing area, that player is sent off for misconduct.
Penalty: A penalty kick is awarded at the place where play is restarted.

4.6 WEARING OTHER CLOTHING
The referee must not allow any player to leave the playing area to change items of clothing, unless these are bloodstained.

Law 5 Time

5.1 DURATION OF A MATCH
A match lasts no longer than eighty minutes plus time lost, extra time and any special conditions. A match is divided into two halves each of not more than forty minutes playing time.

5.2 HALF TIME
After half time the teams change ends. There is an interval of not more than 10 minutes. The length of the interval is decided by the match organiser, the Union or the recognised body which has jurisdiction over the game. During the interval the teams, the referee and the touch judges may leave the playing enclosure.

5.3 TIME KEEPING
The referee keeps the time but may delegate the duty to either or both the touch judges and/or the official time-keeper, in which case the referee signals to them any stoppage of time or time lost. In matches without an official time-keeper, if the referee is in doubt as to the correct time the referee consults either or both the touch judges and may consult others but only if the touch judges cannot help.

5.4 TIME LOST
Time lost may be due to the following:
(a) Injury. The referee may stop play for not more than one minute so that an injured player can be treated, or for any other permitted delay. The referee may allow play to continue while a medically trained person treats an injured player in the playing area or the player may go to the touchline for treatment. If a player is seriously injured and needs to be removed from the field of play, the referee has the discretion to allow the necessary time to have the injured player removed from the field-of-play.
(b) Replacing players' clothing. When the ball is dead, the referee allows time for a player to replace or repair a badly torn jersey, shorts or boots. Time is allowed for a player to re-tie a boot-lace.
(c) Replacement and substitution of players. Time is allowed when a player is replaced or substituted.
(d) Reporting of foul play by a touch judge. Time is allowed when a touch judge reports foul play.

5.5 MAKING UP FOR TIME LOST
Any playing time lost is made up in the same half of the match.

5.6 PLAYING EXTRA TIME
A match may last more than eighty minutes if the Match Organiser has authorised the playing of extra time in a drawn match in a knock-out competition.

5.7 OTHER TIME REGULATIONS
(a) In international matches, play always lasts eighty minutes plus lost time.
(b) In non-international matches a Union may decide the length of a match.
(c) If the Union does not decide, the teams agree on the length of a match. If they cannot agree, the referee decides.
(d) The referee has the power to end the match at any time, if the referee believes that play should not continue because it would be dangerous.
(e) If time expires and the ball is not dead, or an awarded scrum or lineout has not been completed the referee allows play to continue until the next time that the ball becomes dead. If time expires and a mark, free kick or penalty kick is then awarded, the referee allows play to continue.
(f) If time expires after a try has been scored the referee allows time for the conversion kick to be taken.
(g) When weather conditions are exceptionally hot and/or humid, the referee, at his discretion, will be permitted to allow one water break in each half. This water break should be no longer than one minute. Time lost should be added on at the end of each half. The water break should normally be taken after a score or when the ball is out of play near the half way line.

Law 6 Match Officials

6.A. REFEREE

BEFORE THE MATCH

6.A.1 APPOINTING THE REFEREE
The referee is appointed by the match organiser. If no referee has been appointed the two teams may agree upon a referee. If they cannot agree, the home team appoints a referee.

6.A.2 REPLACING THE REFEREE
If the referee is unable to complete the match, the referee's replacement is appointed according to the instructions of the match organiser. If the match organiser has given no instructions, the referee appoints the replacement. If the referee cannot do so, the home team appoints a replacement.

6.A.3 DUTIES OF THE REFEREE BEFORE THE MATCH
(a) Toss. The referee organises the toss. One of the captains tosses a coin and the other captain calls to see who wins the toss. The winner of the toss decides whether to kick off or to choose an end. If the winner of the toss decides to choose an end, the opponents must kick off and vice versa.

DURING THE MATCH

6.A.4 THE DUTIES OF THE REFEREE IN THE PLAYING ENCLOSURE
(a) The referee is the sole judge of fact and of Law during a match. The referee must apply fairly all the Laws of the Game in every match.
(b) The referee keeps the time.
(c) The referee keeps the score.
(d) The referee gives permission to the players to leave the playing area.
(e) The referee gives permission to the replacements or substitutes to enter the playing area.
(f) The referee gives permission to the team doctors or medically trained persons or their assistants to enter the playing area, as and when permitted by the Law.
(g) The referee gives permission to each of the coaches to enter the playing area at half time to attend their teams during the interval.

6.A.5 PLAYERS DISPUTING A REFEREE'S DECISION
All players must respect the authority of the referee. They must not dispute the referee's decisions. They must stop playing at once when the referee blows the whistle except at a kick off.
Penalty: Penalty Kick at the place of infringement or where play would next commence.

6.A.6 REFEREE ALTERING A DECISION
The referee may alter a decision when a touch judge has raised the flag to signal touch or an act of foul play.

6.A.7 REFEREE CONSULTING WITH OTHERS
(a) The referee may consult with touch judges in regard to matters relating to their duties, the Law relating to foul play, or timekeeping.
(b) A match organiser may appoint an official who uses technological devices. If the referee is unsure when making a decision in in-goal involving a try being scored or a touch down, that official may be consulted.
(c) The official may be consulted if the referee is unsure when making a decision in in-goal with regard to the scoring of a try or a touch down when foul play in in-goal may have been involved.
(d) The official may be consulted in relation to the success or otherwise of kicks at goal.
(e) The official may be consulted if the referee or touch judge is unsure if a player was or was not in touch when attempting to ground the ball to score a try.
(f) The official may be consulted if the referee or touch judges are unsure when making a decision relating to touch-in-goal and the ball being made dead if a score may have occurred.
(g) A match organiser may appoint a timekeeper who will signify the end of each half.
(h) The referee must not consult with any other persons.

6.A.8 THE REFEREE'S WHISTLE
(a) The referee must carry a whistle and blow the whistle to indicate the beginning and end of each half of the match.
(b) The referee has power to stop play at any time.
(c) The referee must blow the whistle to indicate a score, or a touch down.
(d) The referee must blow the whistle to stop play because of an infringement or for an offence of foul play. When the referee cautions or sends off the offender, the referee must whistle a second time when

the penalty kick or penalty try is awarded.

(e) The referee must blow the whistle when the ball has gone out of play, or when it has become unplayable, or when a penalty is awarded.

(f) The referee must blow the whistle when the ball or the ball carrier touches the referee and either team gains an advantage from this.

(g) The referee must blow the whistle when it would be dangerous to let play continue. This includes when a scrum collapses, or when a front row player is lifted into the air or is forced upwards out of a scrum, or when it is probable that a player has been seriously injured.

(h) The referee may blow the whistle to stop play for any other reason according to the Laws.

6.A.9 THE REFEREE AND INJURY

(a) If a player is injured and continuation of play would be dangerous, the referee must blow the whistle immediately.

(b) If the referee stops play because a player has been injured, and there has been no infringement and the ball has not been made dead, play restarts with a scrum. The team last in possession throws in the ball. If neither team was in possession, the attacking team throws in the ball.

(c) The referee must blow the whistle if continuation of play would be dangerous for any reason.

6.A.10 THE BALL TOUCHING THE REFEREE

(a) If the ball or the ball carrier touches the referee and neither team gains an advantage, play continues.

(b) If either team gains an advantage in the field of play, the referee orders a scrum and the team that last played the ball has the throw in.

(c) If either team gains an advantage in in-goal, if the ball is in possession of an attacking player the referee awards a try where the contact took place.

(d) If either team gains an advantage in in-goal, if the ball is in possession of a defending player, the referee awards a touch down where the contact took place.

6.A.11 THE BALL IN IN-GOAL TOUCHED BY NON-PLAYER

The referee judges what would have happened next and awards a try or a touch down at the place where the ball was touched.

AFTER THE MATCH

6.A.12 SCORE

The referee communicates the score to the teams and to the match organiser.

6.A.13 PLAYER SENT-OFF

If a player is sent off the referee gives the match organiser a written report on the foul play infringement as soon as possible.

6.B. TOUCH JUDGES

BEFORE THE MATCH

6.B.1 APPOINTING TOUCH JUDGES

There are two touch judges for every match. Unless they have been appointed by or under the authority of the match organiser, each team provides a touch judge.

6.B.2 REPLACING A TOUCH JUDGE

The match organiser may nominate a person to act as a replacement for the referee or the touch judges. This person is called the reserve touch judge and stands in the perimeter area.

6.B.3 CONTROL OF TOUCH JUDGES

The referee has control over both touch judges. The referee may tell them what their duties are, and may overrule their decisions. If a touch judge is unsatisfactory the referee may ask that the touch judge be replaced. If the referee believes a touch judge is guilty of misconduct, the referee has power to send the touch judge off and make a report to the match organiser.

DURING THE MATCH

6.B.4 WHERE THE TOUCH JUDGES SHOULD BE

(a) There is one touch judge on each side of the ground. The touch judge remains in touch except when judging a kick at goal. When judging a kick at goal the touch judges stand in in-goal behind the goal posts.

(b) A touch judge may enter the playing area when reporting an offence of dangerous play or misconduct to the referee. The touch judge may do this only at the next stoppage in play.

6.B.5 TOUCH JUDGE SIGNALS

(a) Each touch judge carries a flag or something similar with which to signal decisions.

(b) Signalling result of kick at goal. When a conversion kick or a penalty kick at goal is being taken, the touch judges must help the referee by signalling the result of the kick. One touch judge stands at or behind each goal post. If the ball goes over the cross-bar and between the posts, the touch judge raises the flag to indicate a goal.

(c) Signalling touch. When the ball or the ball carrier has gone into touch, the touch judge must hold up the flag. The touch judge must stand at the place of the throw in and point to the team entitled to throw in. The touch judge must also signal when the ball or the ball carrier has gone into touch-in-goal.

(d) When to lower the flag. When the ball is thrown in, the touch judge must lower the flag, with the following exceptions:

Exception 1: When the player throwing in puts any part of either foot in the field of play, the touch judge keeps the flag up.

Exception 2: When the team not entitled to throw in has done so, the touch judge keeps the flag up.

Exception 3: When, at a quick throw in, the ball that went into touch is replaced by another ball, or after it went into touch or it has been touched by anyone except the player who takes the throw in, the touch judge keeps the flag up.

(e) It is for the referee, and not the touch judge, to decide whether or not the ball was thrown in from the correct place.

(f) Signalling foul play. A touch judge signals that foul play or misconduct has been seen by holding the flag horizontally and pointing infield at right angles to the touchline.

6.B.6 AFTER SIGNALLING FOUL PLAY

A match organiser may give authority to the touch judge to signal for foul play. If a touch judge signals foul play, the touch judge must stay in touch and continue to carry out all the other duties until the next stoppage in play. The touch judge may then enter the playing area to report the offence to the referee. The referee may then take whatever action is needed. Any penalty awarded will be in accordance with Law 10 – Foul Play.

AFTER THE MATCH

6.B.7 PLAYER SENT-OFF

If a player has been sent-off following a touch judge's signal, the touch judge submits a written report about the incident to the referee as soon as possible after the match and provides it to the match organiser.

6.C. ADDITIONAL PERSONS

6.C.1 RESERVE TOUCH JUDGE

When a reserve touch judge is appointed, the referee's authority regarding replacements and substitutions may be delegated to the reserve touch judge.

6.C.2 THOSE WHO MAY ENTER THE PLAYING AREA

The match doctor and the non-playing members of the team may enter the playing area as authorised by the referee.

6.C.3 LIMITS TO ENTERING THE PLAYING AREA

In the case of injury, these persons may enter the playing area while play continues, provided they have permission from the referee. Otherwise, they enter only when the ball is dead.

Law 7 Mode of Play

7.1 PLAYING A MATCH

A match is started by a kick off. After the kick off, any player who is onside may take the ball and run with it. Any player may throw it or kick it. Any player may give the ball to another player. Any player may tackle, hold or push an opponent holding the ball. Any player may fall on the ball. Any player may take part in a scrum, ruck, maul or lineout. Any player may ground the ball in in-goal. Whatever a player does must be in accordance with the laws of the game.

LAW 8 Advantage

DEFINITIONS

The Law of advantage takes precedence over most other Laws and its purpose is to make play more continuous with fewer stoppages for infringements. Players are encouraged to play to the whistle despite infringements by their opponents. When the result of an infringement by one team is that their opposing team may gain an advantage, the referee does not whistle immediately for the infringement.

8.1 ADVANTAGE IN PRACTICE

(a) The referee is sole judge of whether or not a team has gained an advantage. The referee has wide discretion when making decisions.

(b) Advantage can be either territorial or tactical.

(c) Territorial advantage means a gain in ground.

(d) Tactical advantage means freedom for the non-offending team to play the ball as they wish.

8.2 WHEN ADVANTAGE DOES NOT ARISE

The advantage must be clear and real. A mere opportunity to gain advantage is not enough. If the non-offending team does not gain an advantage, the referee blows the whistle and brings play back to the place of infringement.

8.3 WHEN THE ADVANTAGE LAW IS NOT APPLIED

(a) Referee contact. Advantage must not be applied when the ball, or a player carrying it, touches the referee.

(b) Ball out of tunnel. Advantage must not be applied when the ball comes out of either end of the tunnel at a scrum without having been played.

(c) Wheeled scrum. Advantage must not be applied when the scrum is wheeled through more than 90 degrees (so that the middle line has passed beyond a position parallel to the touchline).

(d) Collapsed scrum. Advantage must not be applied when a scrum collapses. The referee must blow the whistle immediately.

(e) Player lifted in the air. Advantage must not be applied when a player in a scrum is lifted in the air or forced upwards out of the scrum. The referee must blow the whistle immediately.

8.4 IMMEDIATE WHISTLE WHEN NO ADVANTAGE

The referee blows the whistle immediately once the referee decides an advantage cannot be gained by the non-offending team.

8.5 MORE THAN ONE INFRINGEMENT

(a) If there is more than one infringement by the same team the referee applies the advantage law.

(b) If advantage is being played following an infringement by one team and then the other team commit an infringement, the referee blows the whistle and applies the sanctions associated with the first infringement.

Law 9 Method of Scoring

9.A. SCORING POINTS

9.A.1 POINTS VALUES

Try. When an attacking player is first to ground the ball in the opponents' in-goal, a try is scored.
5 Points

Penalty Try. If a player would probably have scored a try but for foul play by an opponent, a penalty try is awarded between the goal posts.
5 Points

Conversion Goal. When a player scores a try it gives the player's team the right to attempt to score a goal by taking a kick at goal; this also applies to a penalty try. This kick is a conversion kick: a conversion kick can be a place kick or a drop kick.
2 Points

Penalty Goal. A player scores a penalty goal by kicking a goal from a penalty kick.
3 Points

Dropped Goal. A player scores a dropped goal by kicking a goal from a drop kick in general play. The team awarded a free kick cannot score a dropped goal until the ball next becomes dead, or until an opponent has played or touched it, or has tackled the ball carrier. This restriction applies also to a scrum taken instead of a free kick.
3 Points

9.A.2. KICK AT GOAL – SPECIAL CIRCUMSTANCES

(a) If after the ball is kicked, it touches the ground or any team mate of the kicker, a goal cannot be scored.

(b) If the ball has crossed the cross bar a goal is scored, even if the wind blows it back into the field of play.

(c) If an opponent commits an offence as the kick at goal is being taken, but neverthless the kick is successful, advantage is played and the score stands.

(d) Any player who touches the ball in an attempt to prevent a penalty goal being scored is illegally touching the ball.
Penalty: Penalty Kick

9.B CONVERSION KICK

9.B.1 TAKING A CONVERSION KICK

(a) The kicker must use the ball that was in play unless it is defective.

(b) The kick is taken on a line through the place where the try was scored.

(c) A placer is a team mate who holds the ball for the kicker to kick.

(d) The kicker may place the ball directly on the ground or on sand, sawdust or a kicking tee approved by the Union.

(e) The kicker must take the kick within one minute from the time the kicker has indicated an intention to kick. The intention to kick is signalled by the arrival of the kicking tee or sand, or the player makes a mark on the ground. The player must complete the kick within the minute even if the ball rolls over and has to be placed again.
Penalty: The kick is disallowed if the kicker does not take the kick within the time allowed.

9.B.2 THE KICKER'S TEAM

(a) All the kicker's team, except the placer, must be behind the ball when it is kicked.

(b) Neither the kicker nor a placer must do anything to mislead their opponents into charging too soon.

(c) If the ball falls over before the kicker begins the approach to kick, the referee permits the kicker to replace it without excessive delay. While the ball is replaced, the opponents must stay behind their goal line. If the ball falls over after the kicker begins the approach to kick, the kicker may then kick or attempt a dropped goal. If the ball falls over and rolls away from the line through the place where the try was scored, and the kicker then kicks the ball over the cross bar, a goal is scored. If the ball falls over and

rolls into touch after the kicker begins the approach to kick, the kick is disallowed.
Penalty: (a)–(c) If the kicker's team infringes, the kick is disallowed.

9.B.3 THE OPPOSING TEAM

(a) All players of the opposing team must retire to their goal line and must not overstep that line until the kicker begins the approach to kick or starts to kick. When the kicker does this, they may charge or jump to prevent a goal but must not be physically supported by other players in these actions.

(b) When the ball falls over after the kicker began the approach to kick, the opponents may continue to charge.

(c) A defending team must not shout during a kick at goal.
Penalty: (a)–(c) If the opposing team infringes but the kick is successful, the goal stands. If the kick is unsuccessful, the kicker may take another kick and the opposing team is not allowed to charge. When another kick is allowed, the kicker may repeat all the preparations. The kicker may change the type of kick.

Law 10 Foul Play

10.1 OBSTRUCTION

(a) Charging or pushing. When a player and an opponent are running for the ball, either player must not charge or push the other except shoulder-to-shoulder.
Penalty: Penalty Kick

(b) Running in front of a ball carrier. A player must not intentionally move or stand in front of a team mate carrying the ball thereby preventing opponents from tackling the current ball carrier or the opportunity to tackle potential ball carriers when they gain possession.
Penalty: Penalty Kick

(c) Blocking the tackler. A player must not intentionally move or stand in a position that prevents an opponent from tackling a ball carrier.
Penalty: Penalty Kick

(d) Blocking the ball. A player must not intentionally move or stand in a position that prevents an opponent from playing the ball.
Penalty: Penalty Kick

(e) Ball carrier running into team mate at a set-piece. A player carrying the ball after it has left a scrum, ruck, maul or lineout must not run into team mates in front of the player.
Penalty: Penalty Kick

(f) Flanker obstructing opposing scrum half. A flanker in a scrum must not prevent an opposing scrum half from advancing around the scrum.
Penalty: Penalty Kick

10.2 UNFAIR PLAY

(a) Intentionally Offending. A player must not intentionally infringe any law of the game, or play unfairly. The player who intentionally offends must be either admonished, or cautioned that a send off will result if the

offence or a similar offence is committed, or sent off. After a caution a player is temporarily suspended for a period of ten minutes playing time. After a caution, the the player commits the same or similar offence, the player must be sent off.
Penalty: Penalty Kick

A penalty try must be awarded if the offence prevents a try that would probably otherwise have been scored. A player who prevents a try being scored through foul play must either be cautioned and temporarily suspended or sent off.

(b) Time-wasting. A player must not intentionally waste time.
Penalty: Free Kick

(c) Throwing into touch. A player must not intentionally knock, place, push or throw the ball with his arm or hand into touch, touch-in-goal, or over the dead ball line.
Penalty: Penalty Kick on the 15-metre line if the offence is between the 15-metre line and the touchline, or, at the place of infringement if the offence occurred elsewhere in the field of play, or, 5 metres from the goal line and at least 15 metres from the touchline if the infringement occurred in in-goal. A penalty try must be awarded if the offence prevents a try that would probably otherwise have been scored.

10.3 REPEATED INFRINGEMENTS

(a) Repeatedly offending. A player must not repeatedly infringe any law. Repeated infringement is a matter of fact. The question of whether or not the player intended to infringe is irrelevant.
Penalty: Penalty Kick

A player penalised for repeated infringements must be cautioned and temporarily suspended. If that player then commits a further cautionable offence, or the same offence, the player must be sent off.

(b) Repeated infringements by the team. When different players of the same team repeatedly commit the same offence, the referee must decide whether or not this amounts to repeated infringement. If it does, the referee gives a general warning to the team and if they then repeat the offence, the referee cautions and temporarily suspends the guilty player(s) for a period of 10 minutes playing time. If a player of that same team then repeats the offence the referee sends off the guilty player(s).
Penalty: Penalty Kick

A penalty try must be awarded if the offence prevents a try that would probably otherwise have been scored.

(c) Repeated infringements: standard applied by referee. When the referee decides how many offences constitute repeated infringement, the referee must always apply a strict standard in representative and senior matches. When a player offends three times the referee must caution that player.

The referee may relax this standard in junior or minor matches, where infringements may be the result of poor knowledge of the laws or lack of skill.

10.4 DANGEROUS PLAY AND MISCONDUCT

(a) Punching or striking. A player must not strike an opponent with the fist or arm, including the elbow, shoulder, head or knee(s).
Penalty: Penalty Kick

(b) Stamping or trampling. A player must not stamp or trample on an opponent.
Penalty: Penalty Kick

(c) Kicking. A player must not kick an opponent.
Penalty: Penalty Kick

(d) Tripping. A player must not trip an opponent with the leg or foot.
Penalty: Penalty Kick

(e) Dangerous tackling. A player must not tackle an opponent early, late or dangerously.
Penalty: Penalty Kick

A player must not tackle (or try to tackle) an opponent above the line of the shoulders. A tackle around the opponent's neck or head is dangerous play.
Penalty: Penalty Kick

A 'stiff-arm tackle' is dangerous play. A player makes a stiff-arm tackle when using a stiff-arm to strike an opponent.
Penalty: Penalty Kick

Playing a player without the ball is dangerous play.
Penalty: Penalty Kick

A player must not tackle an opponent whose feet are off the ground.
Penalty: Penalty Kick

Advantage may be played, but if the offence prevents a probable try, a penalty try must be awarded.

(f) Playing an opponent without the ball. Except in a scrum, ruck or maul, a player must not hold, or push, or charge into, or obstruct an opponent not carrying the ball.
Penalty: Penalty Kick

(g) Dangerous charging. A player must not charge or knock down an opponent carrying the ball without trying to grasp that player.
Penalty: Penalty Kick

(h) Tackling the jumper in the air. A player must not tackle nor tap, push or pull the foot or feet of an opponent jumping for the ball in a lineout or in open play.
Penalty: Penalty Kick

(i) Dangerous play in a scrum, ruck or maul. The front row of a scrum must not rush against its opponents.
Penalty: Penalty Kick

Front row players must not intentionally lift opponents off their feet or force them upwards out of the scrum.
Penalty: Penalty Kick

Players must not charge into a ruck or maul without binding onto a player in the ruck or maul.
Penalty: Penalty Kick

Players must not intentionally collapse a scrum, ruck or maul.
Penalty: Penalty Kick

(j) Retaliation. A player must not retaliate. Even if an opponent is infringing the laws, a player must not do anything that is dangerous to the opponent.
Penalty: Penalty Kick

(k) Acts contrary to good sportsmanship. A player must not do anything that is against the spirit of good sportsmanship in the playing enclosure.
Penalty: Penalty Kick

(l) Misconduct while the ball is out of play. A player, must not, while the ball is out of play, commit any misconduct, or obstruct or in any way interfere with an opponent.
Penalty: Penalty Kick The penalty is the same as for sections 10.4 (a)–(k) except that the penalty kick is awarded at the place where play would restart. If that place is on the touchline or within 15 metres of it, the mark for the penalty kick is on the 15-metre line, in line with that place. If play would restart at a 5-metre scrum, the mark for the penalty kick is at that place of the scrum. If play would restart with a drop out, the non-offending team may choose to take the penalty kick anywhere on the 22-metre line. If a penalty kick

is awarded but the offending team is guilty of further misconduct before the kick is taken, the referee cautions or orders off the guilty player and advances the mark for the penalty kick 10 metres. This covers both the original offence and the misconduct.

If a penalty kick is awarded to a team but a player of that team is guilty of further misconduct before the kick is taken, the referee will caution or send-off the guilty player, declare the kick disallowed, and award a penalty kick to the opposing team. If an offence is committed outside the playing area while the ball is still in play, and if that offence is not covered by any other part of this law, the penalty kick is awarded on the 15-metre line, in line with where the offence happened. For an offence reported by a touch judge a penalty kick may be awarded where the offence happened, or advantage may be played.

(m) Late-charging the kicker. A player must not intentionally charge or obstruct an opponent who has just kicked the ball.
Penalty: The non-offending team may choose to take the penalty kick either at the place of infringement, where the ball lands, or where it was next played.

Place of infringement. If the infringement takes place in the kicker's in-goal, the penalty kick is taken 5 metres from the goal line in line with the place of infringement but at least 15 metres from the touchline. The non-offending team may also choose to take the penalty kick where the ball lands or is next played and at least 15 metres from the touchline.

Where the ball lands. If the ball lands in touch, the mark for the optional penalty kick is on the 15-metre line, in line with where it went into touch. If the ball lands within 15 metres of the touchline, the mark is on the 15-metre line opposite where it landed.

If the ball lands in the in-goal, in touch-in-goal, or on or over the dead ball line, the mark for the optional penalty kick is 5 metres from the goal line, in line with the place where the ball crossed the goal line and at least 15 metres from the touchline. If the ball hits a goal post or crossbar, the optional penalty kick is awarded where the ball lands on the ground.

(n) Flying Wedge and Cavalry Charge. A team must not use the 'Flying Wedge' or the 'Cavalry Charge'.
Penalty: Penalty Kick at the place of the original infringement.

'Flying Wedge' The type of attack known as a 'Flying Wedge' usually happens near the goal line, when the attacking team is awarded a penalty kick or free kick. The kicker tap-kicks the ball and starts the attack, either by driving towards the goal line or by passing to a team mate who drives forward. Immediately, team mates bind on each side of the ball carrier in a wedge formation. Often one or more of these team mates is in front of the ball carrier. A 'Flying Wedge' is illegal.
Penalty: Penalty Kick at the place of the original infringement.

'Cavalry Charge'. The type of attack known as a 'Cavalry Charge' usually happens near the goal line, when the attacking team is awarded a penalty kick or free kick. Attacking players form a line across the field some distance behind the kicker. These attacking players are usually a metre or two apart. At a signal from the kicker they charge forward. When they get near, the kicker tap-kicks the ball and passes it to one of them. Until the ball is kicked, the defending team must stay at least 10 metres from the mark or behind their goal line, if that is nearer. A 'Cavalry Charge' is illegal.
Penalty: Penalty Kick at the place of the original infringement.

10.5 SANCTIONS

(a) Any player who infringes any part of the Foul Play law must be admonished, or cautioned and temporarily suspended, or sent-off.

(b) A player who has been cautioned and temporarily suspended who then commits a second cautionable offence within the Foul Play law must be sent-off.

10.6 YELLOW AND RED CARDS

(a) When a player has been cautioned and temporarily suspended in an International match the referee will show that player a yellow card.

(b) When a player has been sent off in an International match, the referee will show that player a red card.

(c) For other matches the Match Organiser or Union having jurisdiction over the match may decide upon the use of yellow and red cards.

10.7 PLAYER SENT OFF

A player who is sent-off takes no further part in the match.

Law 11 Offside and Onside in General Play

DEFINITIONS

At the start of a game all players are onside. As the match progresses players may find themselves in an offside position. Such players are then liable to be penalised until they become onside again.

In general play a player is offside if the player is in front of a team mate who is carrying the ball, or in front of a team mate who last played the ball.

Offside means that a player is temporarily out of the game. Such players are liable to be penalised if they take part in the game.

In general play, a player can be put onside either by an action of a team mate or by an action of an opponent. However, the offside player cannot be put onside if the offside player interferes with play; or moves forward, towards the ball, or fails to move 10 metres away from the place where the ball lands.

11.1 OFFSIDE IN GENERAL PLAY

(a) A player who is in an offside position is liable to penalty only if the player does one of three things:

- Interferes with play or,
- Moves forward, towards the ball or Fails to comply with the 10-Metre law (law 11.4).
- A player who is in an offside position is not automatically penalised.
- A player who receives an unintentional throw forward is not offside.
- A player can be offside in the in-goal.

(b) Offside and interfering with play. A player who is offside must not take part in the game. This means the player must not play the ball or obstruct an opponent.

(c) Offside and moving forward. When a team mate of an offside player has kicked ahead, the offside player must not move towards opponents who are waiting to play the ball, or move towards the place where the ball lands, until the player has been put onside.

11.2 BEING PUT ONSIDE BY THE ACTION OF A TEAM MATE

In general play, there are four ways by which an offside player can be put onside by actions of that player or of team mates;

(a) Action by the player. When the offside player runs behind the team mate who last kicked, touched or carried the ball, the player is put onside.

(b) Action by the ball carrier. When a team mate carrying the ball runs in front of the offside player, that player is put onside.

(c) Action by the kicker or other onside player. When the kicker, or team mate who was level with or behind the kicker when (or after) the ball was kicked, runs in front of the offside player, the player is put onside.

(d) When running forward, the team mate may be in touch or in touch-in-goal, but that team mate must return to the playing area to put the other player onside.

11.3 BEING PUT ONSIDE BY OPPONENTS

In general play, there are three ways by which an offside player can be put onside by an action of the opposing team. These three ways do not apply to a player who is offside under the 10-Metre law.

(a) Runs 5 metres with ball. When an opponent carrying the ball runs 5 metres, the offside player is put onside.

(b) Kicks or passes. When an opponent kicks or passes the ball, the offside player is put onside.

(c) Intentionally touches ball. When an opponent intentionally touches the ball but does not catch it, the offside player is put onside.

11.4 OFFSIDE UNDER THE 10-METRE LAW

(a) When a team mate of an offside player has kicked ahead, the offside player is considered to be taking part in the game if the player is in front of an imaginary line across the field which is 10 metres from the opponent waiting to play the ball, or from where the ball lands or may land. The offside player must immediately move behind the imaginary 10-metre line. While moving away, the player must not obstruct an opponent.

Penalty: Penalty Kick

(b) While moving away, the offside player cannot be put onside by any action of the opposing team. However, before the player has moved the full 10 metres, the player can be put onside by any onside team mate who runs in front of the player.

(c) When a player who is offside under the 10-Metre law charges an opponent waiting to catch the ball, the referee blows the whistle at once and the offside player is penalised. Delay may prove dangerous to the opponent.

Penalty: Penalty Kick

(d) When a player who is offside under the 10-Metre law plays the ball which has been misfielded by an opponent, the offside player is penalised.

Penalty: Penalty Kick

(e) The 10-Metre law is not altered by the fact that the ball has hit a goal post or a crossbar. What matters is where the ball lands. An offside player must not be in front of the imaginary 10-metre line across the field.

Penalty: Penalty Kick

(f) The 10-Metre law does not apply when a player kicks the ball, and an opponent charges down the kick, and a team mate of the kicker who was in front

of the imaginary 10-metre line across the field then plays the ball. The opponent was not 'waiting to play the ball' and the team mate is onside.

Penalty: When a player is penalised for being offside in general play, the opposing team chooses either a penalty kick at the place of infringement or a scrum at the place where the offending team last played the ball. If it was last played in that team's in-goal, the scrum is formed 5 metres from the goal line in line with where it was played.

(g) If more than one player is offside and moving forward after a team mate has kicked ahead, the place of infringement is the position of the offside player closest to an opponent waiting for the ball, or closest to where the ball lands.

11.5 BEING PUT ONSIDE UNDER THE 10-METRE LAW

(a) The offside player must retire behind the imaginary 10-metre line across the field, otherwise the player is liable to be penalised.

(b) While retiring, the player can be put onside before moving behind the imaginary 10-metre line by any of the three actions of the player's team listed above in 11.2. However, the player cannot be put onside by any action of the opposing team.

11.6 ACCIDENTAL OFFSIDE

(a) When an offside player cannot avoid being touched by the ball or by a team mate carrying it, the player is accidentally offside. If the player's team gains no advantage from this, play continues. If the player's team gains an advantage, a scrum is formed with the opposing team throwing in the ball.

(b) When a player hands the ball to a team mate in front of the first player, the receiver is offside. Unless the receiver is considered to be intentionally offside (in which case a penalty kick is awarded), the receiver is accidentally offside and a scrum is formed with the opposing team throwing in the ball.

11.7 OFFSIDE AFTER A KNOCK ON

When a player knocks-on and an offside team mate next plays the ball, the offside player is liable to penalty if playing the ball prevented an opponent from gaining an advantage.

Penalty: Penalty Kick

11.8 PUTTING ONSIDE A PLAYER RETIRING DURING A RUCK, MAUL, SCRUM OR LINEOUT

When a ruck, maul, scrum or lineout forms, a player who is offside and is retiring as required by law remains offside even when the opposing team wins possession and the ruck, maul, scrum or lineout has ended. The player is put onside by retiring behind the applicable offside line. No other action of the offside player and no action of that player's team mates can put the offside player onside. If the player remains offside the player can be put onside only by the action of the opposing team. There are two such actions:

Opponent runs 5 metres with ball. When an opponent carrying the ball has run 5 metres, the offside player is put onside. An offside player is not put onside when an opponent passes the ball. Even if the opponents pass the ball several times, their action does not put the offside player onside.

Opponent kicks. When an opponent kicks the ball, the offside player is put onside.

11.9 LOITERING

A player who remains in an offside position is loitering. A loiterer who prevents the opposing team from playing the ball as they wish is taking part in the game, and is penalised. The referee makes sure that the loiterer does not benefit from being put onside by the opposing team's action.

Penalty: Penalty Kick

Law 12 Knock on or Throw forward

DEFINITION

KNOCK ON A knock on occurs when a player loses possession of the ball and it goes forward, or when a player hits the ball forward with the hand or arm, or when the ball hits the hand or arm and goes forward, and the ball touches the ground or another player before the original player can catch it. 'Forward' means towards the opposing team's dead ball line.

EXCEPTION

CHARGE DOWN If a player charges down the ball as an opponent kicks it, or immediately after the kick, it is not a knock on even though the ball may travel forward.

DEFINITION

THROW FORWARD A throw forward occurs when a player throws or passes the ball forward. 'Forward' means towards the opposing team's dead ball line.

EXCEPTION

BOUNCE FORWARD If the ball is not thrown forward but it hits a player or the ground and bounces forward, this is not a throw forward.

12.1 THE OUTCOME OF A KNOCK ON OR THROW FORWARD

(a) Unintentional knock on or throw forward. A scrum is awarded at the place of infringement.

(b) Unintentional knock on or throw forward at a lineout. A scrum is awarded 15 metres from the touchline.

(c) Knock on or throw forward into the in-goal. If an attacking player knocks-on or throws-forward in the field of play and the ball goes into the opponents' in-goal and it is made dead there, a scrum is awarded where the knock on or throw forward happened.

(d) Knock on or throw forward inside the in-goal. If a player of either team knocks-on or throws-forward inside the in-goal, a 5-metre scrum is awarded in line with the place of infringement not closer than 5 metres from the touchline.

(e) Intentional knock or throw forward. A player must not intentionally knock the ball forward with hand or arm, nor throw forward.

Penalty: Penalty Kick. A penalty try must be awarded if the offence prevents a try that would probably otherwise have been scored.

Law 13 KickOff and Restart Kicks

DEFINITION

The kickoff occurs at the start of the match and the restart of the match after half time. Restart kicks occur after a score or a touch down.

13.1 WHERE AND HOW THE KICKOFF IS TAKEN

(a) A team kicks off with a drop kick which must be taken at or behind the centre of the half-way line.

(b) If the ball is kicked off by the wrong type of kick, or from the incorrect place, the opposing team has two choices:

- To have the ball kicked off again, or
- To have a scrum at the centre of the half-way line and they throw in the ball.

13.2 WHO TAKES THE KICKOFF AND RESTART KICK

(a) At the start of the game, the team whose captain elected to take the kick after winning the toss will kickoff, or the opposing team if the winning captain elected to choose an end.

(b) After the half time interval, the opponents of the team who kicked off at the start of the game kick off.

(c) After a score the opponents of the team who scored restart play.

13.3 POSITION OF THE KICKER'S TEAM AT A KICK OFF

All the kicker's team must be behind the ball when it is kicked. If they are not, a scrum is formed at the centre. Their opponents throw in the ball.

13.4 POSITION OF THE OPPOSING TEAM AT A KICK OFF

All the opposing team must stand on or behind the 10-metre line. If they are in front of that line or if they charge before the ball is kicked, it is kicked off again.

13.5 KICK OFF OF 10 METRES

If the ball reaches the opponents' 10-metre line or reaches the 10-metre line and is blown back, play continues.

13.6 KICK OFF OF UNDER 10 METRES BUT PLAYED BY AN OPPONENT

If the ball does not reach the opponent's 10-metre line but is first played by an opponent, play continues.

13.7 KICK OFF OF UNDER 10 METRES AND NOT PLAYED BY AN OPPONENT

If the ball does not reach the opponent's 10-metre line the opposing team has two choices:

- To have the ball kicked off again, or
- To have a scrum at the centre. They throw in the ball.

13.8 BALL GOES DIRECTLY INTO TOUCH

The ball must land in the field of play. If it is kicked directly into touch the opposing team has three choices:

- To have the ball kicked off again, or
- To have a scrum at the centre and they have the throw in, or
- To accept the kick.

If they accept the kick, the lineout is on the half-way line. If the ball is blown behind the half-way line and goes directly into touch, the lineout is at the place where it went into touch.

13.9 BALL GOES INTO THE IN-GOAL

(a) If the ball is kicked into the in-goal without having touched or been touched by a player, the opposing team has three choices:

- To ground the ball, or
- To make it dead, or
- To play on.

(b) If the opposing team grounds the ball, or if they make it dead, or if the ball becomes dead by going into touch-in-goal or on or over the dead ball line, they have two choices:

- To have a scrum formed at the centre, and they throw in the ball, or
- To have the other team kick off again.

(c) If they opt to ground the ball or make it dead, they must do so without delay. Any other action with the ball by a defending player means the player has elected to play on.

13.10 DROP OUT

DEFINITION

A drop out is used to restart play after an attacking player has put or taken the ball into the in-goal, without infringement, and a defending player has made the ball dead there or it has gone into touch-in-goal or on or over the dead ball line.

A drop out is a drop kick taken by the defending team. The drop out may be taken anywhere on or behind the 22-metre line.

13.11 DELAY IN DROP OUT

The drop out must be taken without delay.

Penalty: Free Kick on the 22-metre line.

13.12 DROP OUT INCORRECTLY TAKEN

If the ball is kicked with the wrong type of kick, or from the wrong place, the opposing team has two choices:

- To have another drop out, or
- To have a scrum at the centre of the 22-metre line and they throw in the ball.

13.13 DROP OUT MUST CROSS THE LINE

(a) If the ball does not cross the 22-metre line, the opposing team has two choices:

- To have another drop out, or
- To have a scrum at the centre of the 22-metre line. They throw in the ball.

(b) If the ball crosses the 22-metre line but is blown back, play continues.

(c) If the ball does not cross the 22-metre line, advantage may apply. An opponent who plays the ball can score a try.

13.14 DROP OUT GOES DIRECTLY INTO TOUCH

The ball must land in the field of play. If it is kicked directly into touch, the opposing team has three choices:

- To have another drop out, or
- To have a scrum at the centre of the 22-metre line, and they throw in the ball, or
- To accept the kick. If they accept the kick, the throw in is on the 22-metre line.

13.15 DROP OUT GOES INTO THE OPPONENTS IN-GOAL

(a) If the ball is kicked into the opponent's in-goal without having touched or been touched by a player, the opposing team has three choices:
- To ground the ball, or
- To make it dead, or
- To play on.

(b) If the opposing team grounds the ball, or makes it dead, or if the ball becomes dead by going into touch-in-goal or on or over the dead ball line, they have two choices: To have a scrum formed at the centre of the 22-metre line from where the kick was taken and they throw in the ball, or To have the other team drop out again.

(c) If they opt to ground the ball or make it dead, they must do so without delay. Any other action with the ball by a defending player means the player has elected to play on.

13.16 THE KICKER'S TEAM

(a) All the kicker's team must be behind the ball when it is kicked. If not, a scrum is formed at the centre of the 22-metre line. The opposing team throws in the ball.

(b) However, if the kick is taken so quickly that players of the kicker's team who are retiring are still in front of the ball, they will not be penalised. They must not stop retiring until they have been made onside by an action of a team mate. They must not take part in the game until they have been made onside in this way.
Penalty: Scrum at the centre of the 22-metre line. The opposing team throws in the ball.

13.17 THE OPPOSING TEAM

(a) The opposing team must not charge over the 22-metre line before the ball is kicked.
Penalty: Free Kick at the place of infringement.

(b) If an opponent is on the wrong side of the 22-metre line and delays or obstructs the drop out, the player is guilty of misconduct.
Penalty: Penalty Kick on the 22-metre line.

Law 14 Ball on the Ground – No Tackle

DEFINITION

This situation occurs when the ball is available on the ground and a player goes to ground to gather the ball, except immediately after a scrum or a ruck.

It also occurs when a player is on the ground in possession of the ball and has not been tackled.

The game is to be played by players who are on their feet. A player must not make the ball unplayable by falling down. Unplayable means that the ball is not immediately available to either team so that play may continue.

A player who makes the ball unplayable, or who obstructs the opposing team by falling down, is negating the purpose and spirit of the game and must be penalised.

A player who is not tackled, but who goes to ground while holding the ball, or a player who goes to ground and gathers the ball, must act immediately.

14.1 PLAYER ON THE GROUND

The player must immediately do one of three things:
- Get up with the ball, or
- Pass the ball, or
- Release the ball.

A player who passes or releases the ball must also get up or move away from it at once. Advantage is played only if it happens immediately.
Penalty: Penalty Kick

14.2 WHAT THE PLAYER MUST NOT DO

(a) Lying on or around the ball. A player must not lie on, over, or near the ball to prevent opponents getting possession of it.
Penalty: Penalty Kick

(b) Falling over the player on the ground with the ball. A player must not intentionally fall on or over a player with the ball who is lying on the ground.
Penalty: Penalty Kick

(c) Falling over players lying on the ground near the ball. A player must not intentionally fall on or over players lying on the ground with the ball between them or near them.
Penalty: Penalty Kick

Law 15 Tackle: Ball Carrier Brought to the Ground

DEFINITION

A tackle occurs when the ball carrier is held by one or more opponents and is brought to ground. A ball carrier who is not held is not a tackled player and a tackle has not taken place. Opposition players who hold the ball carrier and bring that player to ground, and who also go to ground, are known as tacklers. Opposition players who hold the ball carrier and do not go to ground are not tacklers.

15.1 WHERE CAN A TACKLE TAKE PLACE

A tackle can only take place in the field of play.

15.2 WHEN A TACKLE CANNOT TAKE PLACE

When the ball carrier is held by one opponent and a team mate binds on to that ball carrier, a maul has been formed and a tackle cannot take place.

15.3 BROUGHT TO THE GROUND DEFINED

(a) If the ball carrier has one knee or both knees on the ground, that player has been 'brought to ground'.
(b) If the ball carrier is sitting on the ground, or on top of another player on the ground the ball carrier has been 'brought to ground'.

15.4 THE TACKLER

(a) When a player tackles an opponent and they both go to ground, the tackler must immediately release the tackled player.
Penalty: Penalty Kick

(b) The tackler must immediately get up or move away from the tackled player and from the ball at once.
Penalty: Penalty Kick

(c) The tackler must get up before playing the ball.
Penalty: Penalty Kick

15.5 THE TACKLED PLAYER

(a) A tackled player must not lie on, over, or near the ball to prevent opponents from gaining possession of it, and must try to make the ball available immediately so that play can continue.
Penalty: Penalty Kick

(b) A tackled player must immediately pass the ball or release it. That player must also get up or move away from it at once.
Penalty: Penalty Kick

(c) A tackled player may release the ball by putting it on the ground in any direction, provided this is done immediately.
Penalty: Penalty Kick

(d) A tackled player may release the ball by pushing it along the ground in any direction except forward, provided this is done immediately.
Penalty: Penalty Kick

(e) If opposition players who are on their feet attempt to play the ball, the tackled player must release the ball.
Penalty: Penalty Kick

(f) If a tackled player's momentum carries the player into the in-goal, the player can score a try or make a touch down.

(g) If players are tackled near the goal line, these players may immediately reach out and ground the ball on or over the goal line to score a try or make a touch down.

15.6 OTHER PLAYERS

(a) After a tackle, all other players must be on their feet when they play the ball. Players are on their feet if no other part of their body is supported by the ground or players on the ground.
Penalty: Penalty Kick

(b) After a tackle any players on their feet may attempt to gain possession by taking the ball from the ball carrier's possession.

(c) At a tackle or near to a tackle, other players who play the ball must do so from behind the ball and from directly behind the tackled player or the tackler closest to those players' goal line.
Penalty: Penalty Kick

(d) Any player who gains possession of the ball at the tackle must play the ball immediately by moving away or passing or kicking the ball.
Penalty: Penalty Kick

(e) Any player who first gains possession of the ball must not go to the ground at the tackle or near to it unless tackled by an opposition player.
Penalty: Penalty Kick

(f) Any player who first gains possession of the ball at the tackle or near to it may be tackled by an opposition player providing that player does so from behind the ball and from directly behind the tackled player or the tackler closest to that player's goal line.
Penalty: Penalty Kick

(g) After a tackle, any player lying on the ground must not prevent an opponent from getting possession of the ball.
Penalty: Penalty Kick

(h) After a tackle, any player on the ground must not tackle an opponent or try to tackle an opponent
Penalty: Penalty Kick

(i) When a tackled player reaches out to ground the ball on or over the goal line to score a try, an opponent may pull the ball from the player's possession, but must not kick the ball.
Penalty: Penalty Kick
Exception: Ball goes into the in-goal. After a tackle

near the goal line, if the ball has been released and has gone into the in-goal any player, including a player on the ground, may ground the ball.

15.7 FORBIDDEN PRACTICES

(a) No player may prevent the tackled player from passing the ball.
Penalty: Penalty Kick

(b) No player may prevent the tackled player from releasing the ball and getting up or moving away from it.
Penalty: Penalty Kick

(c) No player may fall on or over the tackled player.
Penalty: Penalty Kick

(d) No player may fall on or over the players lying on the ground after a tackle with the ball between or near to them.
Penalty: Penalty Kick

(e) Players on their feet must not charge or obstruct an opponent who is not near the ball.
Penalty: Penalty Kick

(f) Danger may arise if a tackled player fails to release the ball or move away from it immediately, or if that player is prevented from so doing. If either of these happens the referee awards a penalty kick immediately.
Penalty: Penalty Kick

15.8 DOUBT ABOUT FAILURE TO COMPLY

If the ball becomes unplayable at a tackle and there is doubt about which player did not conform to Law, the referee orders a scrum immediately with the throw in by the team that was moving forward prior to the stoppage or, if no team was moving forward, by the attacking team.

Law 16 Ruck

DEFINITIONS

A RUCK is a phase of play where one or more players from each team, who are on their feet, in physical contact, close around the ball on the ground. Open play has ended.

Rucking Players are rucking when they are in a ruck and using their feet to try to win or keep possession of the ball, without being guilty of foul play.

16.1 FORMING A RUCK

(a) Where can a ruck take place. A ruck can take place only in the field of play.
(b) How can a ruck form. Players are on their feet. At least one player must be in physical contact with an opponent. The ball is on the ground.

16.2 JOINING A RUCK

(a) All players forming, joining or taking part in a ruck must have their heads and shoulders no lower than their hips.
Penalty: Free Kick

b) A player joining a ruck must bind onto the ruck with at least one arm around the body of a team mate, using the whole arm.
Penalty: Penalty Kick

(c) Placing a hand on another player in the ruck does not constitute binding.
Penalty: Penalty Kick

(d) All players forming, joining or taking part in a ruck must be on their feet.
Penalty: Penalty Kick

16.3 RUCKING

(a) Players in a ruck must endeavour to stay on their feet.
Penalty: Penalty Kick

(b) A player must not intentionally fall or kneel in a ruck. This is dangerous play.
Penalty: Penalty Kick

(c) A player must not intentionally collapse a ruck. This is dangerous play.
Penalty: Penalty Kick

(d) A player must not jump on top of a ruck.
Penalty: Penalty Kick

(e) Players must have their heads and shoulders no lower than their hips.
Penalty: Free Kick

(f) A player rucking for the ball must not ruck players on the ground. A player rucking for the ball tries to step over players on the ground and must not intentionally step on them. A player rucking must do so near the ball.
Penalty: Penalty Kick for dangerous play

16.4 OTHER RUCK OFFENCES

(a) Players must not return the ball into a ruck.
Penalty: Free Kick

(b) Players must not handle the ball in a ruck.
Penalty: Penalty Kick

(c) Players must not pick up the ball in a ruck with their legs.
Penalty: Penalty Kick

(d) Players on the ground in or near the ruck must try to move away from the ball. These players must not interfere with the ball in the ruck or as it comes out of the ruck.
Penalty: Penalty Kick

(e) A player must not fall on or over a ball as it is coming out of a ruck.
Penalty: Penalty Kick

(f) A player must not take any action to make the opposing team think that the ball is out of the ruck while it is still in the ruck.
Penalty: Free Kick

16.5 OFFSIDE AT THE RUCK

(a) The offside line. There are two offside lines parallel to the goal lines, one for each team. Each offside line runs through the hindmost foot of the hindmost player in the ruck. If the hindmost foot of the hindmost player is on or behind the goal line, the offside line for the defending team is the goal line.

(b) Players must either join a ruck, or retire behind the offside line immediately. If a player loiters at the side of a ruck, the player is offside.
Penalty: Penalty Kick

(c) Players joining or rejoining the ruck. All players joining a ruck must do so from behind the foot of the hindmost team mate in the ruck. A player may join alongside this hindmost player. If the player joins the ruck from the opponents' side, or in front of the hindmost team mate, the player is offside.
Penalty: Penalty Kick on the offending team's offside line

(d) Players not joining the ruck. If a player is in front of the offside line and does not join the ruck, the player must retire behind the offside line at once. If a

player who is behind the offside line oversteps it and does not join the ruck the player is offside.
Penalty: Penalty Kick on the offending team's offside line

16.6 SUCCESSFUL END TO A RUCK

A ruck ends successfully when the ball leaves the ruck, or when the ball is on or over the goal line.

16.7 UNSUCCESSFUL END TO A RUCK

(a) A ruck ends unsuccessfully when the ball becomes unplayable and a scrum is ordered. The team that was moving forward immediately before the ball became unplayable in the ruck throws in the ball. If neither team was moving forward, or if the referee cannot decide which team was moving forward before the ball became unplayable in the ruck, the team that was moving forward before the ruck began throws in the ball. If neither team was moving forward, then the attacking team throws in the ball.

(b) Before the referee blows the whistle for a scrum, the referee allows a reasonable amount of time for the ball to emerge, especially if either team is moving forward. If the ruck stops moving, or if the referee decides that the ball will probably not emerge within a reasonable time, the referee must order a scrum.

Law 17 Maul

DEFINITION

A maul occurs when a player carrying the ball is held by one or more opponents, and one or more of the ball carrier's team mates bind on the ball carrier. A maul therefore consists of at least three players, all on their feet; the ball carrier and one player from each team. All the players involved must be caught in or bound to the maul and must be on their feet and moving towards a goal line. Open play has ended.

17.1 FORMING A MAUL

(a) Where can a maul take place. A maul can only take place in the field of play.

17.2 JOINING A MAUL

(a) Players joining a maul must have their heads and shoulders no lower than their hips.
Penalty: Free Kick

(b) A player must be caught in or bound to the maul and not just alongside it.
Penalty: Penalty Kick

(c) Placing a hand on another player in the maul does not constitute binding.
Penalty: Penalty Kick

(d) Keeping players on their feet. Players in a maul must endeavour to stay on their feet. The ball carrier in a maul may go to ground providing the ball is available immediately and play continues.
Penalty: Penalty Kick

(e) A player must not intentionally collapse a maul. This is dangerous play.
Penalty: Penalty Kick

(f) A player must not jump on top of a maul.
Penalty: Penalty Kick

17.3 OTHER MAUL OFFENCES
(a) A player must not try to drag an opponent out of a maul.
Penalty: Penalty Kick
(b) A player must not take any action to make the opposing team think that the ball is out of the maul while it is still in the maul.
Penalty: Free Kick

17.4 OFFSIDE AT THE MAUL
(a) The offside line. There are two offside lines parallel to the goal lines, one for each team. Each offside line runs through the hindmost foot of the hindmost player in the maul. If the hindmost foot of the hindmost player is on or behind the goal line, the offside line for the defending team is the goal line.
(b) A player must either join a maul, or retire behind the offside line immediately. If a player loiters at the side of a maul, the player is offside.
Penalty: Penalty Kick on the offending team's offside line
(c) Players joining the maul. Players joining a maul must do so from behind the foot of the hindmost team mate in the maul. The player may join alongside this player. If the player joins the maul from the opponents' side, or in front of the hindmost team mate, the player is offside.
Penalty: Penalty Kick on the offending team's offside line
(d) Players not joining the maul. All players in front of the offside line and who do not join the maul, must retire behind the offside line at once. A player who does not do so, is offside. If any player who is behind the offside line oversteps it and does not join the maul, the player is offside.
Penalty: Penalty Kick on the offending team's offside line
(e) Players leaving or rejoining the maul. Players who leave a maul must immediately retire behind the offside line, otherwise, they are offside. If the player rejoins the maul in front of the hindmost team mate in the maul, they are offside. The player may rejoin the maul alongside the hindmost team mate.
Penalty: Penalty Kick on the offending team's offside line

17.5 SUCCESSFUL END TO A MAUL
A maul ends successfully when the ball or a player with the ball leaves the maul. A maul ends successfully when the ball is on the ground, or is on or over the goal line.

17.6 UNSUCCESSFUL END TO A MAUL
(a) A maul ends unsuccessfully if it remains stationary or has stopped moving forward for longer than 5 seconds and a scrum is ordered.
(b) A maul ends unsuccessfully if the ball becomes unplayable or collapses (not as a result of foul play) and a scrum is ordered.
(c) Scrum following maul. The ball is thrown in by the team not in possession when the maul began. If the referee cannot decide which team had possession, the team moving forward before the maul stopped throws in the ball. If neither team was moving forward, the attacking team throws in the ball.
(d) When a maul remains stationary or has stopped moving forward for more than 5 seconds, but the ball is being moved and the referee can see it, a

reasonable time is allowed for the ball to emerge. If it does not emerge within a reasonable time, a scrum is ordered. **(e)** When a maul has stopped moving forward it may start moving forward again providing it does so within 5 seconds. If the maul stops moving forward a second time and if the ball is being moved and the referee can see it, a reasonable time is allowed for the ball to emerge. If it does not emerge within a reasonable time, a scrum is ordered.
(f) When the ball in a maul becomes unplayable, the referee does not allow prolonged wrestling for it. A scrum is ordered.
(g) If the ball carrier in a maul goes to ground, including being on one or both knees or sitting, the referee orders a scrum unless the ball is immediately available.
(h) Scrum after a maul when catcher is held. If a player catches the ball direct from an opponent's kick, except from a kick off or a drop out, and the player is immediately held by an opponent, a maul may form. Then if the maul remains stationary, stops moving forward for longer than 5 seconds, or if the ball becomes unplayable, and a scrum is ordered, the team of the ball catcher throws in the ball. 'Direct from an opponent's kick' means the ball did not touch another player or the ground before the player caught it. If a maul moves into the player's in-goal, where the ball is touched down or becomes unplayable, a 5-metre scrum is formed. The attacking team throws in the ball.

Law 18 Mark

To make a mark, a player must be on or behind that player's 22-metre line. A player with one foot on the 22-metre line or behind it is considered to be 'in the 22'. The player must make a clean catch direct from an opponent's kick and at the same time shout "Mark". A mark cannot be made from a kick off, or a restart kick except for a drop out.

A kick is awarded for a mark. The place for the kick is the place of the mark.

A player may make a mark even though the ball touched a goal post or crossbar before being caught.

A player from the defending team may make a mark in in-goal.

18.1 AFTER A MARK
The referee immediately blows the whistle and awards a kick to the player who made the mark.

18.2 KICK AWARDED
The kick is awarded at the place of the mark.

18.3 KICK – WHERE
The kick is taken at or behind the mark on a line through the mark.

18.4 WHO KICKS
The kick is taken by the player who made the mark. If that player cannot take the kick within one minute, a scrum is formed at the place of the mark with the ball thrown in by the player's team. If the mark is in the in-goal, the scrum is 5 metres from the goal line, on a line through the mark.

18.5 HOW THE KICK IS TAKEN
The provisions of Law 21 – Free Kicks – apply to a kick awarded after a mark.

18.6 SCRUM ALTERNATIVE
(a) The team of the player who made the mark may choose to take a scrum.
(b) Where is the scrum. If the mark is in the field of play, the scrum is at the place of the mark, but at least 5 metres from the touchline. If the mark is in-goal, the scrum is 5 metres from the goal line on a line through the mark, and at least 5 metres from the touchline.
(c) Who throws in. The team of the player who made the mark throws the ball in.

18.7 PENALTY KICK AWARDED
(a) An opponent, whether onside or offside, must not charge a player who has made a mark after the referee has blown the whistle.
Penalty: Penalty Kick
(b) Where the penalty kick is taken. If the infringing player is onside, the penalty kick is taken at the place of the infringement. If the infringing player is offside, the penalty kick is taken at the place of the offside line (Law 11 offside and onside in General Play.)
(c) The penalty kick. Any player from the non-offending team may take the penalty kick.

Law 19 Touch and Lineout

'Kicked directly into touch' means that the ball was kicked into touch without landing on the playing area, and without touching a player or the referee.

'The 22' is the area between the goal line and the 22-metre line, including the 22-metre line *but excluding the goal line.*

The line of touch is an imaginary line in the field of play at right angles to the touchline through the place where the ball is thrown in.

The ball is in touch when it is not being carried by a player and it touches the touchline or anything or anyone on or beyond the touchline.

The ball is in touch when a player is carrying it and the ball carrier (or the ball) touches the touchline or the ground beyond the touchline. The place where the ball carrier (or the ball) touched or crossed the touchline is where it went into touch.

The ball is in touch if a player catches the ball and that player has a foot on the touchline or the ground beyond the touchline.

If a player has one foot in the field of play and one foot in touch and holds the ball, the ball is in touch. If the ball crosses the touchline or touch-in-goal line, and is caught by a player who has both feet in the playing area, the ball is not in touch or touch-in-goal. Such a player may knock the ball into the playing area.

If a player jumps and catches the ball, both feet must land in the playing area otherwise the ball is in touch or touch-in-goal.

A player in touch may kick or knock the ball, but not hold it, provided it has not crossed the plane of the touchline. The plane of the touchline is the vertical space rising immediately above the touchline.

19.1 THROW IN

NO GAIN IN GROUND

(a) Outside a team's 22, a team member kicks directly into touch. Except for a penalty kick, when a player anywhere in the field of play who is outside the 22 kicks directly into touch, there is no gain in ground. The throw in is taken either at the place opposite where the player kicked the ball, or at the place where it went into touch, whichever is nearer that player's goal line.

(b) Player takes ball into that team's 22. When a defending player gets the ball outside the 22, takes or puts it inside the 22, and then kicks directly into touch, there is no gain in ground.

GAIN IN GROUND

(c) Player inside that team's 22. When a defending player gets the ball inside the 22, or that player's in-goal and kicks into touch, the throw in is where the ball went into touch.

(d) Kicks indirectly into touch. When a player anywhere in the playing area kicks indirectly into touch so that the ball bounces in the field of play the throw in is taken where the ball went into touch. When a player anywhere in the playing area kicks the ball so that it touches or is touched by an opposition player and then goes indirectly into touch so that the ball bounces in the field of play the throw in is taken where the ball went into touch. When a player anywhere in the playing area kicks the ball so that it touches or is touched by an opposition player and then goes directly into touch the throw in is taken in line with where the opposition player touched the ball or where the ball crossed the touchline if that is nearer the opposition player's goal line.

PENALTY KICK

(e) Penalty kick. When a player kicks to touch from a penalty kick anywhere in the playing area, the throw in is taken where the ball went into touch.

FREE KICK

(f) Outside the kicker's 22, no gain in ground. When a free kick awarded outside the 22 goes directly into touch, the throw in is in line with where the ball was kicked, or where it went into touch, whichever is nearer the kicker's goal line.

(g) Inside the kicker's 22 or in-goal, gain in ground. When a free kick is awarded in the 22 or in-goal and the kick goes directly into touch, the throw in is where the ball went into touch.

19.2 QUICK THROW IN

(a) A player may take a quick throw in without waiting for a lineout to form.

(b) For a quick throw in, the player may be anywhere outside the field of play between the place where the ball went into touch and the player's goal line.

(c) A player must not take a quick throw in after the lineout has formed. If the player does, the quick throw in is disallowed. The same team throws in at the lineout.

(d) For a quick throw in, the player must use the ball that went into touch. If, after it went to touch and was made dead, another ball is used, or if another person has touched the ball apart from the player throwing it in, then the quick throw in is disallowed. The same team throws in at the lineout.

(e) At a quick throw in, if the player does not throw the ball in straight so that it travels at least 5 metres along the line of touch before it touches the ground or a player, or if the player steps into the field of play when the ball is thrown, then the quick throw in is disallowed. The opposing team chooses to throw in at either a lineout where the quick throw in was attempted, or a scrum on the 15-metre line at that place. If they too throw in the ball incorrectly at the lineout, a scrum is formed on the 15-metre line. The team that first threw in the ball throws in the ball at the scrum.

(f) At a quick throw in, a player may come to the line of touch and leave without being penalised.

(g) At a quick throw in, a player must not prevent the ball being thrown in 5 metres.
Penalty: Free Kick on 15-metre line

(h) If a player carrying the ball is forced into touch, that player must release the ball to an opposition player so that there can be a quick throw in.
Penalty: Penalty Kick on 15-metre line

19.3 OTHER THROW INS
On all other occasions, the throw in is taken where the ball went into touch.

19.4 WHO THROWS IN
The throw in is taken by an opponent of the player who last held or touched the ball before it went into touch. When there is doubt, the attacking team takes the throw in.

Exception: When a team takes a penalty kick, and the ball is kicked into touch, the throw in is taken by a player of the team that took the penalty kick. This applies whether the ball was kicked directly or indirectly into touch.

19.5 HOW THE THROW IN IS TAKEN
The player taking the throw in must stand at the correct place. The player must not step into the field of play when the ball is thrown. The ball must be thrown straight, so that it travels at least 5 metres along the line of touch before it first touches the ground or touches or is touched by a player.

19.6 INCORRECT THROW IN
(a) If the throw in at a lineout is incorrect, the opposing team has the choice of throwing in at a lineout or a scrum on the 15-metre line. If they choose the throw in to the lineout and it is again incorrect, a scrum is formed. The team that took the first throw in throws in the ball.

(b) The throw in at the lineout must be taken without delay and without pretending to throw.
Penalty: Free Kick on the 15-metre line

(c) A player must not intentionally or repeatedly throw the ball in not straight.
Penalty: Penalty Kick on the 15-metre line

LINEOUT

DEFINITIONS

The purpose of the lineout is to restart play, quickly, safely and fairly, after the ball has gone into touch, with a throw in between two lines of players.

Lineout players. Lineout players are the players who form the two lines that make a lineout.

Receiver. The receiver is the player in position to catch the ball when lineout players pass or knock the ball back from the lineout. Any player may be the receiver but each team may have only one receiver at a lineout.

Players taking part in the lineout known as participating players. Players taking part in the lineout are the player who throws-in and an immediate opponent, the two players waiting to receive the ball from the lineout and the lineout players.

All other players. All other players who are not taking part in the lineout must be at least 10 metres behind the line of touch, on or behind their goal line if that is nearer, until the lineout ends.

15-metre line. The 15-metre line is 15 metres infield and parallel with the touchline.

Scrum after lineout. Any scrum ordered because of an infringement or stoppage at the lineout is on the 15-metre line on the line of touch.

19.7 FORMING A LINEOUT
(a) Minimum. At least two players from each team must form a lineout.
Penalty: Free Kick on the 15-metre line

(b) Maximum. The team throwing in the ball decides the maximum number of players in the lineout.
Penalty: Free Kick on the 15-metre line

(c) The opposing team may have fewer lineout players but they must not have more.
Penalty: Free Kick on the 15-metre line

(d) When the ball is in touch, every player who approaches the line of touch is presumed to do so to form a lineout. Players who approach the line of touch must do so without delay. Players of either team must not leave the lineout once they have taken up a position in the lineout until the lineout has ended
Penalty: Free Kick on the 15-metre line

(e) If the team throwing in the ball put fewer than the usual number of players in the lineout, their opponents must be given a reasonable time to move enough players out of the lineout to satisfy this Law.
Penalty: Free Kick on the 15-metre line

(f) These players must leave the lineout without delay. They must move to the offside line, 10 metres behind the line of touch. If the lineout ends before they reach this line, they may rejoin play.
Penalty: Free Kick on the 15-metre line

(g) Failure to form a lineout. A team must not voluntarily fail to form a lineout.
Penalty: Free Kick on the 15-metre line

(h) Where the lineout players must stand. The front of the lineout is not less than 5 metres from the touchline. The back of the lineout is not more than 15 metres from the touchline. All lineout players must stand between these two points.
Penalty: Free Kick on the 15-metre line

(i) Two single straight lines. The lineout players of both teams form two single parallel lines each at right angles to the touchline.
Penalty: Free Kick on the 15-metre line

(j) Opposing players forming a lineout must keep a clear space between their inside shoulders. This space is determined when players are in an upright stance.
Penalty: Free Kick on the 15-metre line

(k) Metre gap. Each line of players must be half a metre on their side of the line of touch.

Penalty: Free Kick on the 15-metre line

(l) The line of touch must not be within 5 metres of the goal line.

(m) After the lineout has formed, but before the ball has been thrown in, a player must not hold, push, charge into, or obstruct an opponent.

Penalty: Penalty Kick on the 15-metre line

19.8 BEGINNING AND ENDING A LINEOUT

(a) Lineout begins. The lineout begins when the ball leaves the hands of the player throwing it in.

(b) Lineout ends. The lineout ends when the ball or a player carrying it leaves the lineout. This includes the following:

• When the ball is thrown, knocked or kicked out of the lineout, the lineout ends.

• When the ball or a player carrying the ball moves into the area between the 5-metre line and the touchline, the lineout ends.

• When a lineout player hands the ball to a player who is peeling off, the lineout ends.

• When the ball is thrown beyond the 15-metre line, or when a player takes or puts it beyond that line, the lineout ends.

• When a ruck or maul develops in a lineout, and all the feet of all the players in the ruck or maul move beyond the line of touch, the lineout ends.

• When the ball becomes unplayable in a lineout, the lineout ends. Play restarts with a scrum.

19.9 OPTIONS AVAILABLE IN A LINEOUT

(a) Offside. A lineout player must not be offside. The offside line runs through the line of touch until the ball is thrown in. After the ball has touched a player or the ground, the offside line is a line through the ball.

Penalty: Penalty Kick on the 15-metre line

(b) Players jumping for the ball may take a step in any direction providing they do not step across the line of touch.

Penalty: Penalty Kick on the 15-metre line

(c) Levering on an opponent. A lineout player must not use an opponent as a support when jumping.

Penalty: Penalty Kick on the 15-metre line

(d) Holding or shoving. A lineout player must not hold, push, charge, obstruct or grasp an opponent not holding the ball except when a ruck or maul is taking place.

Penalty: Penalty Kick on the 15-metre line

(e) Illegal charging. A lineout player must not charge an opponent except in an attempt to tackle the opponent or to play the ball.

Penalty: Penalty Kick on the 15-metre line

(f) Levering on a team mate. A jumping lineout player must not use a team mate as a support to jump.

Penalty: Free Kick on the 15-metre line

(g) Lifting. A lineout player must not lift a team mate.

Penalty: Free Kick on the 15-metre line

(h) Support before jumping. A player must not support a team mate before the team mate has jumped.

Penalty: Free Kick on the 15-metre line

(i) Jumping or supporting before the ball is thrown. A player must not jump for the ball or support any player before the ball has left the hands of the player throwing it in.

Penalty: Free Kick on the 15-metre line

(j) Pre-grip below the waist. A player must not

pre-grip any team mate below the waist.

Penalty: Free Kick on the 15-metre line

(k) Support of a player. A player must not support a jumping team mate below the shorts from behind or below the thighs from the front.

Penalty: Penalty Kick on the 15 metre line

(l) Lowering a Player. Players who support a jumping team mate must lower that player to the ground as soon as the ball has been won by a player of either team.

Penalty: Free Kick on the 15-metre line

(m) Blocking the throw in. A lineout player must not stand less than 5 metres from the touchline. A lineout player must not prevent the ball being thrown in 5 metres.

Penalty: Free Kick on the 15-metre line

(n) When the ball has been thrown beyond a player in the lineout, that player may move to the space between the touchline and the 5-metre line. If the player moves into that space the player must not move towards that player's goal line before the lineout ends, except in a peeling off movement.

Penalty: Free Kick on the 15-metre line

(o) Catching or deflecting. When jumping for the ball, a player must use either both hands or the inside arm to try to catch or deflect the ball. The jumper must not use the outside arm alone to try to catch or deflect the ball. If the jumper has both hands above the head either hand may be used to play the ball.

Penalty: Free Kick on the 15-metre line

19.10 OPTIONS AVAILABLE TO PLAYERS NOT IN THE LINEOUT

In general, a player not taking part in a lineout must stay at least 10 metres behind the line of touch, or on or behind that player's goal line if that is nearer, until the lineout ends. There are two exceptions to this:

Exception 1: Long throw in. If the player who is throwing in throws the ball beyond the 15-metre line, a player of the same team may run forward to take the ball. If that player does so, an opponent may also run forward.

Penalty: Penalty Kick on the offending team's offside line, opposite the place of infringement but not less than 15 metres from the touchline.

Exception 2: The receiver may run into the gap and perform any of the actions available to any other player in the lineout. The receiver is liable to penalty for offences in the lineout as would be other players in the lineout.

19.11 PEELING OFF

DEFINITIONS

A lineout player 'peels off' when leaving the lineout to catch the ball knocked or passed back by a team mate.

(a) When: A player must not peel off until the ball has left the hands of the player throwing it in.

Penalty: Free Kick on the 15-metre line, in line with the line of touch.

(b) A player who peels off, must stay within the area from that players' line of touch to 10 metres from the line of touch, and must keep moving until the lineout has ended.

Penalty: Free Kick on the 15-metre line, in line with the line of touch.

(c) Players may change their positions in the lineout before the ball is thrown in.

19.12 OFFSIDE AT THE LINEOUT

(a) When a lineout forms, there are two separate offside lines, parallel to the goal lines, for the teams.

(b) Participating players. One offside line applies to the players taking part in the lineout (usually some or all of the forwards, plus the scrum half and the player throwing in). Until the ball is thrown in, and has touched a player or the ground, this offside line is the line of touch. After that, the offside line is a line through the ball.

(c) Players not taking part. The other offside line applies to the players not taking part in the lineout (usually the backs). For them, the offside line is 10 metres behind the line of touch or their goal line, if that is nearer. The lineout offside Law is different in the case of a long throw in, or in the case of a ruck or maul in the lineout.

19.13 OFFSIDE WHEN TAKING PART IN THE LINEOUT

(a) Before the ball has touched a player or the ground. A player must not overstep the line of touch. A player is offside, if, before the ball has touched a player or the ground, that player oversteps the line of touch, unless doing so while jumping for the ball. The player must jump from that player's side of the line of touch.

Penalty: Penalty Kick on the 15-metre line

(b) If a player jumps and crosses the line of touch but fails to catch the ball, that player is not penalised provided that player gets back onside without delay.

(c) After the ball has touched a player or the ground. A player not carrying the ball is offside if, after the ball has touched a player or the ground, that player steps in front of the ball, unless tackling (or trying to tackle) an opponent. Any attempt to tackle must start from that player's side of the ball.

Penalty: Penalty Kick on the 15-metre line

(d) The referee must penalise any player who, intentionally or not, moves into an offside position without trying to win possession or tackle an opponent.

Penalty: Penalty Kick on the 15-metre line

(e) No player of either team participating in the lineout may leave the lineout until it has ended.

Penalty: Penalty Kick on the 15-metre line

19.14 PLAYER THROWING-IN

There are four options available to the player throwing in (and the thrower's immediate opponent):

(a) The thrower may stay within 5 metres of the touchline.

(b) The thrower may retire to the offside line 10 metres behind the line of touch.

(c) The thrower may join the lineout as soon as the ball has been thrown in.

(d) The thrower may move into the receiver position if that position is empty. If the thrower goes anywhere else, the thrower is offside.

Penalty: Penalty Kick on the 15-metre line

19.15 OFFSIDE WHEN NOT TAKING PART IN THE LINEOUT

(a) Before the lineout has ended. The offside line is 10 metres behind the line of touch, or the player's goal line, whichever is nearer. A player who is not taking part in the lineout is offside if that player oversteps the offside line before the lineout has ended.

Penalty: Penalty Kick on the offending team's offside line opposite the place of infringement, at least 15 metres from the touchline.

(b) Players not yet onside when the ball is thrown in. A player may throw in the ball even if a team mate has not yet reached the offside line. However, if this player is not trying to reach an onside position without delay, this player is offside.

Penalty: Penalty Kick on the offending team's offside line opposite the place of infringement, at least 15 metres from the touchline.

Exception: Long throw in. There is an exception to the Law of offside at the lineout. It applies if the ball is thrown beyond the 15-metre line. As soon as the ball leaves the hands of the player throwing in, any players of the thrower's team may run for the ball. This means that a player taking part in the lineout may run infield beyond the 15-metre line, and a player not taking part in the lineout may run forward across the offside line. If this happens, an opponent may also run infield or run forward. However, if a player runs infield or runs forward to take a long throw in, and the ball is not thrown beyond the 15-metre line, this player is offside and must be penalised.

Penalty: Penalty Kick For players taking part in the lineout: penalty kick is on the 15-metre line. For players not taking part in the lineout: penalty kick is on the offending team's offside line at the place of infringement, at least 15 metres from the touchline.

19.16 OFFSIDE AT RUCKS OR MAULS IN THE LINEOUT

(a) When a ruck or a maul develops in a lineout the offside line for a player taking part in the lineout no longer runs through the ball. The offside line is now the hindmost foot of that player's team in the ruck or maul.

(b) However, for players not taking part in the lineout, the offside line is still 10 metres behind the line of touch. For these players, the lineout does not end when a ruck or maul develops.

(c) It ends when the ruck or maul leaves the line of touch. For this to happen, all the feet of all the players in the ruck or maul must have left the line of touch.

(d) A player taking part in the lineout must either join the ruck or maul, or retire to the offside line and stay at that line, otherwise that player is offside.

Penalty: Penalty Kick on the 15-metre line

(e) The rest of the Law of ruck or maul applies. A player must not join the ruck or maul from the opponents' side. Penalty: Penalty Kick Players must not join it in front of the offside line. If they do, they are offside.

Penalty: Penalty Kick on the 15-metre line

(f) Players not taking part in the lineout. When a ruck or maul develops in a lineout, the lineout has not ended until all the feet of all the players in the ruck or maul have moved beyond the line of touch. Until then, the offside line for players not taking part in the lineout is still 10 metres behind the line of touch, or the goal line if that is nearer. A player who oversteps this offside line is offside.

Penalty: Penalty Kick on the offside line at least 15 metres from the touchline.

Law 20 Scrum

DEFINITIONS

The purpose of the scrum is to restart play quickly, safely and fairly, after a minor infringement or a stoppage.

A scrum is formed in the field of play when eight players from each team, bound together in three rows for each team, close up with their opponents so that the heads of the front rows are interlocked. This creates a tunnel into which a scrum half throws in the ball so that front row players can compete for possession by hooking the ball with either of their feet.

The middle line of a scrum must not be within 5 metres of the goal line. A scrum cannot take place within 5 metres of a touchline.

The tunnel is the space between the two front rows.

The player of either team who throws the ball into the scrum is the scrum half.

The middle line is an imaginary line on the ground in the tunnel beneath the line where the shoulders of the two front rows meet.

The middle player in each front row is the hooker.

The players on either side of the hooker are the props. The left side props are the loose head props. The right side props are the tight head props.

The two players in the second row who push on the props and the hooker are the locks.

The outside players who bind onto the second or third row are the flankers.

The player in the third row who usually pushes on both locks is the No.8. Alternatively, the No. 8 may push on a lock and a flanker.

20.1 FORMING A SCRUM

(a) Where the scrum takes place. The place for a scrum is where the infringement or stoppage happened, or as near to it as is practicable in the field of play, unless otherwise stated in Law.

(b) If this is less than 5 metres from a touchline, the place for the scrum is 5 metres from that touchline. A scrum can take place only in the field of play. The middle line of a scrum must not be within 5 metres of the goal line when it is formed.

(c) If there is an infringement or stoppage in in-goal, the place for the scrum is 5 metres from the goal line.

(d) The scrum is formed in line with the place of the infringement or stoppage.

(e) No delay. A team must not intentionally delay forming a scrum.

Penalty: Free Kick

(f) Number of players: eight. A scrum must have eight players from each team. All eight players must stay bound to the scrum until it ends. Each front row must have three players in it, no more and no less. Two locks must form the second row.

Penalty: Penalty Kick

Exception: When a team is reduced to fewer than fifteen for any reason, then the number of players of each team in the scrum may be similarly reduced. Where a permitted reduction is made by one team, there is no requirement for the other team to make a similar reduction. However, a team must not have fewer than five players in the scrum.

Penalty: Penalty Kick

(g) Front rows coming together. First, the referee marks with a foot the place where the scrum is to

be formed. Before the two front rows come together they must be standing not more than an arm's length apart. The ball is in the scrum half's hands, ready to be thrown in. The front rows must crouch so that when they meet, each player's head and shoulders are no lower than the hips. The front rows must interlock so that no player's head is next to the head of a team mate.

Penalty: Free Kick

(h) The referee will call "crouch" then "touch". The front rows crouch and using their outside arm each prop touches the point of the opposing prop's outside shoulder. The props then withdraw their arms. The referee will then call "pause". Following a pause the referee will then call "engage". The front rows may then engage. The "engage" call is not a command but an indication that the front rows may come together when ready.

Penalty: Free Kick

(i) A crouched position is the extension of the normal stance by bending the knees sufficiently to move into the engagement without a charge.

(j) Charging. A front row must not form at a distance from its opponents and rush against them. This is dangerous play.

Penalty: Penalty Kick

(k) Stationary and parallel. Until the ball leaves the scrum half's hands, the scrum must be stationary and the middle line must be parallel to the goal lines. A team must not shove the scrum away from the mark before the ball is thrown in.

Penalty: Free Kick

20.2 FRONT-ROW PLAYERS' POSITIONS

(a) All players in a position to shove. When a scrum has formed, the body and feet of each front row player must be in a normal position to make a forward shove.

Penalty: Free Kick

(b) This means that the front row players must have both feet on the ground, with their weight firmly on at least one foot. Players must not cross their feet, although the foot of one player may cross a team mate's foot. Each player's shoulders must be no lower than the hips.

Penalty: Free Kick

(c) Hooker in a position to hook. Until the ball is thrown in, the hooker must be in a position to hook the ball. The hookers must have both feet on the ground, with their weight firmly on at least one foot. A hooker's foremost foot must not be in front of the foremost foot of that team's props.

Penalty: Free Kick

20.3 BINDING IN THE SCRUM

DEFINITION

When a player binds on a team mate that player must use the whole arm from hand to shoulder to grasp the team mate's body at or below the level of the armpit. Placing only a hand on another player is not satisfactory binding.

(a) Binding by all front row players. All front row players must bind firmly and continuously from the start to the finish of the scrum.

Penalty: Penalty Kick

(b) Binding by hookers. The hooker may bind either

over or under the arms of the props. The props must not support the hooker so that the hooker has no weight on either foot.

Penalty: Penalty Kick

(c) Binding by loose head props. A loose head prop must bind on the opposing tight head prop by placing the left arm inside the right arm of the tight head and gripping the tight head prop's jersey on the back or side. The loose head prop must not grip the chest, arm, sleeve or collar of the opposition tight head prop. The loose head prop must not exert any downward pressure.

Penalty: Penalty Kick

(d) Binding by tight head props. A tight head prop must bind on the opposing loose head prop by placing the right arm outside the left upper arm of the opposing loose head prop. The tight head prop must grip the loose head prop's jersey with the right hand only on the back or side. The tight head prop must not grip the chest, arm, sleeve or collar of the opposition loose head prop. The tight head prop must not exert any downward pressure.

Penalty: Penalty Kick

(e) Both the loose head and tight head props may alter their bind providing they do so in accordance with this Law.

(f) Binding by all other players. All players in a scrum, other than front-row players, must bind on a lock's body with at least one arm. The locks must bind with the props in front of them. No player other than a prop may hold an opponent.

Penalty: Penalty Kick

(g) Flanker obstructing opposing scrum half. A flanker may bind onto the scrum at any angle, provided the flanker is properly bound. The flanker must not widen that angle and so obstruct the opposing scrum half moving forward.

Penalty: Penalty Kick

(h) Scrum collapse. If a scrum collapses, the referee must blow the whistle immediately so that players stop pushing.

(i) Player forced upwards. If a player in a scrum is lifted in the air, or is forced upwards out of the scrum, the referee must blow the whistle immediately so that players stop pushing.

20.4 THE TEAM THROWING THE BALL INTO THE SCRUM

(a) After an infringement, the team that did not cause the infringement throws in the ball.

(b) Scrum after ruck. Refer to Law 16.7.

(c) Scrum after maul. Refer to Law 17.6.

(d) Scrum after any other stoppage. After any other stoppage or irregularity not covered by Law, the team that was moving forward before the stoppage throws in the ball. If neither team was moving forward, the attacking team throws in the ball.

(e) When a scrum remains stationary and the ball does not emerge immediately a further scrum is ordered at the place of the stoppage. The ball is thrown in by the team not in possession at the time of the stoppage.

(f) When a scrum becomes stationary and does not start moving immediately, the ball must emerge immediately. If it does not a further scrum will be ordered. The ball is thrown in by the team not in possession at the time of the stoppage.

(g) If a scrum collapses or lifts up into the air without penalty a further scrum will be ordered and the team who originally threw in the ball will throw the ball in

again. If a scrum has to be reformed for any other reason not covered in this Law the team who originally threw in the ball will throw the ball in again.

20.5 THROWING THE BALL INTO THE SCRUM

(a) No Delay. As soon as the front rows have come together, the scrum half must throw in the ball without delay. The scrum half must throw in the ball when told to do so by the referee. The scrum half must throw in the ball from the side of the scrum first chosen.

Penalty: Free Kick

20.6 HOW THE SCRUM HALF THROWS IN THE BALL

(a) The scrum half must stand one metre from the mark on the middle line so that player's head does not touch the scrum or go beyond the nearest front row player.

Penalty: Free Kick

(b) The scrum half must hold the ball with both hands, with its major axis parallel to the ground and to the touchline over the middle line between the front rows, mid-way between knee and ankle.

Penalty: Free Kick

(c) The scrum half must throw in the ball at a quick speed. The ball must be released from the scrum half's hands from outside the tunnel.

Penalty: Free Kick

(d) The scrum half must throw in the ball straight along the middle line, so that it first touches the ground immediately beyond the width of the nearer prop's shoulders.

Penalty: Free Kick

(e) The scrum half must throw in the ball with a single forward movement. This means that there must be no backward movement with the ball. The scrum half must not pretend to throw the ball.

Penalty: Free Kick

20.7 WHEN THE SCRUM BEGINS

(a) Play in the scrum begins when the ball leaves the hands of the scrum half.

(b) If the scrum half throws in the ball and it comes out at either end of the tunnel, the ball must be thrown in again unless a free kick or penalty has been awarded.

(c) If the ball is not played by a front row player, and it goes straight through the tunnel and comes out behind the foot of a far prop without being touched, the scrum half must throw it in again.

(d) If the ball is played by a front row player and comes out of the tunnel, advantage may apply.

20.8 FRONT-ROW PLAYERS

(a) Striking before the throw in ('foot up'). All front row players must place their feet to leave a clear tunnel. Until the ball has left the scrum half's hands, they must not raise or advance a foot. They must not do anything to stop the ball being thrown in to the scrum correctly or touching the ground at the correct place.

Penalty: Free Kick

(b) Striking after the throw in. Once the ball touches the ground in the tunnel, any front row player may use either foot to try to win possession of the ball.

(c) Kicking-out. A front row player must not intentionally kick the ball out of the tunnel in the direction from which it was thrown in.

Penalty: Free Kick

(d) If the ball is kicked out unintentionally, the same team must throw it in again.

(e) If the ball is repeatedly kicked out, the referee must treat this as intentional and penalise the offender.

Penalty: Penalty Kick

(f) Swinging. A front row player must not strike for the ball with both feet. No player may intentionally raise both feet from the ground, either when the ball is being thrown in or afterwards.

Penalty: Penalty Kick

(g) Twisting, dipping or collapsing. Front row players must not twist or lower their bodies, or pull opponents, or do anything that is likely to collapse the scrum, either when the ball is being thrown in or afterwards.

Penalty: Penalty Kick

(h) Referees must penalise strictly any intentional collapsing of the scrum. This is dangerous play.

Penalty: Penalty Kick

(i) Lifting or forcing an opponent up. A front row player must not lift an opponent in the air, or force an opponent upwards out of the scrum, either when the ball is being thrown in or afterwards. This is dangerous play.

Penalty: Penalty Kick

20.9 SCRUM – GENERAL RESTRICTIONS

(a) All players: Collapsing. A player must not intentionally collapse a scrum. A player must not intentionally fall or kneel in a scrum. This is dangerous play.

Penalty: Penalty Kick

(b) All players: Handling in the scrum. Players must not handle the ball in the scrum or pick it up with their legs.

Penalty: Penalty Kick

(c) All players: Other restrictions on winning the ball. Players must not try to win the ball in the scrum by using any part of their body except their foot or lower leg.

Penalty: Free Kick

(d) All players: When the ball comes out, leave it out. When the ball has left the scrum, a player must not bring it back in to the scrum.

Penalty: Free Kick

(e) All players: No falling on the ball. A player must not fall on or over the ball as it is coming out of the scrum.

Penalty: Penalty Kick

(f) Locks and flankers: Staying out of the tunnel. A player who is not a front row player must not play the ball in the tunnel.

Penalty: Free Kick

(g) Scrum half: Kicking in the scrum. A scrum half must not kick the ball while it is in the scrum.

Penalty: Penalty Kick

(h) Scrum half: Dummying. A scrum half must not take any action to make the opponents think that the ball is out of the scrum while it is still in the scrum.

Penalty: Free Kick

(i) Scrum half: Holding opposing flanker. A scrum half must not grasp an opposing flanker in order to gain leverage, or for any other reason.

Penalty: Penalty Kick

20.10 ENDING THE SCRUM

(a) The ball comes out. When the ball comes out of the scrum in any direction except the tunnel, the scrum ends.

(b) Scrum in the in-goal. A scrum cannot take place in the in-goal. When the ball in a scrum is on or over the goal line, the scrum ends and an attacker or a defender may legally ground the ball for a try or a touch down.

(c) Hindmost player unbinds. The hindmost player in a scrum is the player whose feet are nearest the team's own goal line. If the hindmost player unbinds from the scrum with the ball at that player's feet and picks up the ball, the scrum ends.

20.11 SCRUM WHEELED

(a) If a scrum is wheeled through more than 90 degrees, so that the middle line has passed beyond a position parallel to the touchline, the referee must stop play and order another scrum.

(b) EXPERIMENTAL LAW VARIATION
This new scrum is formed at the place where the previous scrum ended. The ball is thrown in by the team not in possession at the time of the stoppage. If neither team win possession, it is thrown in by the team that previously threw it in.

20.12 OFFSIDE AT THE SCRUM

(a) When the scrum is set, the scrum half not throwing the ball into the scrum must take up a position either at the same side of the scrum as the scrum half throwing in the ball or behind the offside line defined for other players.

(b) Offside for scrum-halves. When a team has won the ball in a scrum, the scrum half of that team is offside if both feet are in front of the ball while it is still in the scrum. If the scrum half has only one foot in front of the ball, the scrum half is not offside.
Penalty: Penalty Kick

(c) When a team has won the ball in a scrum, the scrum half of the opposing team is offside if that scrum half steps in front of the ball with either foot while the ball is still in the scrum.
Penalty: Penalty Kick

(d) The scrum half whose team does not win possession of the ball must not move to the opposite side of the scrum and overstep the offside line running through the hindmost foot of that player's team in the scrum.
Penalty: Penalty Kick

(e) The scrum half whose team does not win possession of the ball must not move away from the scrum and then remain in front of the offside line running through the hindmost foot of that player's team in the scrum.
Penalty: Penalty Kick

(f) Any player may be scrum half, but a team can have only one scrum half at each scrum.
Penalty: Penalty Kick on the offside line

(g) Offside for players not in the scrum. Players who are not in the scrum, and who are not the team's scrum half, are offside if they remain in front of their offside line or overstep the offside line.
Penalty: Penalty Kick on the offside line

(h) Loitering. When a scrum is forming, players not taking part in it must retire to their offside line without delay. If they do not, they are loitering. Loiterers must be penalised.
Penalty: Penalty Kick on the offside line

Law 21 Penalty and Free Kicks

DEFINITION

Penalty kicks and free kicks are awarded to the non-offending team for infringements by their opponents.

21.1 WHERE PENALTY AND FREE KICKS ARE AWARDED
Unless a Law states otherwise, the mark for a penalty or free kick is at the place of infringement.

21.2 WHERE PENALTY AND FREE KICKS ARE TAKEN
(a) The kicker must take the penalty or free kick at the mark or anywhere behind it on a line through the mark. If the place for a penalty or free kick is within 5 metres of the opponents' goal line, the mark for the kick is 5 metres from the goal line, opposite the place of infringement.
(b) When a penalty or free kick is awarded for an infringement in in-goal, the mark for the kick is in the field of play, 5 metres from the goal line, in line with the place of infringement.
Penalty: Any infringement by the kicker's team results in a scrum at the mark. The opposing team throws in the ball.

21.3 HOW THE PENALTY AND FREE KICKS ARE TAKEN
(a) Any player may take a penalty or free kick awarded for an infringement with any type of kick: punt, drop kick or place kick. The ball may be kicked with any part of the lower leg from knee to the foot, excluding the knee and the heel.
(b) Bouncing the ball on the knee is not taking a kick.
Penalty: Any infringement by the kicker's team results in a scrum at the mark. The opposing team throws in the ball.
(c) The kicker must use the ball that was in play unless the referee decides it was defective.
Penalty: Any infringement by the kicker's team results in a scrum at the mark. The opposing team throws in the ball.

21.4 PENALTY AND FREE KICK OPTIONS AND REQUIREMENTS
(a) Scrum alternative. A team awarded a penalty or free kick may choose a scrum instead. They throw in the ball.
(b) No delay. If a kicker indicates to the referee the intention to kick a penalty kick at goal, the kick must be taken within one minute from the time the player indicates the intention to kick at goal. The intention to kick is signalled by the arrival of the kicking tee or sand, or when the player makes a mark on the ground. The player must complete the kick within one minute even if the ball rolls over and has to be placed again. If the one minute is exceeded, the kick is disallowed, a scrum is ordered at the place of the mark and the opponents throw in the ball. For any other type of kick, the kick must be taken without undue delay.
(c) A clear kick. The kicker must kick the ball a visible distance. If the kicker is holding it, it must

clearly leave the hands. If it is on the ground, it must clearly leave the mark.
(d) Place kicking for touch. The kicker may punt or drop kick for touch but must not place kick for touch.
(e) Kicker's freedom of action. The kicker is free to kick the ball in any direction and may play the ball again.
(f) Kick taken in the in-goal. When a penalty or free kick is taken in the team's in-goal and a defending player by foul play prevents an opponent from scoring a try, a penalty try is awarded.
(g) Out of play in the in-goal. If a penalty or free kick is taken in in-goal and the ball goes into touch-in-goal, or on or over the dead ball line, or a defending player makes the ball dead before it has crossed the goal line, a 5-metre scrum is awarded. The attacking team throws in the ball.
(h) Behind the ball. All the kicker's team at a penalty or free kick must be behind the ball until it has been kicked, except the placer for a place kick.
(i) Kick taken quickly. If the penalty or free kick is taken so quickly that players of the kicker's team are still in front of the ball, they are not penalised for being offside. However, they must retire immediately. They must not stop retiring until they are onside. They must not take part in the game until they are onside. This applies to all players of that team, whether they are inside or outside the playing area.
(j) In this situation, players become onside when they run behind the team mate who took the penalty or free kick, or when a team mate carrying the ball runs in front of them, or when a team mate who was behind the ball when it was kicked runs in front of them.
(k) An offside player cannot be put onside by any action of an opponent.
Penalty: Unless otherwise stated in Law any infringement by the kicker's team results in a scrum at the mark. The opposing team throw in the ball.

21.5 SCORING A GOAL FROM A PENALTY KICK
(a) A penalty goal can be scored from a penalty kick.
(b) If the kicker indicates to the referee the intention to kick at goal, the kicker must kick at goal. Once the kicker has made the intention clear, there can be no change of the intention. The referee may enquire of the kicker as to the intention.
(c) If the kicker indicates to the referee the intent to kick at goal, the opposing team must stand still with their hands by their sides from the time the kicker starts to approach to kick until the ball is kicked.
(d) If the kicker has not indicated an intention to kick at goal but takes a drop kick and scores a goal, the goal stands.
(e) If the opposing team infringes while the kick is being taken but the kick at goal is successful, the goal stands. A further penalty is not awarded for the infringement.
(f) The kicker may place the ball directly on the ground or on sand, sawdust or a kicking tee approved by the Union.

21.6 SCORING FROM A FREE KICK
(a) A goal cannot be scored from a free kick.
(b) The team awarded a free kick cannot score a dropped goal until after the ball next becomes dead, or until after an opponent has played or touched it, or has tackled the ball carrier. This restriction applies also to a scrum taken instead of a free kick.

21.7 WHAT THE OPPOSING TEAM MUST DO AT A PENALTY KICK

(a) Must run from the mark. The opposing team must immediately run towards their own goal line until they are at least 10 metres away from the mark for the penalty kick, or until they have reached their goal line if that is nearer the mark.

(b) Must keep running. Even if the penalty kick is taken and the kicker's team is playing the ball, opposing players must keep running until they have retired the necessary distance. They must not take part in the game until they have done so.

(c) Kick taken quickly. If the penalty kick is taken so quickly that opponents have no opportunity to retire, they will not be penalised for this. However, they must continue to retire as described in 21.7(b) above or until a team mate who was 10 metres from the mark has run in front of them, before they take part in the game.

(d) Interference. The opposing team must not do anything to delay the penalty kick or obstruct the kicker. They must not intentionally take, throw or kick the ball out of reach of the kicker or the kicker's team mates.

Penalty: Any infringement by the opposing team results in a second penalty kick, 10 metres in front of the mark for the first kick. This mark must not be within 5 metres of the goal line. Any player may take the kick. The kicker may change the type of kick and may choose to kick at goal. If the referee awards a second penalty kick, the second penalty kick is not taken before the referee has made the mark indicating the place of the penalty.

21.8 WHAT OPTIONS THE OPPOSING TEAM HAVE AT A FREE KICK

(a) Must run from the mark. The opposing team must immediately run towards their own goal line until they are at least 10 metres away from the mark for the free kick, or until they have reached their goal line if that is nearer the mark. If the free kick is in a defending teams in-goal area, the opposing team must immediately run towards their own goal line until they are at least 10 metres away from the mark and not nearer than 5 metres from the goal line.

(b) Must keep running. Even if the free kick is taken and the kicker's team is playing the ball, opposing players must keep running until they have retired the necessary distance. They must not take part in the game until they have done so.

(c) Kick taken quickly. If the free kick is taken so quickly that opponents have no opportunity to retire, they will not be penalised for this. However, they must continue to retire as described in 21.8(b) above or until a team mate who was 10 metres from the mark has run in front of them, before they take part in the game.

(d) Interference. The opposing team must not do anything to delay the free kick or obstruct the kicker. They must not intentionally take, throw or kick the ball out of reach of the kicker or the kicker's team mates.

(e) Charging the free kick. Once they have retired the necessary distance, players of the opposing team may charge and try to prevent the kick being taken. They may charge the free kick as soon as the kicker starts to approach to kick.

(f) Preventing the free kick. If the opposing team charge and prevent the free kick being taken, the kick is disallowed. Play restarts with a scrum at the mark. The opposing team throw in the ball.

(g) Free kick taken in the in-goal. If a free kick has been awarded in the in-goal or if it has been awarded in the field of play and the player retires to in-goal to take it, and the opponents charge and prevent the kick from being taken, a 5-metre scrum is ordered. The attacking team throw in the ball. If a free kick is taken in the in-goal, an opponent who legitimately plays it there can score a try.

(h) Charged down. If opponents charge down a free kick in the playing area, play continues.

Penalty: Any infringement by the opposing team results in a second free kick, awarded 10 metres in front of the mark for the first kick. This mark must not be within 5 metres of the goal line. Any player may take the kick. If the referee awards a second free kick, the second free kick is not taken before the referee has made the mark indicating the place of the free kick.

21.9 CONTRIVED INFRINGEMENTS AT THE PENALTY KICK

If the referee believes that the kicker's team has contrived an infringement by their opponents, the referee does not award a further penalty but allows play to continue.

21.10 CONTRIVED INFRINGEMENTS AT THE FREE KICK

(a) The kicker must not pretend to kick. As soon as the kicker makes a move to kick, the opponents may charge.

(b) If the referee believes that the kicker's team has contrived an infringement by their opponents, the referee does not award a further free kick but allows play to continue.

Law 22 In-Goal

DEFINITIONS

In-goal is part of the ground as defined in Law 1 where the ball may be grounded by players from either team.

When attacking players are first to ground the ball in the opponents' in-goal, the attacking players score a try.

When defending players are first to ground the ball in in-goal, the defending players make a touch down.

A defending player who has one foot on the goal line or in the in-goal who receives the ball is considered to have both feet in in-goal.

22.1 GROUNDING THE BALL

There are two ways a player can ground the ball:
(a) Player touches the ground with the ball. A player grounds the ball by holding the ball and touching the ground with it, in in-goal. 'Holding' means holding in the hand or hands, or in the arm or arms. No downward pressure is required.

(b) Player presses down on the ball. A player grounds the ball when it is on the ground in the in-goal and the player presses down on it with a hand or hands, arm or arms, or the front of the player's body from waist to neck inclusive.

22.2 PICKING UP THE BALL

Picking up the ball from the ground is not grounding it. A player may pick up the ball in the in-goal and ground it elsewhere in the in-goal.

22.3 BALL GROUNDED BY AN ATTACKING PLAYER

Try. When an attacking player who is onside is first to ground the ball in the opponents' in-goal, the player scores a try. This applies whether an attacking or a defending player is responsible for the ball being in the in-goal.

22.4 OTHER WAYS TO SCORE A TRY

(a) Grounded on the goal line. The goal line is part of the in-goal. If an attacking player is first to ground the ball on the opponents' goal line, a try is scored.

(b) Grounded against a goal post. The goal posts and padding surrounding them are part of the goal line, which is part of in-goal. If an attacking player is first to ground the ball against a goal post or padding, a try is scored.

(c) Pushover try. A scrum or ruck cannot take place in the in-goal. If a scrum or ruck is pushed into the in-goal, an attacking player may legally ground the ball as soon as the ball reaches or crosses the goal line and a try is scored.

(d) Momentum try. If an attacking player with the ball is tackled short of the goal line but the player's momentum carries the player in a continuous movement along the ground into the opponents in-goal, and the player is first to ground the ball, a try is scored.

(e) Tackled near the goal line. If a player is tackled near to the opponents' goal line so that this player can immediately reach out and ground the ball on or over the goal line, a try is scored.

(f) In this situation, defending players who are on their feet may legally prevent the try by pulling the ball from the tackled player's hands or arms, but must not kick the ball.

(g) Player in touch or touch-in-goal. If an attacking player is in touch or in touch-in-goal, the player can score a try by grounding the ball in the opponents' in-goal provided the player is not carrying the ball.

(h) Penalty try. A penalty try is awarded if a try would probably have been scored but for foul play by the defending team. A penalty try is awarded if a try would probably have been scored in a better position but for foul play by the defending team.

(i) A penalty try is awarded between the goal posts. The defending team may charge the conversion kick after a penalty try.

22.5 BALL GROUNDED BY A DEFENDING PLAYER

(a) Touch down. When defending players are first to ground the ball in their in-goal, it results in a touch down.

(b) Player in touch or touch-in-goal. If defending players are in touch-in-goal, they can make a touch down by grounding the ball in their in-goal provided they are not carrying the ball.

(c) Grounded against a goal post. The goal posts and padding surrounding them are part of the goal line. If a defending player is first to ground the ball against a goal post or padding, the result is a touch down.

22.6 SCRUM OR RUCK IS PUSHED INTO IN-GOAL

A scrum or ruck can take place only in the field of play. Therefore, if a scrum or ruck is pushed across the goal line, a defending player may legally ground the ball as soon as the ball reaches or crosses the goal line. This results in a touch down.

22.7 RESTARTING AFTER A TOUCH DOWN

(a) When an attacking player sends or carries the ball into the opponents' in-goal and it becomes dead there, either because a defender grounded it or because it went into touch-in-goal or on or over the dead ball line, a drop out is awarded.

(b) If an attacking player knocks-on or throws-forward in the field of play and the ball goes into the opponents' in-goal and it is made dead there, a scrum is awarded where the knock on or throw forward happened.

(c) If at a kick off the ball is kicked into the opponents' in-goal without having touched or been touched by a player and a defending player grounds it there or makes it dead without delay, the defending team have two choices:

- To have a scrum formed at the centre, and they throw in the ball; or
- To have the other team kick off again.

(d) If a defending player threw or took the ball into the in-goal, and a defending player grounded it, and there has been no infringement, play is restarted by a 5-metre scrum. The position of the scrum is in line with where the ball has been touched down. The attacking side throws in the ball.

22.8 BALL KICKED DEAD IN IN-GOAL

If a team kicks the ball through their opponents' in-goal, into touch-in-goal or on or over the dead ball line, except by an unsuccessful kick at goal or attempted dropped goal, the defending team has two choices:

- To have a drop out, or
- To have a scrum at the place where the ball was kicked and they throw in.

22.9 DEFENDING PLAYER IN IN-GOAL

A defending player who has part of one foot in in-goal is considered to have both feet in in-goal.

22.10 BALL HELD UP IN-GOAL

When a player carrying the ball is held up in the in-goal so that the player cannot ground the ball, the ball is dead. A 5-metre scrum is formed. This would apply if play similar to a maul takes place in in-goal. The attacking team throws in the ball.

22.11 BALL DEAD IN IN-GOAL

(a) When the ball touches the corner post, the touch-in-goal line or the dead ball line, or touches anything or anyone beyond those lines, the ball becomes dead. If the ball was played into in-goal by the attacking team, a drop out shall be awarded to the defending team. If the ball was played into in-goal by the defending team, a 5-metre scrum shall be awarded and the attacking team throws in the ball.

(b) When a player carrying the ball touches the corner post, the touch-in-goal line, the dead ball line, or touches the ground beyond those lines, the ball becomes dead. If the ball was carried into in-goal by the attacking team, a drop out shall be awarded to the defending team. If the ball was carried into in-goal by the defending team, a 5-metre scrum shall be awarded and the attacking team throws in the ball.

(c) When a player scores a try or makes a touch down, the ball becomes dead.

22.12 ATTACKING INFRINGEMENT WITH SCRUM PENALTY

If an attacking player commits an infringement in in-goal, for which the penalty is a scrum, for example, a knock on, play is restarted with a 5-metre scrum. The scrum is formed in line with the place of the infringement and the defending team throws in the ball.

22.13 DEFENDING INFRINGEMENT WITH SCRUM PENALTY

If a defending player infringes in in-goal, for which the penalty is a scrum, for example, a knock on, play is restarted with a 5-metre scrum. The scrum is formed in line with the place of the infringement and the attacking team throws in the ball.

22.14 DOUBT ABOUT GROUNDING

If there is doubt about which team first grounded the ball in the in-goal, play is restarted by a 5-metre scrum, in line with the place where the ball was grounded. The attacking team throws in the ball.

22.15 INFRINGEMENTS IN IN-GOAL

All infringements in the in-goal are treated as if they had taken place in the field of play. A knock on or a throw forward in the in-goal results in a 5-metre scrum, opposite the place of infringement.

Penalty: For an infringement, the mark for a penalty kick or free kick cannot be in the in-goal. When a penalty kick or free kick is awarded for an infringement in the in-goal, the mark for the kick is in the field of play, 5 metres from the goal line, opposite the place of infringement.

22.16 MISCONDUCT OR UNFAIR PLAY IN IN-GOAL

(a) Obstruction by the attacking team.
When a player charges or intentionally obstructs an opponent in the in-goal who has just kicked the ball, the opponent's team may choose to take the penalty kick either in the field of play, 5 metres from the goal line opposite the place of infringement, or where the ball landed. If they make the second choice and the ball lands in or near touch, the mark for the penalty kick is 15 metres from the touchline, opposite where the ball went into touch or where it landed. A try is disallowed and a penalty kick awarded if a try would probably not have been scored but for foul play by the attacking team.

(b) Foul play by the defending team. The referee awards a penalty try if a try would probably have been scored but for foul play by the defending team. The referee awards a penalty try if a try would probably have been scored in a better position but for foul play by the defending team. A penalty try is awarded between the goal posts. The defending team may charge the conversion kick after a penalty try. A player who prevents a try being scored through foul play must either be cautioned and temporarily suspended or sent off.

(c) Any other foul play. When a player commits any other foul play in the in-goal while the ball is out of play, the penalty kick is awarded at the place where the game would otherwise have restarted.

Penalty: Penalty Kick.

UNDER 19 VARIATIONS
STANDARD SET OF VARIATIONS APPROPRIATE TO THE UNDER 19 GAME

Law 3 Number of Players – The Team

3.5 SUITABLY TRAINED AND EXPERIENCED PLAYERS IN THE FRONT ROW

(c) If a team nominates 22 players, it **must** have at least six players who can play in the front row in order that there is replacement cover for the loose head prop, hooker and tight head prop. If a team nominates more than 22 players it **must** have at least six players who can play in the front row in order that there is replacement cover for the loose head prop, hooker and tight head prop. There must also be three players who can play in lock position.

3.12 SUBSTITUTED PLAYERS REJOINING THE MATCH

A player who has been substituted may replace an injured player.

Law 5 Time

5.1 DURATION OF A MATCH

Each half of an Under 19 match lasts 35 minutes playing time. Play in a match lasts no longer than 70 minutes. After a total of 70 minutes playing time, the referee must not allow extra time to be played in the case of a drawn match in a knock-out competition.

Law 20 Scrum

20.1 FORMING A SCRUM

(f) In an 8 person scrum the formation must be 3-4-1, with the single player (normally the Number 8) shoving on the 2 locks. The locks must pack with their heads on either side of the hooker.

Exception: A team must have fewer than eight players in its scrum when **either** the team cannot field a complete team, or a player is sent off for Foul Play, **or** a player leaves the field because of injury.

Even allowing for this exception, each team must always have at least five players in a scrum.

If a team is incomplete, the scrum formation must be as follows: If a team is without one player, then both teams must use a 3-4 formation (i.e. no No.8).

If a team is without two players, then both teams must use a 3-2-1 formation (i.e. no flankers).

If a team is without three players, then both teams must use a 3-2 formation (i.e. only front rows and locks).

When a normal scrum takes place, the players in the three front row positions and the two lock positions must have been suitably trained for these positions.

If a team cannot field such suitably trained players because: either they are not available, **or** a player in one of those five positions is injured **or** has been sent off for Foul Play and no suitably trained replacement is available, then the referee must order uncontested scrums.

In an uncontested scrum, the teams do not compete for the ball. The team putting in the ball must win it.

Neither team is allowed to push the other team away from the mark.

20.1 FORMING A SCRUM
(h) The referee will call "crouch" then "touch". The front rows crouch and using their outside arm each prop touches the point of the opposing prop's outside shoulder. The props then withdraw their arms. The referee will then call "pause". Following a pause the referee will then call "engage". The front rows may then engage. The "engage" call is not a command but an indication that the front rows may come together when ready.
Penalty: Free Kick
Note: *The engagement process above is now identical to senior law.*

No wheeling. A team must not intentionally wheel a scrum.
Penalty: Penalty Kick
If a wheel reaches 45 degrees, the referee must stop play. If the wheel is unintentional, the referee orders another scrum at the place where the scrum is stopped.
Maximum 1.5 metres push. A team in a scrum must not push the scrum more than 1.5 metres towards their opponents' goal line.
Penalty: Free Kick
Ball must be released from scrum. A player must not intentionally keep the ball in the scrum once the player's team has heeled the ball and controls it at the base of the scrum.
Penalty: Free Kick

SEVEN-A-SIDE VARIATIONS
STANDARD SET OF VARIATIONS APPROPRIATE TO THE SEVEN-A-SIDE GAME

Law 3 Number of Players – The Team

3.1 MAXIMUM NUMBER OF PLAYERS ON THE PLAYING AREA
Maximum: each team must have no more than seven players on the playing area.

3.4 PLAYERS NOMINATED AS SUBSTITUTES
A team may nominate no more than five replacements/substitutes. A team can substitute or replace up to three players.

3.12 SUBSTITUTED PLAYERS REJOINING THE MATCH
If a player is substituted, that player must not return and play in that match even to replace an injured player.
Exception: A substituted player may replace a player with a bleeding or open wound.

Law 5 Toss Time

5.1 DURATION OF A MATCH
A match lasts no longer than fourteen minutes plus lost time and extra time. A match is divided into two halves of not more than seven minutes playing time.
Exception: A competition final match may last no longer than twenty minutes plus lost time and extra time. The match is divided into two halves of not more than ten minutes playing time.

5.2 HALF TIME
After half time the teams change ends. There is an interval of not more than one minute. During a competition final there is an interval of not more than two minutes.

5.6 PLAYING EXTRA TIME
When there is a drawn match and extra time is required, the extra time is played in periods of five minutes. After each period, the teams change ends without an interval.

Law 6 Match Officials

6.A. REFEREE

6.A.12 DUTIES OF THE REFEREE AFTER THE MATCH

Add extra paragraph:
Extra Time – Toss.
Before extra time starts, the referee organises a toss. One of the captains tosses a coin and the other captain calls to see who wins the toss. The winner of the toss decides whether to kick off or choose an end. If the winner of the toss decides to choose an end, the opponents must kick off and vice versa.

6.B. TOUCH JUDGES

6.B.8 IN-GOAL JUDGES
(a) There are two in-goal judges for each match.
(b) The referee has the same control over both in-goal judges as the referee has over touch judges.
(c) There is only one in-goal judge in each in-goal area.
(d) Signalling result of kick at goal. When a conversion kick or a penalty kick at goal is being taken, an in-goal judge must help the referee by signalling the result of the kick. One touch judge stands at or behind a goal post and an in-goal judge stands at or behind the other goal post. If the ball goes over the crossbar and between the posts, the touch judge and the in-goal judge raise their flags to indicate a goal.
(e) Signalling touch. When the ball or the ball carrier has gone into touch-in-goal, the in-goal judge must hold up the flag.
(f) Signalling tries. The in-goal judge will assist the referee in decisions on touch downs and tries if there is any doubt in the referee's mind.
(g) Signalling foul play. A match organiser may give authority for the in-goal judge to signal foul play in the in-goal.

Law 9 Method of Scoring

9.B. CONVERSION KICK

9.B.1 TAKING A CONVERSION KICK
Amend
(c) The kick must be a drop kick.
Delete **(d)**
Amend
(e) The kicker must take the kick within forty seconds of a try having been scored. The kick is disallowed if the kicker does not take the kick in the time allowed.

9.B.3 THE OPPOSING TEAM
Amend
(a) All the opposing team must immediately assemble close to their own 10-metre line.
Delete **(b)**
(c) *Delete 3rd paragraph* "When another kick is allowed......."

Law 10 Foul Play

Note: Temporary Suspension: When a player has been temporarily suspended, the players period of suspension will be for a period of two minutes.

Law 13 KickOff and Restart Kicks

13.2 WHO TAKES THE KICK OFF AND RESTART KICK
Amend
(c) After a score, the team that has scored kicks off with a drop kick which must be taken at or behind the centre of the half-way line.
Penalty: Free Kick at the centre of the half-way line.

Amend
13.3 POSITION OF THE KICKER'S TEAM AT THE KICK OFF
All the kicker's team must be behind the ball when it is kicked. If they are not, a free kick is awarded to the non-offending team at the centre of the half-way line.
Penalty: Free Kick at the centre of the half-way line.

Amend
13.7 KICK OFF OF UNDER 10 METRES AND NOT PLAYED BY AN OPPONENT.
If the ball does not reach the opponents' 10-metre line, a free kick is awarded to the non-offending team at the centre of the half-way line.
Penalty: Free Kick at the centre of the half-way line.

Amend
13.8 BALL GOES DIRECTLY INTO TOUCH
The ball must land in the field of play. If it is kicked directly into touch, a free kick is awarded to the non-offending team at the centre of the half-way line.
Penalty: Free Kick at the centre of the half-way line.

Amend
13.9 BALL GOES INTO THE IN-GOAL
(b) If the opposing team grounds the ball, or if they make it dead, or if the ball becomes dead by going into touch-in-goal or on or over the dead ball line a free kick is awarded to the non-offending team at the centre of the half-way line.
Penalty: Free Kick at the centre of the half-way line.

Law 20 Scrum

DEFINITIONS

Amend 2nd paragraph:
A scrum is formed in the field of play when three players from each team, bound together in one row, close up with their opponents so that the heads of the players are interlocked. This creates a tunnel into which a scrum half throws in the ball so that the players can compete for possession by hooking the ball with either of their feet.
Amend 4th paragraph:
The tunnel is the space between the two rows of players.
Amend 6th paragraph:
The middle line is an imaginary line on the ground in the tunnel beneath the line where the shoulders of the two rows of players meet.
Amend 7th paragraph:
The middle player is the hooker
Delete paragraphs 9, 10 and 11.

20.1 FORMING A SCRUM
Amend
(f) Number of players: three. A scrum must have three players from each team. All three players must stay bound to the scrum until it ends.
Penalty: Penalty Kick.
Delete Exception

20.1 FORMING A SCRUM
(h) The referee will call "crouch" then "touch". The front rows crouch and using their outside arm each prop touches the point of the opposing prop's outside shoulder. The props then withdraw their arms. The referee will then call "pause". Following a pause the referee will then call "engage". The front rows may then engage. The "engage" call is not a command but an indication that the front rows may come together when ready.
Penalty: Free Kick
Note: The engagement process above is now identical to senior law.

20.8 FRONT ROW PLAYERS
Amend
(c) Kicking out. A front-row player must not intentionally kick the ball out of the tunnel or out of the scrum in the direction of the opponent's goal line.
Penalty: Penalty Kick.

Law 21 Penalty and Free Kicks

21.3 HOW THE PENALTY AND FREE KICKS ARE TAKEN
Amend
(a) Any player may take a penalty or free kick awarded for an infringement with any kind of kick: punt, drop kick but not a place kick. The ball may be kicked with any part of the leg from below the knee to the toe but not with the heel.

21.4 PENALTY AND FREE KICK OPTIONS AND REQUIREMENTS
Amend
(b) No delay. If a kicker indicates to the referee the intention to kick at goal, the kick must be taken within thirty seconds of the penalty having been awarded. If the 30 seconds is exceeded the kick is disallowed, a scrum is ordered at the place of the mark and the opponents throw in the ball.

EXPERIMENTAL LAW VARIATIONS
AUGUST 2008

VARIATION 1

Law 6 Match Officials

Every match is under the control of match officials who consist of the referee and two touch judges or assistant referees. Additional persons, as authorised by the match organisers, may include the referee, reserve touch judge and/or assistant referee, an official to assist the referee in making decisions by using technological devices, the time keeper, the match doctor, the team doctors, the non-playing members of the teams and the ball persons.

A touch judge may be appointed by a match organiser or a team involved in a match and is responsible for signalling, touch, touch-in-goal and the success or otherwise of kicks at goal.

An assistant referee may be appointed by a match organiser and is responsible for signalling, touch, touch-in-goal, the success or otherwise of kicks at goal and indicating foul play. An assistant referee will also provide assistance to the referee in the performance of any of the referee's duties as directed by the referee.

VARIATION 2

Law 17 Maul

17.2 JOINING A MAUL
Clause (a) removed:
(a) Players joining a maul must have their heads and shoulders no lower than their hips.
Penalty: Free Kick

VARIATION 3

Law 17 Maul

17.5 SUCCESSFUL END TO A MAUL
(a) A maul ends successfully when the ball, or a player with the ball, leaves the maul. A maul ends successfully when the ball is on the ground, or is on or over the goal line.
(b) A player may pull a maul to the ground providing that player does so by pulling another player in the maul down from the shoulders to the hips.
Penalty: Penalty kick

17.6 UNSUCCESSFUL END TO A MAUL
(a) A maul ends unsuccessfully if the ball becomes unplayable, or the maul collapses or is pulled down and the ball does not emerge. A scrum is ordered.

VARIATION 4

Law 19 Touch and Lineout

19.1 THROW IN

NO GAIN IN GROUND
(a) Outside a team's 22, a team member kicks directly into touch. Except for a penalty kick, when a player anywhere in the field of play who is outside the 22 kicks directly into touch, there is no gain in ground.

The throw in is taken either at the place opposite where the player kicked the ball, or at the place where it went into touch, whichever is nearer that player's goal line.

(b) When a team causes the ball to be put into that team's 22. When a defending player plays the ball from outside the 22 and it goes into that player's 22 or in-goal area without touching an opposition player and then that player or another player from that team kicks the ball directly into touch before it touches an opposition player, or a tackle takes place or a ruck or maul is formed, there is no gain in ground. This applies when a defending player moves back behind the 22 metre line to take a quick throw-in and then the ball is kicked directly into touch.

(c) Defending team takes the ball into that team's 22 at a scrum or lineout. When a defending team throws the ball into a scrum or lineout outside that team's 22 and the ball then crosses into the team's 22 without touching an opposition player and then a player from the defending team kicks the ball directly into touch before it touches an opposition player, or a tackle takes place or a ruck or maul is formed, there is no gain in ground.

GAIN IN GROUND

(d) Player takes the ball into that team's 22. When a defending player plays the ball from outside the 22 and it goes into that player's 22 or in-goal area and it touches an opposition player, or a tackle takes place or a ruck or maul is formed, and then the ball is kicked by a player of that team directly in touch, the throw in is where the ball went into touch.

(e) Ball put into a player's 22 by the opposition. When the ball is put into a team's 22 by the opposition, without having touched (or been touched by) a player of the defending team before crossing the 22 and the ball is then kicked into touch by the defending team, the throw in is where the ball went into touch.

(f) Kicks indirectly into touch. When a player anywhere in the playing area kicks indirectly into touch so that the ball bounces in the field of play the throw in is taken where the ball went into touch. When a player anywhere in the playing area kicks the ball so that it touches or is touched by an opposition player and then goes indirectly into touch so that the ball bounces in the field of play the throw in is taken where the ball went into touch. When a player anywhere in the playing area kicks the ball so that it touches or is touched by an opposition player and then goes directly into touch the throw in is taken in line with where the opposition player touched the ball or where the ball crossed the touch line if that is nearer the opposition player's goal line.

VARIATION 5

Law 19 Touch and Lineout

19.2 QUICK THROW IN
(e) At a quick throw in, if the player throws the ball in the direction of the opposition's goal line or if the ball does not travel at least five metres along or behind the line of touch before it touches the ground or a player, or if the player steps into the field of play

---

when the ball is thrown, then the quick throw in is disallowed. The opposing team chooses to throw in at either a lineout where the quick throw in was attempted, or a scrum on the 15-metre line at that place. If they too throw in the ball incorrectly at the lineout, a scrum is formed on the 15-metre line. The team that first threw in the ball throws in the ball at the scrum.
(f) At a quick throw in a player may throw the ball in straight along the line of touch or towards that player's goal line.

VARIATION 6

Law 19 Touch and Lineout

19.7 FORMING A LINEOUT
(a) Minimum. At least two players from each team must form a lineout. A team must not voluntarily fail to form a lineout.
Penalty: Free Kick on the 15-metre line
(b) Maximum. There is no restriction to the number
of players from each team participating in the lineout. Each team can decide how many players participate in the lineout and there is no requirement
for there to be an equal number of participants from each team.

VARIATION 7 & 8

Law 19 Touch and Lineout

19.7 FORMING A LINEOUT
(e) Where the receiver must stand. The receiver must stand at least two metres towards that player's goal line from that player's team-mates who are lineout players and between five and fifteen metres from the touch line.
Penalty: Free Kick on the 15-metre line
(f) Player between touch and five metres. The team not throwing in must have a player standing between the touch line and the 5-metre line on that team's side of the line of touch when the lineout is formed. That player must stand at least two metres from the five metres line.

VARIATION 9

Law 19 Touch and Lineout

19.9 OPTIONS AVAILABLE AT A LINEOUT
(e) Pre-gripping is permitted. Players who are going to lift or support a team-mate jumping for the ball may pre-grip that team-mate providing they do not pre-grip below the shorts from behind and below the thighs from the front.
Penalty: Free Kick on the 15-metre line

VARIATION 10

Law 19 Touch and Lineout

19.9 OPTIONS AVAILABLE AT A LINEOUT
(f) Lifting and supporting. Players may assist a team-mate in jumping for the ball by lifting and supporting that player providing that the lifting and/or supporting players do not support the jumping team-mate below the shorts from behind or below the thighs from the front.
Penalty: Free Kick on the 15-metre line
(h) Jumping, supporting or lifting before the ball is thrown. A player must not jump or be lifted or supported before the ball has left the hands of the player throwing in.
Penalty: Free Kick on the 15-metre line

VARIATION 11

Law 20 Scrum

20.12 OFFSIDE AT THE SCRUM
(g) Offside for players not in the scrum. Players who are not in the scrum and who are not the team's scrum half, are offside if they remain in front of their offside line or overstep the offside line which is a line parallel to the goal lines and 5 metres behind the hindmost player of each team in a scrum.
Penalty: Penalty Kick on the offside line

VARIATION 12

Law 20 Scrum

20.12 OFFSIDE AT THE SCRUM
(d) The scrum half whose team does not win possession of the ball must not move to the opposite side of the scrum and overstep the offside line. For that scrum half that runs through the hindmost foot of that player's team in the scrum.
Penalty: Penalty Kick
(e) The scrum half whose team does not win possession of the ball must not move away from the scrum and then remain in front of the offside line. For that scrum half that runs through the hindmost foot of that player's team in the scrum.
Penalty: Penalty Kick

VARIATION 13

Law 22 In-Goal

22.12 BALL OR PLAYER TOUCHING A FLAG OR FLAG (CORNER) POST
If the ball or a player carrying the ball touches a flag or a flag (corner) post at the intersection of the touch-in-goal line and the goal line or at the intersection of the touch-in-goal line and dead ball line without otherwise being in touch or touch-in-goal, the ball is not out of play, unless it is first grounded against a flag post.

GLOSSARY
DEFINITIONS RELATED TO THE GAME OF RUGBY

A

Actual time: Elapsed time including time lost for any reason.

Advantage: Law 8 – Advantage.

Attacking team: The opponents of the defending team in whose half of the ground play is taking place.

B

Ball carrier: A player carrying the ball.

Beyond or behind or in front of a position: Means with both feet, except where the context makes that inappropriate.

Binding: Grasping firmly another player's body between the shoulders and the hips with the whole arm in contact from hand to shoulder.

C

Captain: The captain is a player nominated by the team. Only the captain is entitled to consult the referee during the match and is solely responsible for choosing options relating to the referee's decisions.

Cavalry charge: Law 10 – Foul Play.

Conversion kick: Law 9 – Method of Scoring.

Converted: A conversion kick that was successful.

D

Dangerous play: Law 10 – Foul Play.

Dead: The ball is out of play. This happens when the ball has gone outside the playing area and remained there, or when the referee has blown the whistle to indicate a stoppage in play, or when a conversion kick has been taken.

Dead ball line: Law 1 – The Ground.

Defending team: The team in whose half of the ground play is taking place; their opponents are the Attacking Team.

Drop kick: The ball is dropped from the hand or hands to the ground and kicked as it rises from its first bounce.

Drop out: Law 13 – Kick-Off and Restart Kicks.

Dropped goal: Law 9 – Method of Scoring.

F

Field of play: Law 1 – The Ground.

Flanker: Forward player who usually wears jersey No.6 or No.7.

Flying wedge: Law 10 – Foul Play.

Foul play: Law 10 – Foul Play.

Free kick: Law 21 – Penalty and Free Kicks. A kick awarded to the non-offending team after an infringement by its opponents. Unless a Law states otherwise, a free kick awarded because of an infringement is awarded at the place of infringement.

Front row players: Law 20 – Scrum. The forward players who are the loose-head prop, the hooker and the tight-head prop. These players usually wear jersey Nos. 1, 2 and 3 respectively.

G

Goal: A player scores a goal by kicking the ball over an opponents' cross bar and between the goal posts from the field of play, by a place kick or drop-kick. A goal cannot be scored from a kick-off, drop-out or free kick.

Goal-line: Law 1 – The Ground.

Grounding the ball: Law 22 – In-Goal.

H

Half time: The interval between the two halves of the game.

Hindmost foot: The foot of the hindmost player in a scrum, ruck or maul which is nearest that player's goal-line.

Hooker:
Hooker: Law 20 – Scrum. The middle front row player in a scrum who usually wears jersey No. 2.

I

In-field: Away from touch and towards the middle of the field.

In-goal: Law 22 – In-Goal.

K

Kick: A kick is made by hitting the ball with any part of the leg or foot, except the heel, from the toe to the knee but not including the knee; a kick must move the ball a visible distance out of the hand, or along the ground.

Kick-off: Law 13 – Kick-off and Restart Kicks.

Knock-on: Law 12 – Knock-on or Throw-forward.

L

Lifting: Law 19 – Touch and Line-out.

Line of touch: Law 19 – Touch and Line-out. An imaginary line at right angles to the touch-line at the place where the ball is thrown in from touch.

Line-out: Law 19 – Touch and Line-out. Line through the mark or place: unless stated otherwise, a line parallel to the touch-line.

Long throw: Law 19 – Touch and Line-out.

Loose-head prop: Law 20 – Scrum. The left front row player in a scrum who usually wears jersey No. 1.

M

Match organiser: The organisation responsible for the match which may be a union, a group of unions or an organisation affiliated to the International Rugby Board.

Mark: Law 18 – Mark.

Maul: Law 17 – Maul.

N

Near: Law 14 – Ball on the Ground – No Tackle. Within one metre.

O

Obstruction: Law 10 – Foul Play.

Off-side in open play: Law 11 – Off-side and On-side in General Play.

Off-side Line: An imaginary line across the ground, from one touch-line to the other, parallel to the goal-lines; the position of this line varies according to the Law.

Off-side the 10-Metre Law: Law 11 – Off-side and On-side in General Play.

On-side: Law 11 – Off-side and On-side in General Play.

Open or Bleeding Wound: Law 3 – Number of Players – The Team.

Out of play: This happens when the ball or the ball-carrier has gone into touch or touch-in-goal, or touched or crossed the dead ball line.

Oversteps: A player steps across a line with one or both feet; the line may be real (for example, goal-line) or imaginary (for example, off-side line).

P

Pass: A player throws the ball to another player; if a player hands the ball to another player without throwing it, this is also a pass.

Peeling off: Law 19 – Touch and Line-Out.

Penalty goal: Law 9 – Method of Scoring.

Penalty kick: Law 21 – Penalty and Free Kicks – A kick awarded to the non-offending team after an infringement by its opponents. Unless a Law says otherwise, a penalty kick is awarded at the place of infringement.

Penalty try: Law 10 – Foul Play.

Place kick: The ball is kicked after it has been placed on the ground for that purpose.

Placer:
Placer: A player who holds the ball on the ground for a team mate to kick.

Played: The ball is played when it is touched by a player.

Playing area: Law 1 – The Ground.

Playing enclosure: Law 1 – The Ground.

Playing time: The time that has been played excluding time lost as defined in Law 5 Time.

Possession: This happens when a player is carrying the ball or a team has the ball in its control; for example, the ball in one half of a scrum or ruck is in that team's possession.

Pre-gripping: Law 19 – Touch and Line-out. Gripping a team mate in the line-out prior to the ball being thrown in.

Prop: Law 20 – Scrum. A front row player to the left or right of the hooker in a scrum. These players usually wear jersey Nos. 1 and 3.

Punt: The ball is dropped from the hand or hands and kicked before it touches the ground.

Pushover try: Law 22 – In-Goal.

R

Receiver: Law 19 – Touch and Line-Out.

Red Card: A card, red in colour shown to a player who has been sent off for contravening Law 10 – Foul Play, Law 4.5(c).

Referee: Law 6 – Match Officials.

Repeated infringements: Law 10 – Foul Play.

Replacements: Law 3 – Number of Players – The Team.

Ruck: Law 16 – Ruck.

S

Scrum: Law 20 – Scrum. This happens when players from each team come together in scrum formation so that play can be started by throwing the ball into the scrum.

Scrum-half: A player nominated to throw the ball into a scrum who usually wears jersey No. 9.

Sin Bin: The designated area in which a temporarily suspended player must remain for 10 minutes playing time.

Substitutes: Law 3 – Number of Players – The Team.

T

Tackle: Law 15 – Tackle: Ball-Carrier Brought to the Ground.

Team mate: Another player of the same team.

Temporarily suspended: Law 10 – Foul Play.

The plan: Law 1 – The Ground.

The 22: Law 1 – The Ground.

Throw-forward: Law 12 – Knock-On or Throw-Forward.

Throw-in: The act of the player who throws the ball into a scrum or a line-out.

Tight-head prop: Law 20 – Scrum. The right front row player in a scrum who usually wears jersey No. 3.

Touch: Law 19 – Touch and Line-Out.

Touch down: Law 22 – In-goal.

Touch-line: Law 1 – The Ground.

Touch-in-goal line: Law 1 – The Ground.

Touch judge: Law 6 – Match Officials.

Try: Law 9 – Method of Scoring.

U

Union: The controlling body under whose jurisdiction the match is played; for an International match it means the International Rugby Board or a Committee of the Board.

Y

Yellow card: A card, yellow in colour shown to a player who has been cautioned and temporarily suspended for 10 minutes' playing time.

A GAME FOR EVERYONE

Rugby union is reputed to have begun in England when Rugby School pupil William Webb Ellis caught the ball and ran with it in 1823. Many versions of football games were played before that time and certainly a great deal of rugby union since, with the William Webb Ellis Cup now presented to winners of the Rugby World Cup.

England has more rugby players and more rugby clubs in its membership than any other country in the world. And a complete cross section of the community is involved in the sport of rugby union, with over 2¼ million players, 2,000 rugby clubs, 3,000 schools, 30,000 referees, 40,000 coaches and some 40,000 volunteers involved.

The RFU tries to ensure that everyone has the chance to be involved in rugby and helps to adapt the sport to suit a variety of needs – whether that be wheelchair rugby, non-contact tag rugby or the full blown XV-a-side game.

Children do not play the same form of rugby union as older players but acquire the skills and understanding to play the game to their full potential in adapted versions, with the Laws of the Game altered to suit the development level of each age group.

Girls can play rugby alongside boys until they're 12 and then they can join all-girls teams, with 500 registered women's clubs across the country and all but two playing out of men's RFU member clubs.

All of which seems to confirm that rugby really is a game for everyone.

ENGLAND RUGBY®

rfu.com